WORTH A
DETOUR

NORTH ISLAND

WORTH A DETOUR

NORTH ISLAND

Hidden places and unusual destinations off the beaten track

PETER JANSSEN

First published in 2019 by New Holland Publishers
Sydney • Auckland

Level 1, 178 Fox Valley Road, Wahroonga 2076, Australia
5/39 Woodside Ave, Northcote, Auckland 0627, New Zealand

newhollandpublishers.com

Copyright © 2019 New Holland Publishers
Copyright © 2019 in text: Peter Janssen
Copyright © 2019 in images: Peter Janssen

All rights reserved. No part of this publication may be reproduced, stored in a retrieval system or transmitted, in any form or by any means, electronic, mechanical, photocopying, recording or otherwise, without the prior written permission of the publishers and copyright holders.

A catalogue record for this book is available from the National Library of New Zealand.

ISBN 9781869665265

Group Managing Director: Fiona Schultz
Publisher: David Brash
Project Editor: Duncan Perkinson
Designer: Yolanda La Gorcé
Production Director: Arlene Gippert

Printed in China

10 9 8 7 6 5 4 3

Keep up with New Holland Publishers:
 NewHollandPublishers
 @newhollandpublishers

Contents

Dedication		11
Acknowledgements		11
Introduction		12

NORTHLAND — 14

1. Cape Reinga	15	
2. Bartlett's Rata	16	
3. Te Paki Sandhills	16	
4. Henderson Bay and Rarawa Beach	17	
5. Ninety Mile Beach	18	
6. Gum Diggers Park	18	
7. *St Jean Baptiste* Anchor, Museum@Te Ahu/Far North Regional Museum, Kaitaia	19	
8. Doubtless Bay and Rangikapiti Pa	20	
9. Whangaroa Harbour	21	
10. Matauri Bay	22	
11. The Pear Tree, Kerikeri	22	
12. Marsden Estate	23	
13. Christ Church Russell	24	
14. Flagstaff Hill, Russell	24	
15. Putopu bird, Russell Museum	25	
16. Kawiti Glow-worm Caves	26	
17. Mimiwhangata Coastal Park	27	
18. Ruapekapeka Pa	28	
19. Hone Heke Memorial Park, Tokoreireia/Kaikohe Hill	28	
20. Hokianga Harbour	29	
21. Horeke Hotel	31	
22. Trounson Kauri Park	32	
23. Kai Iwi Lakes	33	
24. Poutu Ki Rongomaeroa, Dargaville Museum/Te Whare Taonga o Tunatahi	33	
25. Pouto Point, Kaipara Harbour	34	
26. Tokatoka Peak	35	
27. Maungaraho Rock	36	
28. Matakohe the Kauri Museum and the Kauri Bushman's Reserve	37	
29. Pahi	38	
30. Skelton's Drapery Paparoa	39	
31. Tutukaka Coast and the Poor Knights Islands	40	
32. Whangarei Heads	40	
33. Clapham Clock Museum	42	
34. Whangarei Quarry Gardens	43	
35. Packard Motor Museum	44	
36. Marsden Point Oil Refinery	45	
37. Waipu	46	
38. Waipu Caves	46	
39. Te Arai Point	47	
40. Utopia Café, Kaiwaka	48	

AUCKLAND – North — 49

1. Brick Bay Winery	50	
2. Parry Kauri Park	51	
3. Warkworth Cement Works	52	
4. Puhoi	53	
5. Dacre Cottage and Okura Bush	53	
6. Glow-worm grotto. Awaruku Bush Reserve	54	
7. Disappearing Gun, North Head Historic Reserve	55	
8. Smith's Bush/Northcote Domain	56	
9. Kauri Point Beach, Fitzpatrick Bay	56	
10. Under the Auckland Harbour Bridge	57	

AUCKLAND – City — 58

11. Auckland's 'Old City'	58	
12. Tepid Baths	62	
13. 1YA Radio Station	62	
14. The Civic Theatre	63	
15. Tiny Auckland Houses	64	
16. Karangahape Road/K'Rd	65	
17. Grafton Bridge and the Symonds Street Cemetery	67	

18. The Auckland Domain	67	
19. The Container Port, Auckland	69	
20. Highwic House	69	
21. Eden Gardens	70	
22. Parnell Pool	71	
23. Savage Memorial Park	71	
24. Melanesian Mission	72	
25. Cornwall Park and One Tree Hill Domain/Maungakiekie	73	
26. Coast to Coast Walkway	75	
27. Avondale Spiders	75	
28. Avondale Market	76	
29. The Pah, Hillsborough	77	
30. Onehunga Blockhouse	77	
31. Auckland Potters Studio, Onehunga	78	
32. Otahuhu War Memorials	79	
33. One city, 55 Volcanoes	80	

AUCKLAND - East 82

34. Ash bank, Farm Cove Walkway	82
35. All Saints Anglican Church, Howick	83
36. Fo Guang Shan Temple	84
37. Ayrlies Garden	84
38. Duders Regional Park	85
39. Tawhitokino Bay	86

AUCKLAND - West 87

40. South Kaipara Head	87
41. Bethells Beach/Te Henga, O'Neill Bay and Lake Waimanu	89
42. Totara Waters	90
43. Hobson's Gum Hobsonville	91
44. Te Ahua Point	92
45. Waikumete Cemetery	93
46. Mazuran's Wines	93
47. Babich Winery	94
48. The Huia to Whatipu Road	95

AUCKLAND - South 97

49. Otara Market	97
50. Rainbow's End Rollercoaster	98
51. Otuataua Stonefields	99
52. Ihumatao Fossilised Forest	100
53. Kentish Hotel	101
54. The Awhitu Peninsula	101

HAURAKI GULF ISLANDS 104

1. Great Barrier Island/Aotea	105
2. Little Barrier Island/Hauturu	106
3. Kawau Island	107
4. Waiheke	108
5. Rotoroa Island	111
6. Motutapu Island	112
7. Motuihe	113

THAMES AND COROMANDEL 115

1. Totara Vineyard	116
2. Hoffman's Pool, Kauaeranga Valley	117
3. Thames School of Mines and Mineralogical Museum	117
4. Historic Thames Hotels	118
5. Bella Street Pumphouse	119
6. Goldmine Experience	120
7. Rapaura Water Gardens	121
8. Square Kauri	121
9. The 309 Road	121
10. Coromandel Town	122
11. Coromandel Seafood	124
12. Coromandel Coastal Walkway	124
13. Opito Pa	125
14. Coromandel Beaches	125
15. Whitianga Pa	128
16. The Coroglen Tavern	129
17. Te Pare Historic Reserve Hahei	130
18. Paku Peak, Tairua	130
19. Broken Hills Gold Town	131
20. Pauanui	132

BAY OF PLENTY 133

1. Martha Mine, Waihi	134
2. Victoria Battery and Museum	134
3. Waitewheta Tramway	135
4. Waihi Beach – Orokawa and Homunga Bays Walk	136
5. Haiku Park, Katikati	137

6. The Cider Factorie, Te Puna	137	
7. Te Puna Quarry Park	138	
8. Macrocarpa Tree, Bethlehem	139	
9. Patrick's Pie/Gold Star Bakery Bethlehem	140	
10. The Elms Mission House	140	
11. Central Tauranga	141	
12. Gate Pa	146	
13. The Historic Village	148	
14. Yatton Park	149	
15. The Rising Tide and the Mount Brewing Co, Mt Maunganui	150	
16. Classic Flyers Museum	150	
17. The Lion and Tusk – Museum of the Rhodesian Services Association	151	
18. Mayor Island	152	
19. McLarens Falls Park	153	
20. Kaiate Falls	154	
21. Karangaumu Pa, Papamoa Hills Regional Park, Te Puke	154	
22. Maketu	155	
23. White Island	156	
24. Moutohora/Whale Island	157	
25. Matahina Dam	157	
26. Kaputerangi/Toi's Pa, Whakatane	158	
27. Whakatane River and Historical Walk	159	
28. Ohope Scenic Reserve – Fairbrother Loop Walk	160	
29. Ohiwa Oyster Farm	161	
30. Burial Tree/Hukutaia Domain, Opotiki	161	
31. Hiona St Stephen's Church, Opotiki	162	
32. Royal Hotel, Opotiki	163	
33. Shalfoon's Store and the De Luxe Theatre – Opotiki Museum	164	
34. Tirohanga Dunes Trail	164	

WAIKATO, HAURAKI PLAINS AND THE KING COUNTRY 165

1. Whakatiwai Regional Park	166	
2. Kaiaua Fish and Chip Shop	167	
3. The Cheese Barn Matatoki	168	
4. The Big Lemon and Paeroa Bottle	168	
5. Te Aroha	169	
6. Waiorongomai Valley	171	
7. Wairere Falls	171	
8. Morrinsville Cows	172	
9. Te Miro Mountain Bike Park	173	
10. Firth Tower	174	
11. Okoroire Hotel and Hot Springs	174	
12. Blue Springs and Waihou River	175	
13. Railway Station Water Tower, Tirau	176	
14. Over the Moon Cheese, Putaruru	176	
15. The Chainsaw Collection - Putaruru Timber Museum	177	
16. Pine Man, Tokoroa	178	
17. Pokeno Ice Creams	179	
18. Vivian Falls, Kohanga	179	
19. Port Waikato	180	
20. *HMS Pioneer* Gun Turrets - Mercer and Ngaruawahia	181	
21. DEKA Sign Huntly	182	
22. Lake Puketirini, Huntly	182	
23. Taupiri Mountain	183	
24. Maori Parliament Building, Ngaruawahia	185	
25. Hamilton Model Engineers Miniature Railway, Minogue Park, Hamilton	186	
26. Frankton Junction Railway House Factory	187	
27. Classics Museum	188	
28. Taitua Arboretum	189	
29. The Church of Jesus Christ of the Latter-day Saints (Mormon Temple)	190	
30. Good George, Somerset Street, Frankton	190	
31. Ice Age Mini-golf	191	
32. It's Astounding! Riff Raff Statue	192	
33. Duck Island Ice Cream	193	
34. Punnet, Tamahere	194	
35. New Zealand's Tallest Native Tree	194	
36. Matakitaki Pa, Pirongia	195	
37. Alexandra Redoubt, Pirongia	196	
38. Vilagrad and Three Brothers Winery	197	
39. Battle of Hingakaka, Lake Ngaroto	198	
40. Uenuku Te Awamutu Museum	199	
41. Te Awamutu Space Centre	200	
42. Kakepuku	201	
43. Kawhia	202	
44. Karam and John Haddad Menswear, Otorohanga	203	
45. The Road from Waitomo to Mokau via Markopa	204	

46. The Mokau Mine	205	
47. Madonna Falls	206	
48. Pureora Forest	206	
49. Omaru Falls	209	
50. Mapara Scenic Reserve	209	

ROTORUA 211

1. Mamaku Blue — 212
2. Mt Ngongotaha — 212
3. Kuirau Park — 214
4. Princes Gate Hotel — 214
5. Maori Rock Art, Lake Tarawera — 215
6. Tree of Hinehopu — 216
7. Te Koutu Pa, Lake Okataina — 217
8. Tarawera Falls — 218
9. Waikiti Valley Thermal Pools — 219
10. Rainbow Mountain/Maungakaramea — 220
11. Kerosine Creek — 221
12. Wai-o-tapu Boardwalk Mud Pools — 221
13. The Bridge Hot Pool, Wai-o-tapu — 222
14. Kaingaroa Forest — 222

TAUPO AND THE CENTRAL PLATEAU 224

1. Hatupatu's Rock/Te Kohatu O Hatupatu — 225
2. Pohaturoa — 225
3. Ohaaki Power Station — 226
4. Wairakei Steamfields — 226
5. Craters of the Moon — 227
6. Huka Falls Walkway — 227
7. AC Baths — 228
8. Te Kooti at Taupo. Opepe Reserve and Te Porere Redoubt — 228
9. Mine Bay Māori Rock Carvings — 230
10. Tongariro River – Turangi — 230
11. Tongariro National Trout Centre — 231
12. Pihanga and Lake Rotopounamu — 232
13. Raurimu Spiral — 233
14. The Old Coach Road — 233
15. Team Carrot Park — 234
16. The Tangiwai Memorial — 235

EAST CAPE, GISBORNE AND TE UREWERA 236

1. East Cape Highway — 237
2. Gisborne Beaches — 241
3. Kaiti Hill — 242
4. Te Poho O Rawiri Wharenui — 244
5. The Star of Canada – Te Moana Maritime Gallery, Tairawhiti Museum, Gisborne — 244
6. Gray's Bush Scenic Reserve — 245
7. Millton Vineyard, Manutuke — 245
8. Manutuke — 246
9. Eastwoodhill Arboretum — 247
10. Rere Falls and Rere Rockslide — 249
11. Morere Hot Springs and Nature Reserve — 249
12. Te Urewera — 250

HAWKES BAY 254

1. Kahungunu Wharenui — 255
2. Mahia Peninsula — 255
3. Giant Puka, Waiatai Reserve — 256
4. Gaiety Theatre, East End Café and Saloon Bar — 257
5. Mohaka Viaduct — 257
6. Waikare Beach — 258
7. Shine Falls — 258
8. Lake Tutira and the Gutherie Smith Arboretum — 259
9. Rorookuri Hill, Whakamaharatanga Walkway — 260
10. Pania of the Reef — 261
11. Napier Botanical Gardens — 262
12. Napier Prison — 263
13. Otatara Pa Historic Reserve — 264
14. Tutaekuri River — 265
15. Ocean Beach — 265
16. The Faraday Centre/Hawkes Bay Museum of Technology — 266
17. Arataki Honey — 266
18. Birdwoods Gallery — 267
19. Rush Munro Ice Cream Garden — 268
20. Spanish Mission, Hastings — 269

21. Hawke's Bay Wineries	270
22. Pekapeka Wetlands	273
23. The Public Toilets, Ongaonga	274
24. Norsewood	274
25. The Wop Wops Wetland Park	275
26. Danish Hair Embroidery - Dannevirke Gallery of History	276
27. Fantasy Cave, Dannevike	277
28. Wimbledon Tavern	277
29. Taumatawhakatangihanga-koauauotamateaturipukaka-pikimaungahoronukupokai-whenuakitanatahu	278
30. Waihi Falls	279

TARANAKI — 280

1. Forgotten World Highway	281
2. Pukerangiora Pa	282
3. Awatetake Pa	283
4. Manutahi Taxidermy Museum	283
5. Hillsborough Car Museum	284
6. The Rewa Rewa Bridge and the Coastal Walkway	285
7. Abraham Salaman Tomb, Te Henui Cemetery	286
8. Govett-Brewster Art Gallery and the Len Lye Centre, New Plymouth	287
9. The Swanndri Collection - Puke Ariki Museum	288
10. New Plymouth Power Station Chimney	289
11. Paritutu Rock and the Sugar Loaf Island	290
12. Ratapihipihi Reserve	291
13. The Vineyard Bistro at Okurukuru	291
14. Te Koru Pa, Oakura	292
15. Parihaka Village	293
16. Cape Egmont Lighthouse	294
17. Opunake Beach	295
18. Peter Snell Statue	295
19. Hollard Gardens Kaponga	295
20. Manaia Blockhouse and Redoubt	296
21. Tawhiti Museum	297
22. Elvis Presley Museum	298
23. Butterfly Tree, King Edward Park, Hawera	299
24. Hawera Water Tower	300
25. Aotea Monument Patea	300
26. The Garden of Tutunui, Patea	302
27. EC Dallison and Sons, Waverley	302

WHANGANUI — 304

1. Whanganui River Road	305
2. Waimarie Paddle Steamer and Centre	307
3. Durie Hill Elevator and Tower	308
4. Lindauer Gallery - Whanganui Regional Museum	309
5. Whanganui War Memorial Hall	310
6. Ladies Rest	310
7. Cook's Garden	311
8. Cameron Blockhouse	311
9. Ratana Temple, Ratana	312

MANAWATU/RANGITIKEI/HOROWHENUA — 314

1. Taihape Gumboot Sculpture	315
2. Stormy Point Lookout Rangitikei	316
3. Te Apiti and Tararua Wind Farms	316
4. Railway Houses	317
5. Hoffman Kiln	317
6. The Log Cabin	318
7. The Bald Kiwi - New Zealand Rugby Museum	318
8. Regent on Broadway	319
9. Savage Crescent	320
10. Mini Railway Victoria Esplanade	320
11. Caccia Birch House	321
12. Mt Cleese, Awapuni Landfill	322
13. Feilding Sales Yards	323
14. The Coach House Museum	324
15. De Molen and Nieuwe Stroom	325
16. Foxton Flax Stripper	326
17. Foxton Beach – Manawatu Estuary	326
18. Waitarere Beach Shipwreck	327
19. Mangahao Power Station	328
20. RJ's Licorice	328
21. Lake Papaitonga	329
22. Ohau Wines	331

23. Our Lady of Lourdes, Paraparaumu	331	24. Kapiti Island 332

WAIRARAPA 334

1.	Tui Brewery, Mangatainoka, 'Yeah right'	335	Golden Shears	341
2.	Anzac Bridge, Kaiparoro	336	10. Wairarapa Times Age Building	343
3.	Eketahuna War Memorial Hall	336	11. The Clareville Bakery	343
4.	Mt Bruce Pioneer Museum	337	12. Stonehenge Aotearoa	344
5.	The Alpaca Place	338	13. Papawai Marae	344
6.	Castlepoint Lighthouse and Lagoon	339	14. Mountain Ash Gum Tree, Greytown	345
7.	Ten O'Clock Cookie Bakery and Café	340	15. Tauherenikau Racecourse	346
8.	The Cricket Oval and a Redwood Stump, Queen Elizabeth Park, Masterton	340	16. Fell Locomotive Museum, Featherston	346
			17. Wairarapa Wineries	347
			18. Putangirua Pinnacles	348
			19. Ngawi, South Wairarapa Coast	348
9.	The Wool Shed and the			

WELLINGTON 350

1.	Kaitoke Regional Park	351	21. Old Government Buildings	368
2.	Mangaroa Rail Tunnel	352	22. Old Bank Arcade, Animated Musical Clock	369
3.	Wallaceville Blockhouse	353		
4.	The Weeping Pagoda Tree	353	23. Paddy the Wanderer Memorial Fountain	370
5.	Wainuiomata Hill Tunnel Portal	354		
6.	Pencarrow Coastal Trail	355	24. The Board Room – Wellington Museum	371
7.	Lower Hutt Council Building and Town Hall	356	25. New Zealand Academy of Fine Arts and New Zealand Portrait Gallery	371
8.	Petone Wharf	357		
9.	Battle Hill	358		
10.	Pataka Art + Museum	359	26. Boat Sheds, Clyde Quay Boat Harbour	372
11.	Te Pa o Kapo	360		
12.	Second World War American Officer's Mess	360	27. Cuba Street Bucket Fountain	373
			28. Nairn Street Cottage	374
13.	Johnsonville Line - Wellington Rail	361	29. Otari-Wilton Bush's Native Botanic Garden and Forest Reserve	374
14.	Matiu/Somes Island and Wellington Harbour/Te Whanganui a Tara	362	30. Mrs Chippy Monument	375
			31. Wrights Hill Fortress	376
15.	Katherine Mansfield House and Garden	363	32. Makara Peak Mountain-bike Park	377
16.	Tinakori Road Houses, Thorndon	364	33. Makara Beach and Walkway	377
17.	Harry Holland's Grave, Bolton Street Cemetery	365	34. Brooklyn Wind Turbine	378
			35. Carlucci Land	379
18.	Pinus Radiata Botanic Gardens	366	36. The Container House, Happy Valley	380
19.	Krupp Gun	366		
20.	He Tohu: The Declaration of Independence, The Treaty of Waitangi and Women's Suffrage Petition	367	37. Wellington's South Coast	380
			38. Island Bay Butchery	381
			39. Wellington Airport	382
			40. Ataturk Memorial	382

Glossary 384

Dedication

To all the dedicated volunteers without whom New Zealand's human and natural history would be much diminished.

Acknowledgements

Without all your helpful suggestions this book would have been much shorter. Thank you.

Helen Adams, Winton Bebbington, Kevin Brewer, Rose Carson, Melissa Carson, Grant Hadfield, John Haig, Susan Holmes, Lloyd Houghton, Harry Janssen, Lyn Janssen, Teresa Janssen, Dora Moffit, Jonathan Pierce, Sarah Raman, Peter Rickard, Nick Seaman, Katrina Smith, Wilma Smith, Alison Southby.

Introduction

Over the past few years while researching a number of guidebooks I have travelled just about every road and visited every town and hamlet in New Zealand. I have enjoyed finding the more offbeat attractions, the quirky places bypassed by most travellers and the eccentric characters that have been great stories to tell. Even now I am finding plenty of new places and it's hard just to know when to stop. Many of the places are well known locally, but are unknown to a visitor who is frequently short on time. Even our bigger cities have corners and places that remain unexplored by most. This book is a varied collection of the places throughout the country that I think are worth a small detour. There is something for everyone (I hope), from a taxidermy collection and homemade baking, backcountry pubs to old time wineries, through to empty beaches and obscure country roads.

By its very nature a book of this type comes down to personal choice, but I trust through experience that the choices are good ones, though I'm more than ready to hear about other places I might have missed.

NORTHLAND

1. Cape Reinga
2. Bartlett's Rata
3. Te Paki Sandhills
4. Henderson Bay and Rarawa Beach
5. Ninety Mile Beach
6. Gum Diggers Park
7. St Jean Baptiste Anchor, Museum@Te Ahu/Far North Regional Museum, Kaitaia
8. Doubtless Bay and Rangikapiti Pa
9. Whangaroa Harbour
10. Matauri Bay
11. The Pear Tree, Kerikeri
12. Marsden Estate
13. Christ Church, Russell
14. Flagstaff Hill, Russell
15. Putopu bird, Russell Museum
16. Kawiti Glow-worm Caves
17. Mimiwhangata Coastal Park
18. Ruapekapeka Pa
19. Hone Heke Memorial Park, Tokoreireia/Kaikohe Hill
20. Hokianga Harbour
21. Horeke Hotel
22. Trounson Kauri Park
23. Kai Iwi Lakes
24. Poutu Ki Rongomaeroa, Dargaville Museum/Te Whare Taonga o Tunatahi
25. Pouto Point, Kaipara Harbour
26. Tokatoka Peak
27. Maungaraho Rock
28. Matakohe the Kauri Museum and the Kauri Bushman's Reserve
29. Pahi
30. Skelton's Drapery Paparoa
31. Tutukaka Coast and the Poor Knights Islands
32. Whangarei Heads
33. Clapham Clock Museum
34. Whangarei Quarry Gardens
35. Packard Motor Museum
36. Marsden Point Oil Refinery
37. Waipu
38. Waipu Caves
39. Te Arai Point
40. Utopia Café, Kaiwaka

1. Cape Reinga

In the middle of the summer Cape Reinga can be so packed with visitors, that the magnificent scenery is often diminished by the crowds, yet there are two unique features that are frequently overlooked.

In Maori tradition Cape Reinga is the final departing point for the spirits of the dead on their journey to the underworld domain of Hine-nui-te-po, the goddess of death. The twisted and gnarled vegetation along the coast is where the spirits have desperately attempted to cling to this world. Right at the point is a small battered pohutukawa named Te Aroha clinging to the rocks just above the water. What it lacks in size it more than makes up for in importance, as this tree is the entrance to the world of Hinenui-te-po, the Goddess of Death. Once the departing spirits reach this tree, they use the gnarled roots as steps to make their way down to the sea and the door to the underworld. In Maori, a gentle way to say someone has died is to say they 'have slid down the pohutukawa root'. Said to be over 800 years old, tradition has it that in all those years, the tree has flowered only once.

The other special place is Te Werahi Beach. From the carpark, packed with tour buses where the track leads down to the lighthouse, there is another, seldom used track which leads in the other direction. Only forty-five minutes walk away is Te Werahi Beach, where there is every chance you will find yourself alone. This wide sandy beach on the western side of the cape directly faces the wild Tasman Sea and is frequently exposed to strong westerly winds and rolling surf pounding in from the open ocean. It is a wonderful wild place away from the crowds, and even better the track down to the beach winds along spectacular coastal cliffs that drop hundreds of metres to the rocks below, before dropping into sheltered valley that leads to the beach. The salt-laden spray from the wild waves produces bonsai like manuka, and diminutive pohutukawa.

📍 At the very end of SH 1

2. Bartlett's Rata

New Zealand's rarest native tree, Bartlett's rata is found at Te Paki on the Te Aupouri Peninsula. Just thirty-four trees in three bush remnants survive in the wild and were rediscovered in 1975 by Auckland schoolteacher John Bartlett in Radar Bush near Cape Reinga. The local iwi Ngati, of course knew of the trees and named them rata moehau, 'the big rata asleep on the hill'.

Like northern rata, this tree usually starts life as an epiphyte high in the branches of a large host tree and can grow up to 30 metres in height. In contrast to the other two rata species, it has white flowers instead of bright crimson and fine, paper-like bark that flakes easily, rather than the rough, tough bark of its common cousins.

One theory for the difference is that this species developed in isolation when these volcanic hills were once an island, separated from the mainland for long periods of time in the way, today, offshore islands are home to subspecies of native flora and fauna. The area was once covered in the dense forest, but only isolated patches of bush have survived the arrival of humans and the subsequent clearing for agriculture and timber. The flaky bark may have also helped the tree to survive bush fires set to clear the land for crops and grass.

The track to the tree is signposted to the right on the road between Waitiki Landing and Cape Reinga. It begins as a 4WD track and after about twenty minutes a smaller track branches off to the right. At 300 metres is a gate. Take the track to the left and this follows a ridge dropping steeply downhill. The track is muddy and not well formed. It ends by a single large kauri tree behind which are two specimens of Barlett's rata. Do not take seeds or cuttings.

3. Te Paki Sandhills

Huge sandhills reminiscent of the Sahara Desert are not an image that immediately springs to mind when thinking of the New Zealand landscape. At Te Paki massive sand dunes stretch from Te Paki Stream to

Te Werahi Beach, in places reaching as high as 150 metres. The light gold sand blends with the yellowy-green dune-creeper pingao, which manages to take hold in the shifting sands. The best way to walk the sand hills is to start walking from the car park up the loose sand of the dunes. This is hard work; when you have had enough drop down to Te Paki Stream, which is both flat and shallow, and an easy walk back to the car park. Te Paki Stream serves as a major access route to Ninety Mile Beach, so keep an eye out for speeding vehicles. Sand-surfing on boogie boards is a popular activity here, and there are several places hiring out boards, including one right at the car park during the summer.

> Te Paki Stream Road, off the Cape Reinga Road.

4. Henderson Bay and Rarawa Beach

These two unspoilt beaches are just two among the many beautiful and often empty Northland beaches. What makes these two beaches special is that while they are only a couple of kilometres apart, the sand on the beaches is distinctly different. Henderson Bay is a magnificent long sweep of golden sand and, with its rolling breakers, is very popular with surfers. The sand at Rarawa Beach is a vivid white. The difference is caused by the variation in the amount of silica in the sand. Rarawa and the beaches north of here contain a high amount of silica, giving these beaches a dazzling white colour that on a summer's day will make you reach for the sunnies. The contrast between the white of the sand and the blue of the ocean is just stunning. If getting away from it all is what you are after, then both these beaches fit the bill perfectly.

> 13 km north of Horohora to the Henderson Bay Road turnoff and 15 km to the Rarawa Beach turnoff. From the turnoff it is 6 km to the either beach on an unsealed road.

5. Ninety Mile Beach

Why this beach was named Ninety Mile Beach is a bit of a mystery as the beach is not even 90 kilometres long. If accuracy wasn't important, why not go the whole way and called it One Hundred Mile Beach? For the record the beach is just 54 miles or 88 km long. Precise distances aside, this magnificent sweeping beach has room enough for everyone. Ahipara Beach at the southern end is the most sheltered part of the beach and safest for swimming, while at the other end the giant Te Paki sand hills have become a firm favourite for sand surfing.

The beach is drivable for a few hours both sides of low tide, but only for the experienced. Check your insurance first as many car insurance companies, and nearly all rental car companies exclude off road driving from their policies. The annual Snapper Classic fishing competition is held on the beach in February each year for the heaviest snapper caught by surf casting off the beach. It is the biggest and most lucrative fishing competition of its type in New Zealand, attracting entries from all over New Zealand and Australia. Visit www.snapperclassic.co.nz

📍 There are numerous entry spots along SH 1 north of Kaitaia.

6. Gum Diggers Park

Located on an actual gum field, Gum Diggers Park is a fascinating insight into an industry unique to Northland. The kauri gum had a wide range of uses particularly as a high-quality varnish, but it was hard won by men working in difficult conditions. The footwear used in the extraction of the gum gave rise to the very Kiwi word 'gumboot'.

Workers in this gumfield included Dalmatians from the Croatian coast who first arrived in Northland in 1885 and by 1900 numbered nearly 5000. Many of these men worked hard, saved their money and returned to their homeland, while others moved south to Auckland and became particularly influential in the wine industry, construction and fishing.

This gum field was based on two extinct kauri forests: the first forest may have declined owing to climate change 150,000 years ago, while the second forest was subjected to a more severe event such as a tsunami about 45,000 years ago. Information boards and reconstructions detail both the kauri gum industry and life on the gum field, and the trees in this park are said to be the oldest preserved timber in the world.

In addition to the old gum workings, Diggers Park has a small viewing platform so visitor can look out over the tops of the trees, and the park also breeds Northland green geckos that can be viewed in the Gecko House.

- 171 Heath Road, signposted from SH 1 25 km north of Kaitaia
- Open daily 9 am to 5.30 pm. Summer months only.
- 09 406 7166
- www.gumdiggerspark.co.nz
- Entrance fee.

7. St Jean Baptiste Anchor, Museum@Te Ahu/Far North Regional Museum, Kaitaia

While the voyages of Captain Cook are well documented, what is not so well known is that the French explorer Jean Francois de Surville was exploring New Zealand at the same time as Cook. Considering that New Zealand was virtually unknown to European sailors it is incredible that at one stage both Cook's *Endeavour* and de Surville's *St Jean Baptiste* ships passed within a few kilometres of each other off North Cape in December 1769. At the time bad weather obscured visibility so neither captain was aware that the other was sailing in the very same waters. While sheltering in Doubtless Bay, de Surville was forced to cut both his anchors, and these were later recovered by diver and adventurer Kelly Tarlton. Rusted and a bit worse for wear, but still impressive, one of these huge anchors is here at Kaitaia, while the other is in Te Papa, Wellington.

📍 Corner Matthews Ave and South Road, Kaitaia.
🕐 Open October to May 8.30 am to 4.30 pm, Monday to Friday; June to September 10.30 am to 4.30 pm Monday to Friday.
📞 09 408 9457
🌐 www.teahuheritage.co.nz

8. Doubtless Bay and Rangikapiti Pa

Doubtless Bay, known to Maori as Rangaunu, was first discovered by Kupe who landed at Taipa around 900 AD and encompasses some of the best beaches of the north, including Coopers Beach, Cable Bay, Taipa and Taupo Bay. At the eastern end of the bay is historic Mangonui Harbour, once a thriving whaling station. Sheltering the bay to the west and north is the Karikari Peninsula at the end of which is Matai Bay, without question one of the finest beaches in the area.

Rangikapiti Pa overlooks both Doubtless Bay and inland along the Mangonui Harbour, and was the principal pa in this area. According to Ngati Kahu tradition, it was here that the voyaging waka *Ruakaramea*, commanded by Moehuri, first landed. It is now turned to stone and is still visible just below the pa at low tide. The name Rangikapiti means 'gathered together'.

The *Ruakaramea* was guided by a great shark across the open ocean to the safe harbour. To honour the shark, Moehuri not only named the harbour Mangonui (big shark), but gave orders that the shark was to be protected. Directly in opposition to his father's orders, Moehuri's son Tukiato and a group of friends killed the shark and, as punishment, Tukiato was expelled from the pa to the other end of Coopers Beach where he built the pa Otanenui.

📍 Between Coopers Beach and Mangonui turn off SH 10 into Mill Bay Road and then immediately left into Rangikapiti Road and the pa is at the end.

9. Whangaroa Harbour

The view from SH 10 of the tidal upper reaches of the Whangaroa Harbour doesn't tempt the passing visitor to make the effort of taking a detour, but the harbour has some surprises. In contrast to the upper reaches, towards the entrance the harbour narrows considerably becoming almost an enclosed fiord-like bay, surrounding by rocky peaks and bush-clad hills. Marine fossils found in the area date from the early Permian era (270 million years ago), making them some of the oldest fossils in the North Island, and rising sea levels over the last 5000 years flooded an older river valley to create the inland waterway.

The small settlement has a fine old pub and is the sheltered base for fishing boats. High above the town an old volcanic plug known as St Paul's Rock gives spectacular views over the harbour and out to Stephenson Island just beyond the entrance.

The origin of this rock has a lively Maori legend. Taratara was a handsome mountain, and being handsome he had two loving wives who took care of his every need. One day Maungataniwha, who lived to the west, and was both a taniwha and a mountain, asked Taratara if he could have one of his wives, as he was still single. Not only did Taratara refuse the request, but he laughed in his face and mocked the bachelor to such a degree that Maungataniwha swung his huge tail and whipped off Taratara's head with such force that it sailed over the harbour and landed on the hill now known as Ohakiri or St Pauls Rock. The headless Taratara still stands today as the flat-topped mountain to the west of Whangaroa harbour.

Tauranga Bay just beyond the entrance to the bay is a beautiful but isolated stretch of beach with just small huddle of baches and a camping ground.

📍 Whangaroa village is 6 km off SH 10, north of Kerikeri.

10. Matauri Bay

The long sweep of sandy beach fronting Matauri Bay (30 km north of Kerikeri) is largely undeveloped, and the bay is now best known as the final resting place of the Greenpeace ship the *Rainbow Warrior*, sunk first by French saboteurs in Auckland harbour in 1985. A monument to the ship is on the bluff at the northern end of the bay, while the ship itself lies in the clear waters between the beach and the Cavalli Islands. The *Rainbow Warrior* is now appropriately an artificial reef sheltering sea life, and a very popular diving spot.

 At the end of Matauri Bay Road, 17km off SH 10.

11. The Pear Tree, Kerikeri

Several towns claim to be New Zealand's oldest European settlements, but just what constitutes a settlement is certainly up for discussion and some claims are based on just a single person or family arriving to stay permanently in a given area. Working on the basis that a town can be founded by very few people, Kerikeri, settled between 1818 and 1822, is the front runner with two other Northland towns not far behind: Rawene (1825) and Russell (1829).

As well as building a house, establishing a garden and orchard was a high priority for the first settlers and these vegetable and fruit trees were especially valued by local Maori whose local plant diet was severely limited.

Pear trees are long-lived and it is not surprising the oldest surviving fruit tree brought by Europeans to New Zealand is a pear. Once part of a much larger orchard, it is no coincidence that the fruit trees were planted just below the pa of Hongi Hika on whose patronage the settlers relied. Most sources attribute the planting of the tree in 1819 to Samuel Marsden but another missionary, John Butler, recorded in his journal in August 1819 that he and local Maori workers had planted over 300 fruit trees, so just who placed the tree in the ground will forever remain a mystery.

The pear is even older than New Zealand's oldest buildings, sitting side by side across the road. Now looking its age, the tree is surprisingly healthy, though the trunk is largely hollow and the base of the tree looks more like a lava flow than a living thing. One story tells of the tree in its prime producing fruit so large that just four pears filled a bucket. Largely protected by a fence within the carpark, there is no reason this tree will not continue to fruit and flourish for a long time yet, though damage to the tree roots beyond the fence is a concern. Happy 200th Birthday, Tree.

📍 The pear tree is in the car park at the end of opposite the Stone Store, Kerikeri.

12. Marsden Estate

The humid north is not the kindest place to grow grapes for wine, but one exception is Marsden Estate. Established in 1993, the winery takes its name from Samuel Marsden, an early missionary who planted the first vines in New Zealand to make altar wine. Set in the lush countryside just out of Kerikeri amid orchards of oranges and olive groves, this four-hectare vineyard produces single-estate wines including pinot gris, chardonnay, syrah, chambourcin, muscat and tempranillo and pinotage, with sauvignon blanc grapes brought in from Marlborough and viognier from Mangawhai. Most of the estate's wine is sold through the cellar door and restaurant.

Popular with the locals, the restaurant and winery are an attractive country-inn style building by local architect Martin Evans. The Mediterranean influenced menu, focussing on fresh local product, suits the relaxed dining atmosphere both on the beautiful, wide terrace overhung with grapevines in the summer, and indoors with a cosy open fire in winter. The view is over the spacious garden and lily pond to the vineyard on the gentle slopes beyond.

📍 56 Wiroa Road, Kerikeri.
🕐 Open Summer 10 am to 5 pm, plus Friday and Saturday nights. Winter 10 am to 4 pm.
📞 09 407 9398
🌐 www.marsdenestate.co.nz

13. Christ Church, Russell

Like the oldest European building, New Zealand's oldest church is in Northland at Russell. Also known as Te Whare Karakia o Kororareka, Christ Church was built in 1835 with the first service held in January 1836. Simply designed with a hipped roof, the church was significantly altered in 1871. The church survived the sacking of Kororareka by Hone Heke in 1845 but bears the scars of the battle that raged around the church and several bullet holes are still visible. Notable Ngapuhi chief Tamati Waka Nene is buried in the church's graveyard. The church was designated a World Heritage Site in 1983.

Keeping up with the time and although no longer used for services, the church is still consecrated ground and in 2018 the ordination of the first Anglican New Zealander in an openly gay relationship was held in the church.

📍 Church St, Russell.

14. Flagstaff Hill, Russell

Russell began life as Kororareka, and the early settlement, known as the 'hellhole of the Pacific', was notorious for grog shops, brothels and general lawlessness. Despite its reputation it was even the capital of the fledgling colony for a brief nine-month period.

As tensions grew between the Maori and the British, mainly over trade and the imposition of duties and tariffs, Ngapuhi chief Hone Heke was well aware of the symbolic nature of the British flag flying over Russell, regardless of the fact that he had actually gifted the flagpole in the first place. Inspired by talk of revolution by American Captain William Mayhew, Heke hacked down the pole for the first time on 8 July 1844. When it was replaced, he cut it down again in January 1845 and actually flew the US flag from his waka.

The fourth time the flagpole was erected, the lower portion was clad in iron, but this did not deter Hone from cutting down the pole on 11 March 1845; and then, for good measure, he followed this up by sacking the town and burning down many buildings including the Duke of Marlborough Hotel.

Later, in an act of reconciliation, those involved in cutting down the pole erected a new flagstaff in 1857; and in January 1958 a British flag was raised, with the flagpole being named Whakakotahitanga or 'Being at one with the Queen'. This flagpole still stands today.

📍 End of Flagstaff Road, Russell.

15. Putopu bird, Russell Museum

In a simple case in the Russell Museum sits a rather ordinary stuffed bird looking a bit like a weka. It is, however, the only example of an extinct member of rail family and the story of how this bird came to be in the museum is an intriguing tale. Tension was high in Russell in early March 1845 and on March 11 it was decided to immediately evacuate the European residents of the town to Auckland by ship. Hurriedly packing up precious possessions, four year old Catherine Flowerday desperately tried to find her cat Ginger. Boarding the boat, Ginger emerged from the creek and Catherine swept up the cat in her arms, taking little notice of the bird firmly clenched in the cat's mouth. On board, the ship's mate, an amateur taxidermist, removed the bird which sadly was dead and on leaving the ship in Auckland presented the stuffed bird in a glass case. Years later, Catherine's great niece, Mrs Elsie Wilkinson presented the bird to the Russell Museum, the only example of the long extinct Putopu.

- 📍 2 York Street, Russell.
- 🕐 Open daily 10 am to 4 pm, to 5 pm January only.
- 📞 09 403 7701
- 🌐 www.russellmuseum.org.nz
- 💲 Entrance fee.

16. Kawiti Glow-worm Caves

Located near the historic Kawiti marae, these caves combine history, glow-worms and limestone formations. The caves were discovered in the seventeenth century by Roku, the runaway wife of chief Haumoewarangi who successfully used the caves to hide from her husband and his family. Over 200 m in length, up to 20 m at their highest point and 12 m wide, the caves feature delicate stalactites and stalagmites and clusters of glow-worms. Set in a bush-clad limestone valley, the caves are surrounded by cliffs, boulders, caverns and rock pillars. The famous fighting chief Kawiti, who held the British at Ruapekapeka, is an ancestor of this marae. Entrance to the caves is by guided tour only. They depart every 20-30 minutes and includes a short bush walk.

- 📍 56 Waiomio Road, 5 km south of Kawakawa on SH1.
- 🕐 Open daily 9 am to 5 pm, guided tours only.
- 📞 09 404 0583
- 🌐 www.kawiticaves.co.nz
- 💲 Entrance fee.

17. Mimiwhangata Coastal Park

Beautiful but isolated, this sprawling farm park covers the rolling hills of Mimiwhangata Peninsula. While there are tracks, the signage is erratic, but you can't get lost as it is all open farmland. There are several sandy beaches, the pick of which is the long Mimiwhangata Beach, which is more sheltered and north facing. Attracting few visitors, it is a long drive to get here and the only facilities at the park are toilets.

The peninsula was also the site of a great battle between Ngapuhi and Ngati Manaia.

Mimiwhangata was originally settled by people arriving on the waka Mahuhukiterangi, who eventually formed the iwi Ngati Manaia. Although they later intermarried with Ngapuhi, the relationship was not always an easy one.

Tensions boiled over when Te Waero of Ngapuhi deliberately destroyed a fishing net belonging to Ngati Manaia and, in an act of utu, was killed by Ngati Manaia. Ngapuhi were incensed at the murder and in reply planned to attack the three Ngati Manaia Pa on the Mimiwhangata peninsula: Te Rearea, Taraputa and Kaituna.

To create the greatest confusion, Ngapuhi under their rangatira Te Rangitamaru, decided to attack all three pa simultaneously in the middle of the night. Te Rearea was attacked from the land, while the other two pa were invaded by sea and totally caught by surprise. Ngati Manaia suffered a devastating defeat with a huge loss of life, though their rangatira and some people managed to escape. Kaituna Beach is still considered tapu today.

📍 From Helena Bay take Webb Road for 5.5 km and turn left into Mimiwhangata Road. Continue for another 5 km along this narrow, winding gravel road to the carpark.

18. Ruapekapeka Pa

Ruapekapeka Pa or 'the bat's nest', was the site of the final battle in war of the north in 1845. The British, outnumbering the Maori three to one, were confounded by Kawiti's innovative defences. Realising that the traditional fortified pa offered little protection from modern weapons, Ruapekapeka featured underground bunkers linked by tunnels and fox holes to protect the defenders from cannon and musket fire. The pa only fell when the Maori, believing the British would not attack on a Sunday, were caught off guard and were forced to abandon it. The outline of the pa is very clear and complemented by good information boards. The pa site has great views over the surrounding countryside. Note that the car park is a little way from the site, and the British position is not be confused with the actual pa, the entrance of which is marked by a fine carved gateway.

📍 35 km north of Whangarei on SH 1 turn right at Towai into Ruapekapeka Rd. The pa site is 4 km down this road, which is unsealed and narrow in places.

19. Hone Heke Memorial Park, Tokoreireia/Kaikohe Hill

The name Kaikohe is a short version of kaikohekohe or 'to eat the berries of the kohekohe tree'. This name stems from the aftermath of a battle when the Pakinga Pa fell to attacking Ngapuhi led by Tuohu, and the survivors subsisted on kohekohe trees growing on the hill now known as Tokareireia. It was also on this hill where the warrior Hone Heke Pokai retreated to mourn the fall of Ruapekapeka in 1846 and the death of his friends killed in the battle.

Now the hill is crowned with a monument and gardens in honour of Hone Heke Ngapua, the great nephew of Hone Heke and great great nephew of Hongi Hika. Graduating as a lawyer, Hone began working for the Native Land Court in 1891 and as a staunch supporter of the Kotahitanga (Unity) Movement, he became leader of the Federated Tribes of New Zealand in 1892. From there he became MP for Northern Maori, a position which he held until his death in 1909. Hone is credited with introducing rugby to the North, and today local teams still compete for the Hone Heke cup.

The entrance to the park starts through a fine carved gateway that incorporates both Maori and Pakeha motifs. It slopes gently uphill past magnificent old trees and through gardens to the monument.

📍 End of Monument Road, Kaihoke.

20. Hokianga Harbour

Discovered by the legendary explorer Kupe, the full name of the harbour is Hokianga-Nui-A-Kupe, The Place of Kupe's great return. Narrow and long, the harbour winds a surprisingly long way inland as far as Mangamuka Bridge on SH 1, and the sheltered waters were once an important transport link for both Maori and Pakeha travelling west to east.

While geologists will tell us that the harbour is a river valley drowned by rising sea levels, the traditional story of how the Hokianga was formed is a good deal more interesting. There are two different versions of the creation of the harbour, and both involve two taniwha.

The first story is relatively simple, and tells that two taniwha lived on either side of the harbour entrance: Niwa made his home on the high sandhills on the north head; Araiteuru lived in a cave on the south head. These two taniwha have just one important task: using their long and very powerful tails, together they stir the water at the entrance to the harbour, creating treacherous waves and strong currents and thereby protecting the people of the Hokianga from enemies invading by sea.

The second story involves just Araiteuru and her children, of which she had eleven and, like all big families, the children found their home in a cave above the beach just too crowded and started to fight among themselves.

One of the children, Waihou, decided to leave home and off he went, burrowing his way far inland until finally he was so tired that he made himself a hole, lay down and slept. This hole filled with water and became Lake Omapere. When Waihou didn't return, his brother Waima began searching for him, creating inlets as he went, until he became hopelessly lost and remains forever in the Punakitere swamp. Next Utakura left to find his brothers ... and on it went until all the taniwha's children had left home, never to return, and in the course of their travels created the eleven major waterways of the Hokianga.

A short walk on the south head known as the Arai Te Uru Coastal Walkway meanders through wind stunted manuka, flax and toi toi and has incredible views north over the giant golden sand hills on the northern shore, and west along the inland waterway of the harbour. Like the north head the hard sandy soil has been shaped by persistent wind, and below the lookout is a lovely sandy cove ideal for a swim on a hot day. But like so many west coast harbours, Hokianga has a treacherous sand bar just offshore from the harbour mouth. Especially dangerous on a southwesterly swell, a pilot service and a signal station were built in 1832 by John Martin, the earliest such service in New Zealand, which continued to operate until 1951. The signal station is still there, though the flagstaff was commandeered for other uses and now graces the Opononi RSA. The access to the south head is via Signal Hill Rd off the state highway 12.4 km east of Omapere.

On the north head are huge golden sand hills, and exposure for millennia to a combination of wind and rain has shaped the hard sand into deep gullies and wind blasted cliffs and intriguing formations. They are a great place to walk, though be aware that these sand hills are much larger close up than they appear from a distance and walking on the sand can be a strain – so don't be too ambitious. Devoid of any vegetation they are exposed to harsh winds so make sure you take plenty of water in the hot weather and thick clothing in cooler weather. The magnificent golden sand hills are well worth a visit and Hokianga Express Charters runs a water taxi from Opononi wharf on the hour depending on demand.

The statue of Opo the Dolphin outside the Opononi pub commemorates the friendly dolphin whose antics attracted huge crowds and publicity in 1955 before she met an untimely death trapped between rocks. The small museum inside the Hokianga Visitor Centre at Omapere has an Opo display.

Rawene is New Zealand's third-oldest European settlement and is the access point for the ferry to Kohukohu on the northern shore. Among its many old buildings is historic Clendon House built in the 1860s, the home of Captain James Clendon, the first US consul to New Zealand. Several of the older stores are built on tall piles over the water including the lovely Boatshed Café where is not difficult to while away the time doing not much at all.

On Clendon Esplanade is the Te Ara Manawa Walkway, a short boardwalk complete with information boards that takes only around 20 minute and allows visitors to walk through mangroves – a common feature of shallow northern harbours. Usually associated with the tropics, the single New Zealand species *Avicennia marina*, subspecies Australiasica, is the southernmost in the world but it is only in the Far North that mangroves grow to the size of small trees.

Tucked away in the upper reaches of the harbour beyond Rawene is the Mangungu Mission House. Built on a hill with a great view down the harbour, the mission house itself has changed very little from the time when the house was built in 1838, though most of the outbuildings have long gone. The house is stylish in its simplicity with a wide veranda running across the front of the building, an ideal spot to survey comings and goings on the harbour below. The mission still houses the old table on which the third and largest signing of the Treaty of Waitangi took place in February 1840, when the Hokianga chiefs assembled to add their marks to the treaty.

◉ Motukiore Road, 3 km from Horeke.
◷ Limited summer opening hours.

21. Horeke Hotel

There is much contention regarding the oldest pub in New Zealand and as many as six pubs stake a claim. The problem arises over the definition of pub or hotel. Many earlier hotels in New Zealand were very basic buildings and in some cases, especially on the goldfields, were merely a wooden façade for a large tent. The lethal and often fatal combination of naked flames and alcohol resulted in many pubs burning down either totally or partially, though some hotels were rebuilt in exactly the same style. Many other hotels, particularly in areas that went 'dry', changed their function entirely, while others seesawed between hotel and tavern and back again. Remodelling was, and still is, popular and some hotels have been altered and modernised to such an extent that they no longer resemble the original.

All that aside, the Horeke Hotel on the upper Hokianga harbour definitely existed in 1833 and may even date back to the late 1820s when the area was a thriving shipbuilding yard. Substantially altered and extended throughout the nineteenth century, how much of the hotel is original is up for a lively discussion, but the floor in the heart of the hotel definitely dates from 1833 as it is constructed with home-made nails and hand-sawn timber.

📍 End of Horeke-Taheke Road, 15 km off SH 12 from Taheke.

22. Trounson Kauri Park

Tronson Kauri Park is often bypassed in favour of the better known and more accessible Waipoua forest, but this is a real gem and not at all difficult to get to. This forest remnant was set aside as reserve by local landowner James Trounson, and now covers over 450 hectares of virgin kauri forest. The loop walk is through impressive groves of mature kauri with an under storey of nikau, fern and kiekie, and with fewer visitors the forest retains a quiet and primeval feel. The forest is also a mainland island reserve where intense control of predators has seen a recovery of many species including kiwi and kereru. The walk through the forest is an easy loop that takes around 45 minutes and suits even very small children.

📍 Trounsen can be accessed by a 15 km loop clearly marked off SH 12 south of Waipoua.

23. Kai Iwi Lakes

These three small lakes are basin-type dune lakes formed in consolidated sand with no outlets or inlets, relying entirely on rain to maintain the level of water. The small beaches have dazzling white sand the consistency of powder, while the water varies from a light aqua to a deep blue where the shallows suddenly drop off into very deep water. This is a spot for swimming and water skiing, with a camping ground and basic facilities available.

📍 From Dargaville take SH 12, 23 km north to Omamari Road and follow this road for 11 km to the lakes.

24. Poutu Ki Rongomaeroa, Dargaville Museum/Te Whare Taonga o Tunatahi

Situated on a hill just west of the town with great views over the Northern Wairoa River, this museum is easily recognised by the two masts of the *Rainbow Warrior* in front of the main building and holds one of this country's most intriguing and mysterious carvings.

A carving named Poutu Ki Rongomaeroa was uncovered during a wild storm on the Kaipara Harbour near Poutu and found by a local woman. Nearly three metres tall, the kauri carving is of a woman, but bears no resemblance to local carving styles or for that matter any other Maori carving style. For some this is a clear link to the proposition that New Zealand was occupied much earlier by the mysterious Waitaha people, an ancient Polynesian culture overwhelmed by the much later immigration by Maori. For others the carving provides a link to the Ainu people of Northern Japan who also created similar totem poles in the same carving style and who may have arrived in New Zealand on Chinese voyages of discovery lead by Zhou Man.

The Maori section of the museum also holds the largest pre-European waka in the country at 16.2 metres long and carved by stone tools from a single totara trunk.

- 📍 Harding Park, 32 Mount Wesley Road, Dargaville.
- 🕐 Open daily 9 am to 4 pm.
- 📞 09 439 7555
- 🌐 www.dargavillemuseum.co.nz
- 💲 Entrance fee.

25. Pouto Point, Kaipara Harbour

The Kaipara tends to be dismissed as a dirty, shallow expanse of water but this harbour was once an important waterway giving access far inland via long tidal rivers and estuaries. Around 1350 AD, after first landing at Kawhia, the waka *Tainui* voyaged north and entered Kaipara Harbour, beginning a long settlement of Maori in the area. In 1772 French explorer Marion du Fresne discovered the entrance but did not enter the harbour and it wasn't until 1836 that the first ships safely negotiated the bar.

The Kaipara can claim the most shipwrecks in New Zealand. In Maori tradition the first wreck was the waka *Mahuhu* which capsized at the entrance and the captain Rongomai was drowned. Since 1840 no fewer than 113 ships have come to grief here, and the entrance to the harbour is known as 'the ship's graveyard'. Even with the building of the three storey wooden lighthouse at Pouto in 1884 the harbour still claimed numerous ships.

The entrance to the harbour is wild, with constantly shifting sandbars and an enormous flow of water volume with each tide through the narrow entrance. While kauri timber trade was king, the Kaipara flourished, but after the timber was exhausted the harbour declined into a quiet backwater and in 1947 was closed as a port of entry.

Today one of the best places to experience what the Kaipara has to offer is Pouto. The small seaside settlement is tucked inside the harbour entrance, protected from the worst of the westerly wind, but looking out over the channel near the entrance where the water is surprising clean and clear. From here it is possible to drive along the hard sand at low tide (if you know what you're doing), to the entrance itself, but is is also a great place to go for a long, long walk in a special and wild place. Facilities are limited (there is a camping ground), but if it is peace and solitude you are looking for, then Pouto is a great place to start.

📍 60 km south of Dargaville on a road that includes a 20 km stretch of gravel.

26. Tokatoka Peak

Tokatoka Peak and its nearby neighbour Maungaraho are both cores of old volcanos that erupted millions of years ago and where, over eons, the outer volcanic material has eroded away. The distinctive shape is impossible to miss on the road from Ruawai to Dargaville and from a distance the peak looks quite difficult to climb. However, the track through regenerating bush is not that hard and takes about twenty minutes one way, though it is rough in patches with a bit of a rocky scramble near the top. It is worth the effort as the views from the top are superb. Below the languid Wairoa River snakes through the flat landscape as it wends its way to the Kaipara Harbour to the south. To the east the views are inland to rugged bush-clad ranges.

During the bitter and bloody war that raged between Ngapuhi and the Te Roroa people, a hapu of Ngati Whatua, this pa above the Wairoa River was a Te Roroa stronghold under the rangatira Taoho. Ever alert to attack, Taoho knew when he saw smoke columns from Maunganui Bluff that the scouts he posted there were warning that Ngapuhi warriors were invading up the long beach. Knowing a battle was imminent, Taoho sang a war song that urged his warriors 'to be as firm as the rock on Tokatoka'. It was Taoho who turned the tide of the battle of Moremonui when he killed the Ngapuhi chief Pokaia, though he himself was wounded during the fight.

Below the peak, sitting on a bluff alongside the river, is the distinct shape of an old pa site, ideally situated for both protection and to keep an eye on the comings and going on the river. In the nineteenth century a pilot service for the river operated below the peak and the pilot would climb the peak to scout the wide river for arriving vessels.

> At Tokatoka Tavern north of Ruawai turn right into Tokatoka Road. The track begins about 1.5 km on the left by the 'Scenic Reserve' sign.

27. Maungaraho Rock

Maungaraho Rock lies the north east of Tokatoka Peak and is more a challenging climb. From the car park, the solid wall of rock rising 222 metres from the surrounding farmland seems unclimbable, but a rough track circles the rock, with the track to the top beginning from the other side. There is a short difficult section at the base of the rock, made easier by cables. Once past this tricky bit, the climb to the top isn't that hard. The views and the satisfaction of reaching the top make it all worthwhile. Discovered only in 2008 is a rare native hebe which on grows on this rock outcrop and nowhere else.

> Continue north on SH 12 from Tokatoka for 6 km, then turn right into Mititai Road, following the signs for 7 km to the end of Maungaraho Rock Road.

28. Matakohe the Kauri Museum and the Kauri Bushman's Reserve

Opened in 1962, originally set up to celebrate 100 years of local European settlement, this large museum now focuses on every aspect of the kauri tree and the associated timber industry, especially important with the new threat of kauri dieback disease.

The collection of kauri furniture, and the display of kauri panelling, clearly demonstrates why this beautiful timber was so widely used. Its clean even grain, together with the warm golden glow makes this timber instantly appealing and for the timber industry massive trees produced vast amounts of useable timber. The Amber Room, with its enormous display of kauri gum and carved kauri objects, positively glows with soft yellowish light. On show are lumps of gum containing fossilised seeds, a spider and a flea trapped aeons ago as the sticky gum oozed from the tree. In the central hall is a massive slab of kauri 22.5 m in length and cut from the heart of a single tree, along with Warawara kauri plank that is over 4000 years old.

A new section of the museum includes a replica boarding house, a humble gum digger's hut, a working steam mill and a display of machinery, both hand and machine driven, including a vintage 1929 Caterpillar 60, the type of machine that replaced the bullock teams formerly used to haul logs.

- The museum is on Church Road, well sign posted off SH 12, 26 km from SH 1 on the road to Dargaville.
- Open daily 9 am to 5 pm.
- www.kauri-museum.com
- Entrance fee.

Just a short distance from the museum is the Kauri Bushman Memorial Reserve, a tiny reserve of just a few hectares set aside in 1954 as a memorial to the old-time bushmen who worked the kauri forest. Despite the destructive nature of their work, this was a tough life with bushmen living in rough conditions in rugged bush country trying to make a modest living. This easy 15 minute walk, mostly on boardwalk to protect the delicate roots of the kauri trees, meanders through a handsome stand of good sized trees; the best bit is this reserve is little known and you are very likely to have it to yourself.

◉ The reserve is five kilometres from Matakohe on Sterling Road, 2 km off SH 12. The road is narrow, winding and gravel.

29. Pahi

Pahi lies on the Kaipara Harbour occupying the tip of long peninsula at the head of the Arapapa River and flanked on either side by the Pahi River and the Paparoa Creek, and very different from Pouto on Kaipara North Head.

The Kaipara is easily New Zealand's largest harbour and one of the largest in the world. At high tide it covers 947 square kilometres, which reduces by 57 per cent at low tide to just 409 square kilometres (the next largest, the Manukau is 394 sq km). On the scale of international harbours, Kaipara is up there with the largest, and while there is no consensus on the exact ranking, San Fransico Bay is largest at just over 1000 square kilometres (but then is it a bay or harbour?). Not only does it cover a huge area, but has over 2800 km of coastline and when the tide is running hard it can reach a speed of 6 knots (9 kph) at the harbour entrance.

Governed by the tides, this bucolic seaside village was once a transport hub with a regular steamer service to Helensville. Established in 1865 by the nonconformist religious group known as Albertlanders (their main settlement was at Port Albert further south, also on the Kaipara), the settlement never flourished and Pahi quickly became a quiet backwater, the fine old pub long closed and now a private house. Today Pahi is best known for the annual regatta, first held in 1887 and still a popular event in January each year, and its enormous Moreton Bay fig tree, Ficus macrophyllia. Growing in a park at the heart of this small settlement, this tree, recognised as one of New Zealand's ten most important exotic trees, is a native of Queensland, Australia and really is gigantic. Planted around 1840 the tree has a spread of over 42 metres, is 26 metres high and the huge snake-like roots support massive horizontal branches the easily weigh several tonnes.

📍 End of Pahi Road, 7 km off SH 12 near Paparoa.

30. Skelton's Drapery Paparoa

Drapery and haberdashery are two words no longer associated with modern retailing, but in an era when most women made the family clothes, such stores where just as important as the butcher or greengrocer. All is not lost, as here in rural Papamoa Skelton's Drapery still provides its local community (and loyal customers as far south as Auckland) with everything they need either to make or knit clothing, along with an extensive range of ready to wear modern clothing. Established in 1967 by Doreen and Ron Skelton, the drapery is now run by their daughter Robyn for whom the store has been part of her entire life. While other businesses and the bank have long shut up shop, Skelton's remains at the heart of this small township. The range is incredible; gifts, fashionwear, pattern books, school uniforms, bolts of material workwear, cards, wool, shoes and handbags and of course haberdashery defined in the dictionary as 'small items used in sewing, such as buttons, zips, and thread'. Call in, you are bound to find something you need.

📍 2008 Paparoa Valley Road/SH 12, Paparoa.
🕐 Open Monday to Friday 8.30 am to 5 pm.
   Saturday 9 am to 12 noon.
📞 09 431 7306

31. Tutukaka Coast and the Poor Knights Islands

Lying northeast of Whangarei, Tutukaka is the base for trips to the Poor Knights Islands. Considered one of the top diving spots in the world, the islands are now a marine reserve and are famous for their deep clear waters, underwater caverns and rock formations. Situated between warm tropical and cooler southern currents, the waters surrounding the islands have a spectacular variety of sea life, and boat operators cater for novice snorkellers as well as experienced divers.

North of Tutukaka are the superb beaches of Matapouri, Whale Bay and Sandy Bay.

📍 Tutukaka lies 30 km northeast of Whangarei on a good road.

32. Whangarei Heads

Whangarei Heads is an area of outstanding coastal beauty with sandy beaches, dense bush and rugged peaks rising to 476 m at Bream Head and 420 m at Mt Manaia. These peaks are part of a massive volcano that erupted around 20 million years ago with the remaining sections of the volcano being Bream Head, Mt Lion, Mt Manaia and the Hen and Chickens Islands a few kilometres off the coast. The Bream Head Scenic Reserve is the largest remaining area of coastal forest in the region and contains rare flora and fauna including kiwi, kaka and red-crowned parakeets.

Mt Manaia is easily recognised by the numerous volcanic outcrops that define the peak. In Maori legend the rocky peaks are the figures of the rangatira Manaia, his two daughters and his wife, pursued by the chief from whom Manaia stole his wife, and all turned to stone by the god of thunder. From the top the views are spectacular in all directions, especially over the harbour, Bream Head and far to the south. In the bush near the peak keep an eye out for the rare kaka parrots who you will hear before you see. The track is well formed and takes around two and half hours return. The historic school at the base of the mountain was established in 1858 and the pupils were originally taught in Gaelic, a reflection of the strong Scottish background of the early settlers. The track to the top is from the carpark of the Mt Manaia Club.

Smugglers Cove was once a real smugglers' hideout and not just a fancy name. Imported liquour then, as now, was subject to duties and taxes. Wily Scot's settlers, less than keen on paying the duty to the Customs at Whangarei, rowed out to ships anchored off shore, and smuggled crates of whisky, hiding them in the sand dunes to be recovered later. The ships then sailed on to dock at Whangarei Harbour. This beautiful white sandy beach, overhung with pohutukawa, is only accessible by a twenty minute walk from Urquharts Bay, a walk just far enough to keep this beach uncrowded and often empty during the weekdays even in summer. On Busby Head overlooking the bay is an ancient pa site, and on the headland on the harbour side are the remains of a gun emplacement built during the Second World War to protect the harbour. The track to the cove begins at the car park at the very end of Urquharts Bay Road, Whangarei Heads.

Named Te Whara by Maori after Manaia's principal wife, and Bream Head by Captain Cook when he mistook tarakihi for bream, the coastal views from the summit are nothing short of extraordinary, with only the visibility of the day limiting how far you can see north and south. Out to sea in the distance are Little Barrier and Great Barrier Islands, the Mokohinau Islands and the Coromandel Peninsula, while closer in shore are the Hen and Chickens and the Poor Knights Islands. During the Second World War a top-secret surveillance station was established on Bream Head with radar to scan the waters to the north and warn of any possible attack. This was after the *RMS Niagara* struck a German mine off Bream Head in June 1940; although no lives were lost, a large amount of gold sank with the ship. It is a hard uphill slog, but Ocean Beach below the head is a magnificent surf beach and is an ideal spot for a swim on a summer's day after a tough walk. The track entrance is from the beach access carpark at Ocean Beach.

Whangarei Heads is 30 km east of Whangarei City.

33. Clapham Clock Museum

With over 1700 clocks on display this incredible collection is the largest in the southern hemisphere. Begun by local man, Archibald Clapham in 1900 and gifted to the city in 1961, the huge variety of clocks includes everything from long case and cuckoo clocks through to alarm clocks and wristwatches.

Nineteenth-century clocks make up a significant part of the collection and many of the clocks were brought to this country by early settlers, including the intriguing 1820 Ballet Clock, which was a music box to which a clock was later added. The oldest dated clock is a Charles Gretton Longcase clock from 1690, though a clock built by a blacksmith is thought to be much older. Particularly appealing is the Rolling Ball Clock from 1970, and more recently the collection has expanded to include 400 wristwatches.

The collection includes the Speakers Clock. Made especially for the New Zealand Parliament, this simple clock didn't tell the time as such, but allowed the speaker of the house to time parliamentary speeches with one hour being the maximum. Only marked with quarter, half, and three-quarter the clock was controlled by a switch next to the speaker's chair.

The museum is in the attractive Town Basin, a collection of cafes and shops alongside the yacht-lined inner harbour.

- Town Basin, Dent St, Whangarei.
- Open daily 9 am to 5 pm.
- 09 438 3993
- www.claphamsclocks.com
- Entrance fee.

34. Whangarei Quarry Gardens

Whangarei has a definite subtropical climate; moist all year round, ground frosts are rare and summer temperatures seldom go over 30°C. Combine this climate with an old quarry with heat-reflecting rocks and sheltered from cooling breezes and you have the perfect environment to grow a very unique garden. Established as a stone quarry in 1944, the enterprise came to an end in 1974 when flooding made the operation unviable and the owners then donated the 25-hectare site to the Whangarei District Council as part of their parks and reserves network. Clearly the donation wasn't particularly welcome, as for the next twenty years, the old quarry was ignored, overgrown with weeds and used as dumping ground for rubbish.

Local Laughton King clearly had a much greater vision and approached the council for permission to create a public garden, which they quickly agreed to, and a 'Friends of the Quarry Garden' was established. Not daunted by the herculean task ahead, a band of enthusiastic volunteers set to work to clear the quarry of weeds and rubbish, aided by local contractors who donated machinery and labour to the formidable task. Over the next five years, the Trust created a small lake, two waterfalls, two bridges and planted thousands of plants.

Much of that work went up in smoke when in 2005 an arsonist set four fires in the steep hillsides resulting in the loss of a large section of native trees. Used to hard work in difficult situations, in one day in May 2006 a small army of volunteers planted 10,000 trees.

Gradually the gardens took shape with tender trees and shrubs flourishing in the benign climate and sheltered valley, and today the former old quarry once abandoned and full of weeds and rubbish, is one of this country's most delightful public gardens. There are even kiwi roaming the native bush surrounding the main gardens.

The five key plantings are the Native Forest, Arid Garden, Fragrant Camellia Garden, Five Senses Garden and the Bromeliad Garden, but the range of plants is much wider than this. A series of easy paths links the gardens with plenty of places to sit in the shade in summer or enjoy the sun in winter. The quarry's industrial past is not forgotten, and concrete foundations and some machine has been retained.

In November 2015, the Visitors Centre – which includes a café – was opened, making this the perfect destination for a half day out.

📍 37a Russell Road, Kensington, just off SH 1, Whangarei.
🕐 Open daily 9 am to 5 pm.
   Café open Wednesday to Sunday 9 am to 3 pm.
📞 09 437 7210
🌐 www.whangareigardens.org.nz

35. Packard Motor Museum

Let's face it, this is going to be the only collection of 125 historic potato mashers you are ever going to see and to be honest, potato mashers are last thing you would expect in the museum called the Packard Motor Museum. Or is that the Packard and Pioneer Museum? Even the name is a bit confused. The potato mashers and the name are a good clue as to what this extraordinary museum, just outside Whangarei, is all about. Yes, there are Packards, lots of them, but there is also a lot of everything else so come prepared for the unusual, the unexpected and the downright odd and that's why the potato mashers fit right in.

Machines are at the heart of this sprawling museum in an old dairy factory, ranging from the Packard collection which started the whole thing off in the early 1950s, through to motorbikes, tractors, steam engines, fire engines, earth moving machines and every agriculture machine you can think of. However, there are also sewing machines, old telephones, money boxes, vacuum cleaners and radios. There is rarely just one of anything and some of the collections are would fill a small museum on their own. Most of the material is well displayed, but it does get a little piled up in the back shed. Gems are everywhere, but there are helpful staff you help you pick your way through it.

Finally, saving the best till last, there is one exhibit that really demonstrates how incredible this collection is and that is the 4" gun turret from the legendary battleship the *HMS Achilles*. The *Achilles* ended up in the Indian

Navy in 1948 and was scrapped in 1978. At the time another gun turret was presented to the New Zealand Navy Museum in Devonport and how these guns ended up in Maungatapere is a whole other story.

- 📍 Old Dairy Factory SH 14, Maungatapere, Whangarei.
- 🕒 Open Wednesday to Saturday 10 am to 4 pm.
- 🌐 www.packardmuseum.co.nz
- 📞 09 434 8214
- $ Entrance fee.

36. Marsden Point Oil Refinery

New Zealanders are not used to seeing large industrial complexes and this oil refinery does sit oddly in the stunning landscape of Whangarei Heads. Opened in May 1964, the site at Marsden Point was chosen primarily for its access to a deep water port, but also the availability of flatland, its low earthquake risk and proximity to the larger population in the North Island.

It was expanded in 1973 and again in 1981 when a 168 km underground pipeline was constructed from the refinery to a holding depot in Wiri, Auckland. Marsden Point refinery imports medium-sour oils and produces 70 per cent of New Zealand's oil needs including premium and regular gasoline, automotive and marine diesel, aviation and lighting kerosene, fuel oils and bitumen. Oddly New Zealand does produce light-sweet oil, but this can't be refined at Marsden Point and is exported to refineries in Australia.

The visitor centre has extensive displays on the history and operation of the the refinery, including a large scale model of the complex.

- 📍 Marsden Point Road, Ruakaka.
- 🕒 Open 10 am to 5 pm Monday to Friday.

📞   09 432 8311
🌐   www.refiningnz.com

37. Waipu

Waipu is one small town that takes its history seriously, and so it should as it has the most unusual and unique story of any New Zealand town. Charismatic religious leader Norman McLeod left Scotland in 1817 and settled in Nova Scotia, Canada where over the next thirty-five years hundreds more followers joined him, and they became known as Normanites. Finding Canada too tough, the band moved first to Australia before finally arriving in the Waipu area in 1853. While most settled in the Waipu area, many families also settled in Leigh, and around Whangarei Heads. By the end of 1860 nearly 900 people from nineteen Scottish clans had arrived in the area. Norman McLeod died in 1866. The local museum, known as the House of Memories, houses an extensive collection related to the extraordinary double migration and in the main street a tall pillar topped by a Scottish Lion commemorates the early settlers.

Over time the Gaelic influence waned, but every New Year's Day, Waipu hosts the largest highland games in the southern hemisphere. Held annually since 1871 and attracting visitors both locally and internationally, the games feature Highland dancing, piping, drumming, tossing the caber, hammer throwing and tossing the sheaf.

📍   Waipu is just off SH 1, 40 km south of Whangarei.

38. Waipu Caves

This cave system, just a short walk from the road, features limestone formations, stalactites and stalagmites; and, deep within the cave, glow-worms. Glow-worms are lavae of the insect *Arachnocampa luminosa* or the fungus gnat. The lavae produce a light that attracts other insects on which the glow-worms feed. In a particularly clever evolutionary adaption, the hungrier the lavae, the brighter the light, though interestingly the adult insect has no mouth and doesn't eat at all, living only a few days. A torch is essential as the caves are quite deep and it is necessary to wade through shallow water to see the glow-worms, which are about 100 m to the left from the cave entrance.

> 13 km from SH 1 – clearly signposted at several points between Waipu and Whangarei.
> (the last 5 km of the road is unsealed and narrow.)

39. Te Arai Point

Te Arai Point is a large rocky outcrop, the only break in the huge sweep of beach and dunes that run from Mangawhai in the north to Pakiri in the south. Cleared of forest by Maori, the vast area became a landscape of shifting dunes until pine trees were planted in the 1930s.

With only 15 per cent of Auckland's dune habitat remaining, the area north and south of Te Arai Point is the largest expanse of dune country in the region. Unlike other Auckland/east coast beaches, this stretch of coast is not protected from inclement weather by the islands of the gulf and the beaches experience greater swells and surf than beaches further south.

From the main car park on the north side of the point, it is a short 30-minute walk to the southern beach and from the headland there are stunning views over the beaches and the gulf. A tiny cove on the rocky peninsula provides a safe swimming hole away from the open beach. This stretch of coast is also the only place you are likely to see the critically endangered Fairy Tern (*Sterna nereis davisae*). One of New Zealand's most endangered birds, with less than ten breeding pairs in existence (in 1984 just three pairs remained), Fairy terns only breed only along this coast and the very top of the South Head of the Kaipara. However, they do range over a wide area to feed and are easily distinguished by their small size, distinctive black caps, yellow bill and orange legs with a white chest and contrasting grey body.

Facilities are limited, just a small car park, toilets and limited camping with a permit. Although busy on weekends over summer, the beaches are often deserted the rest of the year.

📍 End of Te Arai Point Road (most of this road is unsealed).

40. Utopia Café, Kaiwaka

Familiar to anyone travelling regular north of Auckand, the Utopia Café at Kaiwaka appears interesting, but somehow never seems worth pulling over for. Built by wizard and artist Peter Harris, the style is 1960s hippy with a good deal of Hobbiton thrown in. Utopia never really took off and was eventually sold to another local artist Marjike Valkenburg and then things really looked up. Now well worth the stop, Utopia will not fail to raise a smile in even the most jaded heart. The tiny alcoves and fountain courtyard, with not a straight line in sight, are highly decorated with glass mosaics, paintings and sculptures. The result is an appealing fantasy world with a surprise in every corner and the toilets are a treat.

However, decoration counts for little if the food is not good and here Utopia has really picked up the game with great organic coffee and excellent food with a focus on fresh seasonal ingredients.

It's now time to stop driving past Utopia.

📍 1955 State Highway 1, Kaiwaka.
🕐 Open Tuesday to Sunday 7.30 am to 4 pm.
📞 09 431 2222

AUCKLAND

1. Brick Bay Winery
2. Parry Kauri Park
3. Warkworth Cement Works
4. Puhoi
5. Dacre Cottage and Okura Bush
6. Glow-worm grotto. Awaruka Bush Reserve
7. Disappearing Gun, North Head Historic Reserve
8. Smith's Bush/Northcote Domain
9. Kauri Point Beach, Fitzpatrick Bay
10. Under the Auckland Harbour Bridge
11. Auckland's 'Old City'
12. Tepid Baths
13. 1YA Radio Station
14. The Civic Theatre
15. Tiny Auckland Houses
16. Karangahape Road/K'Rd
17. Grafton Bridge and the Symonds Street Cemetery
18. The Auckland Domain
19. The Container Port, Auckland
20. Highwic House
21. Eden Gardens
22. Parnell Pool
23. Savage Memorial Park
24. Melanesian Mission
25. Cornwall Park and One Tree Hill Domain/ Maungakiekie
26. Coast to Coast Walkway
27. Avondale Spiders
28. Avondale Market
29. The Pah, Hillsborough
30. Onehunga Blockhouse

31. Auckland Potters Studio, Onehunga
32. Otahuhu War Memorials
33. One city, 55 volcanoes
34. Ash bank, Farm Cove Walkway
35. All Saints Anglican Church, Howick
36. Fo Guang Shan Temple
37. Ayrlies Garden
38. Duders Regional Park
39. Tawhitokino Bay
40. South Kaipara Head
41. Bethells Beach/Te Henga, O'Neill Bay and Lake Waimanu
42. Totara Waters
43. Hobson's Gum Hobsonville
44. Te Ahua Point
45. Waikumete Cemetery
46. Mazuran's Wines
47. Babich Winery
48. The Huia to Whatipu Road
49. Otara Market
50. Rainbow's End Rollercoaster
51. Otuataua Stonefields
52. Ihumatao Fossilised Forest
53. Kentish Hotel
54. The Awhitu Peninsula

North

1. Brick Bay Winery

Bush, wine, art and food is the perfect combination for any day out. Brick Bay Winery is nestled in a steep-sloped valley behind Snells Beach and the first grove of olives was planted in 1992 and two years later a vineyard was laid out on either side of the valley. In 1998 the winery produced its first vintage and today Brick Bay offers a range of wines including chardonnay, pinot gris and their signature wine, Pharos, a blend of red grapes.

At the heart of the vineyard is the immensely stylish 'Glasshouse', designed by Auckland architect Noel Lane. As the name suggests this glass building, with warm Tasmanian oak floors, is a restaurant, and straddles a pond fringed with large swathes of waterlilies. A grape arbour on the slope above is perfect for summer dining (lunch only).

What makes this place even more special, is not only have the surrounding bush remnants been preserved, but over 30,000 trees, both native and exotic, have been planted over the last thirty years. Now well-formed easy tracks wind through bush, past wetlands and ponds, under a grove of mature kahikatea trees and across grassy clearings.

If that is not enough, the bush trail has been turned into an outdoor gallery of works (around seventy) by leading New Zealand artists which are also for sale. There is an entry fee to the sculpture garden which includes a list of all the works on display and a guide to flora and fauna. The walk through the bush and sculptures takes around one hour.

- Arabelle Lane, Snells Beach.
- Open daily 10 am to 5 pm.
- www.brickbay.co.nz
- Entrance fee to sculpture park

2. Parry Kauri Park

Covering just two hectares, this tiny reserve is the best example of kauri forest in the Auckland region. Parry Kauri Park is unusual in the Auckland area, in that the bush is dominated by kauri, and sizeable ones at that. More importantly, it is now one of the very few places that the public can see mature kauri trees, as the track is largely on boardwalks and remains open as the forest has so far escaped kauri dieback disease.

Right by the carpark and at the entrance to the loop track is the majestic McKinney kauri, named for the original European landowner, the local Presbyterian Minister Reverend McKinney. Reaching a height of 38 metres, it is almost 12 metres to the first limb and over seven and a half metres in circumference. The Mckinney kauri is estimated to be approximately 800 years old and the largest kauri tree on the east coast.

In addition to kauri there are numerous kahikatea and good examples of rewarewa, rimu, tanekaha, kohekohe, taraire, karaka and totara, many of which are marked to assist in identification. The loop walk takes about twenty minutes. The park is adjacent to the Warkworth Museum and in the carpark are relics of the early saw milling operations.

From SH 1, 2 km south of Warkworth, turn into Mckinney Road and then right into Thompson Road and continue to the Warkworth Museum.

3. Warkworth Cement Works

New Zealanders are good at making do. In the absence of hilltop castles, ancient churches and ruined abbeys, we make do with the ruin of an old cement works and in reality it is not a bad substitute.

Cement production began here as early as the 1850s and, located on the banks of the Mahurangi River, was shipped south to Auckland, then the capital of New Zealand. Expanding over the years, and now known as the Wilson's Portland Cement Works, the complex produced 20,000 tonnes of cement annually by 1903. However, in 1918, the company amalgamated with the New Zealand Portland Cement Company and with production shifted to the Whangarei works, the Mahurangi operation finally closed in 1929.

At the peak of their operation, the works covered the entire flat area alongside the river, but gradually the timber and corrugated iron buildings were demolished and only the substantial brick kilns and tower chimneys remain today. The site is a Heritage New Zealand, Category 1 historic place and an IPENZ Engineering Heritage site.

Overgrown but still impressive, the deep lime pit on the western side of the works is now full of water and a very popular swimming hole. Around the crumbling brick ruins are wide grassy areas and shady trees which, together with the swimming hole, make this an ideal summer destination.

📍 End of Wilson Road, Warkworth.

4. Puhoi

Puhoi is certainly the original New Zealand 'detour'. The popular Kiwi slang saying 'Up the boohai', meaning the back of beyond, is said to have been derived from 'Up the Puhoi' and reflects how isolated the area was in the nineteenth century.

In 1863 a small group of settlers from villages near Pilsen in Bohemia settled along the Puhoi River north of Auckland. With help from local Maori, who supported the settlers through their first year, the number of Bohemians eventually numbered around 200 by 1881, and the area still retains a strong Bohemian flavour. A small museum has been set up in the old convent school (the settlers were Roman Catholic), and the church of St Peter and St Paul, built 1881, has stained-glasses windows featuring local family names such as Schollum, Rauner, Schischka, Wenzlick, Bayer and Straka. The historic Puhoi Pub, first named the German Hotel, is a firm local favourite, as is the Puhoi Valley Cheese Factory 3 km up the road from the village. The village is also a popular starting point for kayaking on the Puhoi River.

📍 1 km off SH 1, 8 km north of Orewa.

5. Dacre Cottage and Okura Bush

In 1848 retired sea captain Ranulph Dacre purchased the land around Karepiro Bay along the tidal Weiti River. Later, sometime in the early 1850s, his son Henry built a small cottage in the bay that is unusual in both style and construction. The house, consisting of just two rooms, was built of brick at a time when wood was the common choice of building material, being both cheap and readily available. The square floor plan and hip roof also differs from the usual gable roof line and veranda style of most New Zealand colonial cottages and is more Australian in style. Now restored, the cottage is only accessible on foot (or by water) along the attractive Okura Bush Walkway (two hours return). However, extensive housing development on the slopes behind the cottage is likely to change the access to this quiet picturesque bay. The cottage is unfortunately closed due to continued vandalism, but the bay is a good spot for a picnic and at high tide is good for swimming.

📍 Drive north from the intersection of East Coast Bays Road and Oteha Valley Road; after 4.5 km turn right into Haigh Access Road and the track begins at the end of the road.

6. Glow-worm grotto. Awaruku Bush Reserve

The glow-worm/titiwai is common throughout New Zealand and can be found in clusters in caves, the banks of streams and almost any damp overhang, although it is usually in caves that they are the most impressive.

Here in a small abandoned quarry in the Awaruku Reserve behind Torbay, the conditions are ideal for this fascinating little insect. Set aside as a reserve in the late 1960s, this small patch of bush contains ancient kahikatea, kohekohe, rewarewa, tanekaha towai and several huge old puriri, with one tree around 500 years old. Thriving in the wet, mild climate the understory is dense with nikau, kiekie and ferns. In the early 1900s a small quarry was developed, but as the stone was unsuitable for road works, it was quickly abandoned. Today it is a damp grotto of dripping water and lush with mosses, the perfect environment for the New Zealand glow-worm. There are not lots of glow-worms so don't come expecting a mini Waitomo, but the night here is pitch black and scattered on the old rockface are tiny pinpricks of sparkling light.

There isn't a map at the entrance or any other direction signage in the reserve, but it is only 3 ha so it is impossible to get lost during the day, but at night a torch is essential.

📍 17 Awaruku Road, Torbay.

7. Disappearing Gun, North Head Historic Reserve

Formed by an eruption 50,000 years ago, this area attracted Maori with its rich volcanic soil and easy access to seafood, but despite its superb location, North Head/Maunguika was never fortified and the main pa in the area was on nearby Mt Victoria/Takarunga.

A pilot station was established as early as 1836 but it wasn't until 1885, with the threat of a Russian attack, that the government constructed three batteries to protect the approaches to Auckland. Most of the tunnels and underground rooms visible today were built at this time, as were the two oldest buildings on the summit, a small stone kitchen and army barracks.

The disappearing gun still intact on the South Battery was one of three placed on North Head in 1887. Weighing 23.5 tonnes it was built in Britain in 1886 at the Elswick Ordinance Works, though this particular model was only used in Australia and New Zealand. Originally placed on the summit, the gun fired 95 kg shells a distance of 2.5 kilometres and, once it was fired, the recoil of the huge gun pushed it below ground level to be reloaded undercover.

Only ever fired in practice, this gun is one of very few left in the world and was saved from scrap in 1953 and moved to its present position as a war memorial to gunners.

Below North Head at Torpedo Bay is the excellent Naval/Navy Museum and ideal spot to wrap up a walk around North Head.

📍 Main entrance at end of Takarunga Road, Cheltenham.

📍 North Head is an easy 2 km walk from the Devonport ferry.

8. Smith's Bush/Northcote Domain

Botanically Smith's Bush is a curiosity. The bush is dominated by kahikatea, a tree that favours swamp land, but the area is not wet and most of the trees are not more than one hundred years old indicating that the kahikatea are more recent colonisers. Dispersed among the kahikatea are much older puriri, one of which has five huge trunks, and, very surprising for this coastal location, there are no pohutukawa or kauri.

Familiar to those who frequently travel on the Northern Motorway, this tiny bush remnant has struggled to survive. Originally milled for timber, the reserve was devastated by the creation of the motorway in the late fifties which cut right through the heart of the bush. The reserve was further reduced with the recent widening of the motorway for the bus lane so now just a narrow sliver of trees survives on eastern side of the motorway; despite this Smith's Bush still remains magnificent.

📍 Near to the Takapuna Cricket Club, Northcote Road, Northcote.

9. Kauri Point Beach, Fitzpatrick Bay

First consult your tide tables before setting out for Kauri Point Beach, unless of course you are just walking the dog or feel like a pleasant stroll. At high tide however, this is a lovely swimmable beach in a hidden cove just 10 km from central Auckland. Officially this is Fitzpatrick Bay in Kauri Point Domain, but ask locals directions to Fitzpatrick Bay and you are very likely to receive blank stares. Most people know this bay as Kauri Point Beach in Balmain Domain; in the end it's all the same place.

Only accessible on foot, it's an easy 10-minute walk from the end of Balmain Road through regenerating bush to a large swath of grass above a small sandy beach. Facing south west, it's a bit exposed to westerly winds but it also captures all the heat of the sun late in the day. The shallow water is ideal for small children and as this is also a dog park, your pooch can run around and swim all it likes.

Parking is very limited at the end of Balmain Road so you might have to walk a bit to the start of the track.

📍 End of Balmain Road off Waipa Street, Chatswood.

10. Under the Auckland Harbour Bridge

Needing no introduction to both locals and visitors alike, the Auckland Harbour Bridge is one of this city's most striking icons. A huge undertaking, the bridge was stretched to capacity from the day it opened in May 1959, with over 13,000 vehicles crossing the bridge daily in the first year, when planners had expected daily usage to reach 8500 only by 1965. However, by 1965, 10 million vehicles crossed the bridge each year, three times the forecast. Within ten years of opening, the bridge expanded another four lanes with the addition of the 'Nippon Clippon' in 1969, but the numbers kept growing to 80,000 vehicles daily in 1970 and to 165,000 by 2000.

It is extremely likely that every Aucklander and every visitor has crossed the bridge at some time, but few people take the time to go under the bridge when it meets Northcote Point. The first surprise is how many houses there are and how close they are to the traffic deck of the bridge; the rumble of vehicles must be constant, and they must all surely have triple glazing, but even so the grit and grim from exhausts must be a constant problem.

Another surprise is that right on the point are the remains of the old Onewa Pa. Through the two centuries before the European settlement, the pa was hotly contested turf passing through the hands of Ngati Tai, Ngati Whatua and Ngati Paoa before being sold to the Government in 1840. Just the defensive ditch remains of the pa, but carved pou by artist Reuben Kirkwood was erected in February 2018 when the council upgraded the area under the bridge.

Unlike the southern end of the bridge, visitors on this side can get right under the structure and at one point, cars, trucks and buses thunder just a few metres above your head. Here the scale and detail of the structure is laid bare, with the tall concrete pylons rising out of the water and huge iron girders bearing the weight of the constant traffic. It doesn't bear thinking about that the clippon was estimated to have a life of fifty years in 1969. An appealing touch is the literary quotes that adorn a series of pillars, each becoming longer as the pillars grow taller.

On the western side of point in the lee of the bridge is a small boatyard and boat ramp, a peaceful seaside scene if you block your ears and don't look up.

📍 South end of Princes Street, Northcote.

Auckland City

11. Auckland's 'Old City'

The idea of an 'old town' is very European so it is odd to think of Auckland as having an 'old town', but it does, though naturally it is a good deal younger than its European counterparts.

Both Maori and Europeans settled on what was known to early Europeans as Britomart Point, between Commercial Bay (Lower Queen Street) and Official Bay (Beach Road). Queen Street at the time was a swampy creek, Horotiu Stream. Running through the heart of this headland are three main streets, Shortland, Princes and Anzac Avenue/Symonds Street (previously Jermyn Street) and in this small area are the majority of Auckland's most important historic buildings. Prior to European settlement two pa were known to occupy this area, one where the High Court now stands and the other in Albert Park, though no trace of either pa remains.

The area is packed with historic buildings, the most important of which are the following:

Debretts Hotel

Originally constructed in 1841, the hotel was rebuilt in 1860 and remodelled in the Art Deco style in 1926.

📍 Cnr Shortland Street and High Street.

Colonial Cottage

This lone survivor of a four roomed workers dwelling was built in 1884 and unusual in that it is built of concrete rather than wood.

📍 Bankside Street.

Emily Place

At the heart of the colonial settlement is the Churton Memorial in remembrance of the first vicar of St Pauls Anglican Church. Now known for its spectacular pohutukawa trees.

Eden Hall

Striking mid-1930s Art Deco building, designed by architect Reginald Hammond as quality inner city apartments, highly unusual for the period.

📍 3 Eden Crescent.

The Northern Club

Originally built an hotel in 1841, the building opened in 1867 as government offices and was purchased two years later and became the Northern Club.

📍 19 Princess Street.

Parliament Street

The name Parliament Street is a reminder of Auckland's brief period as New Zealand's capital city from 1841–1865.

Corner Courteville, Middle Courteville and Braemar House, Parliament Street

Three fine examples of early twentieth century flats built for professional city dwellers.

Auckland High Court, Waterloo Quadrant

Constructed between 1865–1868 in the fashionable Gothic Revival style, particular appealing are the carvings of local dignitaries.

St Andrews Church

This Presbyterian Church is built in a simple style of local basalt and is Auckland's oldest surviving church opened in 1850.

📍 2 Symonds Street.

Old Choral Hall

One of the largest surviving nineteenth century buildings in Auckland the hall, built in 1872, could hold over 1000 people.

📍 7 Symonds Street.

Old Government House

Built for the Governor of New Zealand in 1856 when Auckland was still the capital.

📍 Waterloo Quadrant.

Synagogue

Combining Moorish and Romanesque elements, the synagogue was opened in 1885.

📍 19a Princes Street.

Princes Street – Merchant Houses

Princes Street in the late nineteenth century was Auckand's most desirable address and these five houses were built by Auckland's leading merchants.

Old Arts Building, Auckland University

Designed by American architects and opened in 1926, this building was highly controversial at the time and criticised for being 'not English enough'. Highly unusual for the use of New Zealand motifs in the decoration.

📍 22 Princes Street.

Albert Park

Originally the site of the Te Horotiu Pa, in 1845 the Albert Barracks were established and substantially fortified in the 1860s. The park retains a strong Victorian flavour with statues of Queen Victoria and Sir George

Grey, an elegant band rotunda. and the quaint caretakers lodge. The park has a number of notable trees.

○ 33 – 43 Princes Street.

Auckland Art Gallery

Originally the city library, this building in the French Renaissance style was opened in 1887 and finally became a dedicated art gallery in 1971.

○ 1 Kitchener Street.

12. Tepid Baths

A saltwater pool conveniently filled at high tide existed on the waterfront since Victorian times, but in 1914 the covered Tepid Baths were constructed. Originally divided into separate 'male' and 'female' pools, the former 'male' pool is now the main 25-m lap pool and the 'female' pool is a shallow pool for younger swimmers. In 1974, freshwater replaced the saltwater and in 2010 the pools were closed for a renovation that cost over $15 million, and now upgraded with modern facilities, the pool still retains its distinctive Edwardian atmosphere and style.

○ 100 Customs Street, City.

13. 1YA Radio Station

Not only one of Auckland's most unusual buildings, but the former 1YA Radio Station is at the heart of this country's radio and television history. Although built in 1934, this building is designed in the flamboyant

Romanesque style, rather than the streamlined Art Deco that was far more popular at the time. Fortress-like, this was the first purpose-built radio station with massive thick brick walls and no external windows. Internally, the building is more Art Deco in style and particular impressive is the stained-glass dome over the old reception area, while at street level the old 1YA entrance lamps were restored in 2009. Below the building on Shortland Street are several more floors of studios and it was from one of the lower studios that New Zealand's first official television broadcast was made in 1961.

The top floor off Shortland Street is now the Gus Fisher Gallery and open to the public (www.gusfishergallery.auckland.ac.nz).

Q 74 Shortland St.

14. The Civic Theatre

Built in less than a year, the Civic opened in December 1929, New Zealand's first purpose-built picture theatre and the largest surviving 'Atmospheric' theatre in Australasia. This style of theatre moved away from simple box like structures, and aimed to recreate an exotic location and dramatic atmosphere. The Civic's main auditorium is designed to represent an open-air theatre, with eastern arches and a twinkling star-studded ceiling, while the foyer areas are heavily decorated in a faux Oriental style, happily mixing up any number of art styles. The result is eclectic, endearing and just plain mad. In the depression years, the Civic must indeed have lived up to its reputation as a 'picture palace'.

During the Second World War, a nightclub in the basement level was popular with American troops on R&R in Auckland, attracted no doubt by the dancer Freda Stark who was famous for performing clad only in gold paint. Completely restored in recent years, the Civic continues to show films and host live shows.

Q Corner of Wellesley and Queen Streets.

15. Tiny Auckland Houses

At first glance, central Auckland is a modern city of high rise with its older built heritage somewhat lost. Those older surviving buildings are mostly larger public structures, grand houses and elegant buildings. However, hidden away are three groups of working-class houses, each constructed in different materials: wood, stone and concrete.

Nicholas Street

The two wooden houses in Nicholas Street are the most typical of the period, and as such it is extraordinary that they have survived in the middle of city. One room wide, two stories high with a simple but elegant veranda across the front, each cottage sits on less than 75 sq metres of land. Built in the 1890s, the exteriors are largely original, though the interiors are thoroughly modern.

📍 5/7 Nicholas Street, south of Cook Street between Hobson and Nelson.

Airedale Street

Equally small, but quite different are two rare stone terrace houses in Airedale Street. Constructed in three stages, the cottage on the left was built first by stone mason Thomas Rushden around 1856/1857, with the cottage on the right following in the early 1860s. Partly stuccoed, the volcanic stone construction is clearly visible on the left of the building. Initially the both houses were just one room up and one room down with the front door opening directly into the main downstairs room and steep ladder-like stairs to the upper storey. Two rear rooms were finally added in 1882 with few changes since. From the 1940s the houses were used for commercial purposes, but today they are again private residences and beautiful preserved.

📍 30 Airedale Street.

Bankside Street

Of concrete construction, the last house in Bankside Street was built in 1883-1884 when this steep slope below elegant Princes Street was crowded with small working-class cottages. It is likely that an older wooden house previously stood on the site, but why this cottage was built of concrete is a mystery as concrete was both rare and expensive at the time. A possible explanation is that at the time several larger concrete buildings nearby were under construction, making the material readily available. Consisting of just four rooms (a front parlour, kitchen and two tiny bedrooms), the house was initially home to a family of seven. Saved from demolition in 1984, today the tiny cottage has been meticulously restored, including the unique wooden shingle roof.

📍 10 Bankside Street, off Shortland Street.

16. Karangahape Road/K'Rd

Karangahape Road has always been one of Auckland most important streets. It was the beginning of the Great North Road, the main thoroughfare leading west out of the city and by the early and mid 20th century, the street, usually referred to as just K'Rd, became the city's leading shopping street, lined with impressive department stores and the best shops in town.

When the motorways destroyed much of the housing in the area, the street declined, the grand shops closing to be replaced by strip clubs, dodgy bars and street prostitution. Now high-rise apartments are changing the street yet again and today is a mix of eclectic shops, lively cafes, stylish and not so stylish bars, and is a good deal less sleazy.

The fine George Court building at 244 Karangahape Rd was opened in 1926 and modelled on Selfridges in London. Six floors of shopping, linked by lifts and elegant staircases, and crowned by rooftop tearooms, this was the place to shop in Auckland. Converted to apartments in 1993, the store still dominates the street skyline.

Not surprisingly, the busy thoroughfare was the ideal location for city hotels and the first, the Naval Hotel, was built by Patrick Darby in 1862. In 1882 the name changed to the odd combination of Naval and Family Hotel and when the wooden pub went up in flames in 1894, a splendid new hotel rose from the ashes. Three storeys high, it was typical of the late Victorian corner pub and the exterior has changed little over the last 120 years. Inside the hotel is another matter with the configuration of the ground floor substantially altered in the 1930s, and by 1972 the Naval and Family had become a tavern and recently home to Calendar Girls, a strip club which still occupies the first and second floors. Now the ground floor is the Pitt St Pub while, in the intervening years all the other old hotels in the street have been demolished or closed down, and once the first hotel on K'Rd, the Family and Naval is now the last pub standing.

○ Corner Karangahape Road and Pitt Street.

Another great survivor is the intriguing St Kevins Arcade. Constructed in 1924, the arcade was home to tailors, dressmakers and photography studios, while at the north end overlooking Myers Park was a tearoom. Little altered, now nearly 100 years later, a café still looks over the park and the arcade is home to small stores and the popular Gemmayze Street Lebanese Restaurant. In the park below, linked to the arcade by a flight of stairs, is a full-sized statue of Michelangelo's Moses. Made from marble from the same quarry as the original, the statue was imported by Milne and Choyce Department store in 1971 and gifted to the city in 1973. One of a pair, the other statue was the naked David which the city declined on the grounds of 'good taste' and the fate of the David statue is unknown.

Radically different from the older buildings is the former Newton Post Office. Built in 1974 and designed by Ron Sang, it is considered an outstanding example of modernist architecture. Equally notable is the starburst bronze bas-relief sculpture on the exterior created by the leading New Zealand Chinese artist Guy Ngan. The building is on the corner of Karangahape Road and East Street.

17. Grafton Bridge and the Symonds Street Cemetery

Spanning Grafton Gully between Symonds Street and Grafton Road this bridge, opened in 1910, was, at the time, a special feat of modern engineering as the longest reinforced concrete arch in the southern hemisphere. At 97 m long and 43 m high, the bridge is anchored at either end by massive concrete piers with the footpaths cantilevered over the gully and, while ordinary from above, the bridge is much more impressive viewed from below. A perspex barrier is now in place to deter jumpers.

Below the bridge is the old Symonds Street Cemetery originally established by the Church of England in 1846 when this area was on the outskirts of the tiny settlement. Closed in 1886, the cemetery straddles both sides of Symonds Street and when the motorway was extended, over 4100 graves were removed. The cemetery is divided into different religious denominations as was common at the time, including Presbyterian, Roman Catholic, Anglican and the distinctive Jewish section on the corner of Symonds Street and Karangahape Road.

Many notable people are buried in the cemetery including New Zealand's first Governor, Captain William Hobson, who died on 10 September 1842. His grave is located between Grafton Bridge and the on-ramp to the Southern Motorway.

📍 Intersection of Symonds Street, Grafton Bridge and Karangahape Road.

18. The Auckland Domain

Although the Auckland War Memorial Museum attracts around one million visitors each year, far fewer take time to stroll around this huge 75-ha park which holds several surprises.

Auckland oldest public park (established 1843) is it also Auckland's oldest volcano dating back 130,000 years and the magnificent museum (opened 1929) sits on its northern rim from where the views of the Hauraki Gulf are spectacular.

The park has strong Maori connections, containing a major pa site (Pukekawa) and a tribute to the first Maori king, Potatau Te Wherowhero, a totara tree enclosed by a fence stands on the top of the old pa.

In 1913-14 a huge temporary pavilion was erected in the Domain for the Great Industrial Exhibition; the only surviving reminder is the 'ideal New Zealand House' which is now the restaurant by the duck ponds.

The elegant Winter Gardens comprise two large glasshouses linked by a formal courtyard and ornamental pond. Recently restored, the houses were completed in 1921 but lack of funds delayed the opening of the complex until 1928. The northern 'cool' house contains temperate plants and has a continual and stunning display of flowering plants, while the southern 'hot' house contains tropical plants. Behind the pool is a deep hole, originally an old quarry and now the site of the Fernery. Incredibly the 'hot' house contains 2000 plants including a large cocoa tree, a plant normally found in the tropics and within this warm environment is the only such tree in the country to actual produce fruit.

The gateway arch to the park off Grafton Road, built in 1935, and the statue on top attracted great controversy. Created by New Zealand artist Richard Gross, the council were unaware that the statue of an athlete man was to be totally nude and depict his genitals. While there was no doubt regarding its artistic merits, the nude man was perceived by many to have a corrupting influence on the youth at that time. The Council voted to erect the statue unaltered and genitals intact by defeating a proposal to 'modify the statue to conform to public good taste' by 14 votes to 5.

Within the park are a mixture of bush walks, playing fields, formal gardens, an eclectic collection of old statuary and new sculpture, and hidden behind the hospital a couple of small paddocks still contain cattle and are a reminder of the Domain's origin as a farm. Popular with local runners, several of the tracks have acquired curious nicknames, such as the Red Path and the Ho Chi Minh Trail.

The Symphony under the Stars concert in February holds the record for the largest classical music concert in the world, attracting around 200,000 people. Naturally the theme is classical music and a firm favourite, Tchaikovsky's 1812 Overture, is complete with cannon fire supplied by the New Zealand Army.

📍 The main entrance to the Domain is in Park Street, Grafton.

19. The Container Port, Auckland

Once at the very heart of the city, modern container shipping has now moved to the fringes, or as in many cities, completely removed from central city. In Auckand the shipping wharves have moved just to east of the business district, but with increased security, public access is no longer possible. However, if you have time on your hand, this small parking area in Gladstone Road, Parnell is the perfect spot to watch great ships slide in and out of the port and to observe the frantic business of unloading and moving thousands of containers.

📍 Gladstone Road, Parnell.

20. Highwic House

It's hard to conceive of building a house from a 'pattern book', yet that is precisely the genesis of Highwic House, which is described as one of New Zealand's 'finest timber Gothic houses'. Still in print today and mainly used for renovation, AJ Downing's *The Architecture of the Country House* contained thirty-four designs for model houses with floor plans, elevations and detailed information on design, function and construction. Although published in the United States, the book took its inspiration from Europe, primarily Britain with Gothic, French and Italian designs thrown in for good measure. First published in 1850, by 1866 it had been through nine editions. Key to the success of the plans were that they focussed on stylish, efficient, yet low-priced house that included features that previously were only found in the mansions of the rich.

Like many early houses, Highwic expanded considerably over the years, with the original house constructed in 1862 by Alfred and Eliza Buckland to house their twenty-one children; Highwic House remained in the same family until 1978.

- Corner of Gillies Avenue and Mortimer Pass, Newmarket.
- Open Wednesday to Sunday 10.30 am to 4.30 pm.
- Entrance fee.

21. Eden Gardens

Hidden away on the eastern side of Mt Eden are Eden Gardens. This botanical haven was established in 1964 in a former quarry, with the hard work of dedicated volunteers the dry barren quarry of scoria rock has been turned into a verdant tropical paradise. Covering over two hectares, plants include palms, camellias, rhododendrons, hibiscus, clivias, bromeliads, fuchsias and an extensive collection of native plants. The gardens has an extensive collection of camellias and the rocky quarry provides ideal conditions for the sub-tropical vireya rhododendrons. If that is not enough attraction, the gardens also have an excellent café.

- 24 Omana Ave off Mountain Road, Epsom.
- Open daily 9 am to 4.30 pm.
- www.edengarden.co.nz
- Entrance fee.

22. Parnell Pool

Original a tidal swimming pool enclosed by a rock wall, the Parnell Pool is Auckland's only saltwater pool and a popular destination for both the serious swimmer and for family fun. Most people would hardly notice the plaque of the wall indicating that the building was awarded a Gold Medal in 1957 by the New Zealand Institute of Architects. The pool was the work of Serbian born Tibor Donner, the Auckland city architect, and was refurbished in the Lido style in 1955. The building is rather plain, but the outstanding feature is the stylish coloured glass and stone mosaic that graces the front of the building. Designed by James Turkington, the mosaic technique is said to be inspired by Donner's visit to Mexico in 1956 and by the Matisse painting *The Swimming Pool*. For some unknown reason the pool is 60 m long, which doesn't match the usual swimming pool lengths of 25, 33 or 50 m.

- Judges Bay Road, Parnell.
- Summer only Labour Weekend to Easter.
  Open 6 am to 8 pm Monday to Friday,
  8 am to 8 pm Saturday, Sunday and public holidays.
- $ Entrance fee.

23. Savage Memorial Park

Just where is Michael Joseph Savage? Elected as New Zealand's first Labour Prime Minister in 1935, the government of Michael Joseph Savage introduced many key aspects of the welfare state and for many decades was regarding as the hero of the New Zealand working class. It was not unusual for a photograph of Michael Savage to have pride of place above the mantlepiece in the living room in many New Zealand homes. At the time of his death in 1940, over 200,000 Aucklanders lined the streets to watch the funeral procession make its way to his burial site on a bluff called Takaparawha above Tamaki Drive. The grand memorial consists of an obelisk, formal gardens and a reflecting pool and has wide views over the city and harbour. However, the whereabouts of his remains are a mystery. In the room under the obelisk is the original tomb (visible through a window in the door) but was found to be empty. Further investigation has revealed another coffin beneath this tomb. It is yet not known if this in fact contains the remains of Michael Joseph Savage. This leaves the question as to why he is buried in the coffin and not in the purpose-built tomb, or is the body in the coffin even the remains of the beloved Prime Minister?

⚲ Hapimana Street, Mission Bay.

24. Melanesian Mission

In the heart of busy Mission Bay is one of Auckland's most historic buildings and one that is usually overlooked, for at a glance the simple stone building just doesn't look that old. It is also unusual that is it built of stone for, while Auckland abounds in walls and the occasional garage or shed built from lava stone, larger buildings are very rare. Despite the abundance of volcanic rock, it is a difficult stone to work and especially difficult to achieve a uniform, flat surface. Even more unusual is that the stones for the mission building are not large blocks but small rocks, not much larger than a fist, and neatly fitted to present a smooth finish, made more striking by the vivid white mortar.

Founded by the Bishop of New Zealand George Selwyn the short-lived Melanesian Mission began life in 1859 with the arrival of thirty-eight Melanesian students on the ship Southern Cross (these islands were at that time part of the bishop's diocese). The purpose of the mission was to train missionaries who were then to return to their homelands and spread the word of the Lord, though some also received medical and agricultural training. The mission, however, was a disaster and after outbreak of dysentery which killed fourteen students, the mission at Auckland was closed and shifted to Norfolk Island in 1864.

The mission buildings were either dismantled or fell into disrepair and were demolished and today only the distinctive dining hall, with its volcanic stone walls and shingle roof remains, now, appropriately, as part of a larger restaurant and bar complex.

📍 44 Tamaki Drive, Mission Bay.

25. Cornwall Park and One Tree Hill Domain/ Maungakiekie

Now a popular picnic destination, One Tree Hill or Mangakiekie (mountain of the kiekie, a native vine) has always held attraction for Aucklanders. Despite all the visitors, the two adjoining parks hide some surprising stories.

In pre-European times this was the most populous pa on the Auckland isthmus and covering 45 ha it is the largest pa in New Zealand, though not all of the hill would have been fortified at any one time. Most pa were tiny in comparison. Maungakiekie was for a long period occupied by the iwi Te Wai o Hua until the early seventeenth century, when Ngati Whatua invaders from the Kaipara became the dominant iwi on the isthmus. However, Tamaki Makarau was devastated by the subsequent invasion by Ngapuhi heavily armed with muskets. When European settlers began to arrive, the pa on Maungakiekie was abandoned and the entire isthmus was only lightly populated.

The tree after which One Tree Hill is named has itself had a turbulent past. Originally a totara tree, 'Te Totara i Ahua', stood on the summit. It was cut down in the nineteenth century – though at this point the story becomes murky. One version goes that the tree was cut down by a settler for firewood; however, according to two other sources, the totara had already disappeared and it was a pohutukawa that was cut down. Yet another variation of the same story says that the tree was cut down by a drunken European in an act of sheer vandalism; while yet another version says that the tree was cut down by workmen protesting the lack of food rations.

John Logan Campbell tried to replace the native tree on the summit, using pines as a shelterbelt; but while the native trees failed to take hold, two of the pine trees flourished. One of the pair was cut down in 1960 with no fuss, leaving just the single tree to match the name. It was this lone tree that was attacked by a Maori activist in 1994. The tree was later removed by the Auckland City Council because it was unstable, and it then took local authorities and iwi representatives more than twenty years to agree on replacements. Now the hill is variably known as Gone, None or No Tree Hill.

Sir John Logan Campbell, who named the area One Tree Hill after the totara tree and donated the park to Auckland City, is buried on the summit next to the obelisk, which is dedicated to the Maori people. Acacia Cottage, originally situated in Shortland Street in the city and occupied by John Campbell and his business partner, John Brown, in 1841, is Auckland's oldest surviving building. Moved to the park in 1920, the house is restored, contains period furniture and is open to the public.

Tucked away behind a cascading waterfall is a very rare relic of a Maori shrine. Kumara was vital to Maori for their survival, and to ensure the success of the crop a carving – occasionally in stone – of Rongo, the god of cultivation, was erected near to the gardens to enlist the help of the god with the growth of the crop. This narrow column of stone originally formed part of a shrine on Te Tatua o Riukiuta (Three Kings) and was called Te Toka-i-tawhio, 'the stone that has travelled around', as it was originally located in the upper Waitemata Harbour and was later moved. The stone had been dumped on the side of a road where it was found by John Logan Campbell, who then had it placed on a plinth in the park.

One Tree Hill became part of Campbells extensive estate of 400 ha. Along with cattle and sheep farming he was also well ahead of his time and experimented with grapes and olives. The grapes have long gone but many of the olives have flourished, clinging to well-drained and sun-drenched slopes above the picturesque cricket ground. These trees are over 145 years old with twisted, sun-toughened trunks and matched by the hard grey-green leaves. Along with the olives the twin parks are also noted for other exceptional trees planted later including oak, gingko, kauri, eucalypt and the magnificent avenue of pohutukawa at the Greenlane Road entrance.

📍 The two vehicle entrances to the park are on Green Lane East and Manukau Road near Royal Oak.

26. Coast to Coast Walkway

Starting at the Ferry Building on the Waitemata Harbour, this walk takes in many of Auckland's best-known landmarks such as Mt Eden and One Tree Hill, but also includes several lesser-known gardens and parks such as the University of Auckland gardens and Jellicoe Park. Meandering through back streets and parks, 16 kilometres might sound a long way, but the variety of landscapes provides plenty of interest and, apart from a couple of uphill climbs, the walking is easy. The final leg of the walk finishes at the restored Onehunga Lagoon on the Manukau Harbour.

It is the perfect walk for fitter first-time visitors to the city but even if you are a long time Auckland resident, this walk will still provide you with pleasant surprises and is ideal on a sunny winter's day when more challenging walks are muddy and wet. The signage along the way can be erratic in parts, so if you are not familiar with Auckland streets, make sure you have a good map on your phone or print one out.

📍 At Onehunga regular bus and train services run back to the city centre.

27. Avondale Spiders

Large but harmless, the spider now known as Avondale spiders is a huntsman spider *Delena cancerides Walckenaer*. Accidently introduced to New Zealand, and Avondale specifically, the first spider was found in 1924 and is very likely to have hitched a ride on wooden railway sleepers imported from Australia.

Nocturnal and shy, the spiders favour dark, dry places to hide out during the day and are most likely to be found in sheds, garages and under houses. They do a great job keeping down insect pests as they feed mainly on flies, cockroaches and moths. The mostly likely time the shy spiders are spotted is during the summer months when the male spiders are out looking for female company.

However, if you are an arachnophobe, these spiders are especially challenging as they can grow up to 20 cm wide and when disturbed can move incredibly fast. These are the spiders that starred in the 1990 spider horror film Arachnophobia.

The curious thing about these spiders is they just love Avondale and haven't moved beyond the suburb in almost 100 years, a feature which has clearly endeared them to the locals who have erected a huge model spider in the small Avondale shopping centre.

28. Avondale Market

In recent years the inner-west suburbs of Auckland have become a human melting pot for immigrants from around the world. This very popular Sunday market reflects and caters for the wide diversity of immigrant cultures and, while strongly Asian and Polynesian in flavour, both the stallholders and shoppers cover just about every nationally under the sun. This market is where the locals come to do their weekend shopping and and this is in turn reflected by the exotic food available, from live catfish to an amazing array of Asian vegetables and all at very good prices. However, it also has a very lively second hand market in goods ranging from crockery and books to tools and clothing. Reflecting the diversity of its customers, the Avondale Market provides the widest choices in ethnic food stalls of any market in Auckland.

- Avondale Racecourse, Ash Street, Avondale.
- Sunday only 6 am to noon.

29. The Pah, Hillsborough

James Williamson had great ambitions when he built The Pah on a spectacular site on the southern outskirts of Auckland in 1879. Designed as a 'gentleman's residence' by Thomas Mahony, the grand house was modelled on Queen Victoria's country estate – Osborne House on the Isle of Wight. Constructed on an abandoned pa, with extensive vistas over the Manukau Harbour to the south, and One Tree Hill to the north, a grand drive through huge exotic trees sweeps up to one of the country's finest houses.

Plastered brick to resemble stone, the Italianate style house, with its broad verandas and bay windows is crowned by a small tower to take in the views. The interior was no less lavish, with intricate plastered ceilings, Italian marble fireplaces and sumptuous wooden panelling from Gillow and Sons, the royal cabinet makers. Despite all the changes over the years, the exterior remains largely unchanged and most of the fine interior detailing is intact.

What didn't remain intact was James Williamson's fortune and following the 1886 land crash, both the house and all the exquisite furniture was sold. Heartbroken, Williamson died in 1888. It is a great irony that in more recent times, the grand house became a refuge for the homeless and new immigrants. Purchased by the Auckland City Council in 2002, the house and estate were renovated and restored and, now open to the public, houses the James Wallace Trust art collection and a lovely café. Although the Trust has a permanent collection, the exhibitions are constantly changing, most lasting less than two months.

Delargey Ave, off Hillsborough Road.

30. Onehunga Blockhouse

As the relationship between Maori and Pakeha deteriorated during the 1850s, a string of ten protective forts, known as block houses, were built to protect the southern approaches to the city from Howick through Panmure, Otahuhu, Onehunga to Blockhouse Bay. Most were built of wood and all have long since disappeared with the exception of the brick blockhouse built at Onehunga in 1860. Situated on a strategic high point on what was then called Green Hill, the Onehunga Blockhouse has a wide view to the south and across the Manukau, as an attack was most likely to come from that direction. That attack never came and in the end it was the British who moved south into the Waikato and attacked the Maori. Subsequently the blockhouse was used as the Council Chambers and then a school and today the building is well preserved and the feature of the very pleasant Jellicoe Park. A careful inspection of the brick walls reveals a single vertical brick at regular spaces in the exterior walls. These were originally the loopholes from which the muskets were fired.

Two other buildings also on the Onehunga site are Laishley House, built in 1856 and originally situated at 44 Princes Street, Onehunga, along with replica Fencible House, built in 1959.

The only other remaining fortification from this period is Stockade Hill in Howick. Built in 1863, the stockade was only used for a few months during the New Zealand Wars. While all that remains of the stockade are ditches and earthworks, the views over the Hauraki Gulf are magnificent and well worth the short walk up the hill. A monument to the soldiers from the district now stands in the centre of the stockade.

◉ Jellicoe Park, Corner Quadrant Road and Grey Street, Onehunga.

31. Auckland Potters Studio, Onehunga

At this end of Captain Springs Road, you have come for just one of two things: the rubbish tip or the Auckland Potters Studio. Established in 1961 the APS moved an old house onto vacant council land in Onehunga in 1975 and built a kiln shortly after. The addition, in 1994, of a purpose-built teaching studio provided space for nineteen potting wheels and today the site has no fewer than thirteen kilns.

This place is a treat and here you can see potters at work, pick up some great pottery at excellent prices, and view the small but intriguing collect of pottery by some of this country's finest potters. What makes this collection unique is that all the pieces were created in short workshops, resulting in 'unfinished' works that can be viewed up close and even handled. It's not a particularly organised place, but it is certainly welcoming and friendly and will have immense appeal to anyone interested in art and pottery.

📍 96 Captain Springs Road, Onehunga.

🕐 Open Monday to Thursday 1 pm to 5 pm, Friday 1 pm to 4 pm, Saturday 1 am to 4 pm.

📞 09 634 3622

🌐 www.ceramics.co.nz

32. Otahuhu War Memorials

On the busy intersection of Great South Road and Mangere Road in the heart of Otahuhu are two of Auckland's most important war memorials. Most striking of these is the soldier riding a rearing horse set on a high plinth above the rushing traffic. Unveiled on Anzac Day 1928, the bronze statue of a New Zealand mounted rifleman is a tribute to all those who served in the First World War and was gifted by local businessman Alfred Trenwith.

Right behind this statue is a much older and simpler memorial, the Nixon Monument. Highly unusual, and one of just three monuments to survive from this era, the obelisk was erected to Marmaduke Nixon and three other soldiers who died at the battle of Rangiaowhia in the Waikato during the New Zealand Wars. In more recent years, there have been calls to have the monument removed as the battle of Rangiaowhia was an attack on a lightly defended pa that mainly sheltered women and children. The one-sided fight resulted in many deaths including those trapped in a whare that was set on fire.

With its very diverse population, the Otahuhu town centre is like no other in Auckland with the shops and eateries catering for both recent immigrants along with long established Polynesian and European residents. A stroll along the main street is an experience.

📍 The monuments are busy junction of Great South Road and Mangere Road, Otahuhu.

33. One city, 55 Volcanoes

Auckland is the only city in the world to be sited right on top of an active volcanic hot spot or plume. Situated 100 kilometres below the city, the temperatures are hot enough to melt rock and create an eruption at the surface. The field covers an area of 350 square kilometres and the fifty-three volcanic cones concentrated within Auckland's boundaries make this the city with the most volcanic cones anywhere in the world. And this is not including the older volcanic fields in the Waitakere Ranges, Franklin district or Waiheke Island.

Geologically young, Auckland's volcanoes began erupting less than 100,000 years ago and twenty have erupted in the last 20,000 years. While most of the volcanic eruptions have been relatively small, Rangitoto Island, the youngest volcano, active 600 years ago, was also the largest. The eruptions on average lasted only for a short time – anywhere between a few months to a few years. The nature of the volcanic field is such that there is every possibility of a new volcano anywhere within the field, existing volcanoes are unlikely to erupt again.

Many of the volcanoes are easily recognisable such as Mt Eden, One Tree Hill, Mt Victoria and Mangere, while others are less obvious, water-filled craters such as Lake Pupuke and Orakei Basin or modest hillocks such as the Big King. Nearly all cones have signs of quarrying and some volcanos have completely disappeared. Lava flows have defined the shape of the city and some of Auckland's best-known streets such as Karangahape Road, Ponsonby Road and Symonds Street follow the line of old lava flows.

Auckland residents could visit a different volcano every weekend for a year, though some would be a challenge to find.

For those who like such things here are some Auckland volcanic facts:

* The oldest volcano is Auckland Domain erupting 130,000 years ago.
* The newest volcano is Rangitoto Island last erupting about 600 years ago.
* All the volcanos are extinct. Any new eruption will be in a new location.
* The tallest volcano is Rangitoto at 260 m. On the mainland the tallest is Mt Eden at 196 m.
* Merely 30 metres high, Puketapapa is Auckland's smallest volcano.
* The largest and most intact cone is Mangere Mountain which also has a lava dome in one of the craters.
* Lake Pupuke is the only crater with freshwater.
* Meola Reef, especially visible at low tide and extending well into the Waitemata harbour, is an old flow from the eruption of the Mt Saint John eruptions. The lava flow halted when it reached a river in the valley which is now Waitemata Harbour. It is possible to walk out onto the reef at very low tides, but it covered in rock oysters and you will need strong shoes.
* Maar craters are common in Auckand and the best preserved and largest 'maar' craters is the Puhunui crater in South Auckland. A maar crater is formed when hot magma meets shallow ground water, producing a violent steam explosion which pulverise the ground above. The resulting debris flies straight up into the air and when falls creates a shallow crater with steep sides.
* Between Thorne Bay and Takapuna Beach are clear examples of lava moulds and lava casts, created when lava encountered trees. At Takapuna and visible at low tide are the moulds of standing trees trunks destroyed by lava.
* There are three main types of lava flow: pillow, pahoehoe and a'a. Pahoehoe lava is formed when molten lava breaks through the

congealed surface crust and is characterised by a billowy, smooth or rope like surfaces. Pillow lava is formed by underwater eruptions, the rapid cooling effect of the water caused the lava to billow out and then cool in rounded pillow shapes. A'a lava forms when liquid lava beneath a solid crust of cooling lava breaks through, and twists the hard surface into rough and jagged rocks.

* Hochstetter's Pond in suburban Onehunga looks like a crater but is in fact a collapsed lava lake from the Mt Smart eruption. This volcanic oddity takes its name from a map created by Ferdinand von Hochstetter in 1864.

* On Withell Drive, Epsom is a tiny remnant of unique lava forest. Lava forests once covered over 5000 hectares on the Auckland Isthmus but today less than 29 hectare remain, most of it unprotected. The basalt lava landscape is a tough place to grow; there is very little soil and plants must survive in pockets of humus built up by leaf fall.

Auckland East

34. Ash bank, Farm Cove Walkway

It certainly doesn't look like much, a crumbly white bank two to three metres high, barely worth a second glance, but this bank represents an incredibly violent chapter in Auckland's geological history. Imagine an eruption in the central North Island so enormous that it deposited a layer of fine pumice 300 kilometres away that even today it is three metres deep, many thousands of years later. A massive cloud of pumice and ash swept across the island at such a speed that it would have taken just sixty minutes to reach Auckland. What's more is that the flow was still so hot by the time it reached Auckland that it left a layer of charred vegetation below the ash.

Huge explosive eruptions throw vast amounts of material high into the air above a volcano within a very short space of time. Much of the material immediately falls back to earth and creates a massive, extremely hot cloud known as a pyroclastic flow. This flow of ash, pumice and gas sweeps outward from the volcano at an incredible speed usually following the contours of the surrounding land and incinerates anything in its path. The ash at Farm Cove represents just one eruption, but there is evidence that over time the Auckland region has been subject to several such eruptions, though mostly smaller than the one that created the pumice cliffs at Farm Cove. Ignimbrite flows are pyroclastic flows in which pumice is the main material.

A modern-day eruption of this magnitude doesn't bear thinking about.

📍 Access to the pumice banks is down a short walkway off Fisher Parade opposite Holly Way.

35. All Saints Anglican Church, Howick

Today Howick is a suburb of Auckland, but it was once a distant frontier settlement and the largest of the fencible towns, populated by soldier/settlers to protect the fledging town of Auckland. One of Auckland's oldest churches, All Saints, was Howick's first European building built and the opening service was held her on 21 November 1847 when the building consisted of only the walls and rafters with no roof. Constructed under the instructions of Bishop Selwyn at the cost of 47 pounds, 3 shillings and ninepence, the church was designed by notable colonial architect Frederick Thatcher and it is even said that Bishop Selwyn himself helped with the actually building. The stained-glass window was presented by Robert McLean and dedicated on 20 December 1891, and a small but sad memorial to the children who died in the scarlet fever epidemic of 1851 can be found on the lychgate.

📍 Corner Selwyn Road and Cook Street, Howick.

36. Fo Guang Shan Temple

While Indian temples (both Hindu and Sihk) and mosques are common and visible in Auckland, there are very few Chinese places of worship, despite Auckland's large Chinese population. This temple in Flat Bush certainly makes up for that lack with its style and sheer size. Opened in 2007 and designed in the architectural style of the Tang Dynasty, this temple took seven years to build and is beautifully constructed.

Flanked by stone lions, a wide flight of stairs leads up to large entrance foyer that features a large bronze Buddha and, in the heart of the vast complex, a spacious courtyard. Directly opposite is the main temple, with an enormous golden Buddha the central feature. Wide galleries enclose the courtyard with statuary, bronze bells and perfectly placed trees and plants. The whole effect is calming and contemplative. On the northern side is a small pagoda and a reflective pool set in a Chinese style garden.

Visitors are welcome at the temple, but please dress respectfully.

Corner of Stancombe and Chapel Road, Flat Bush.
www.fgs.org.nz

37. Ayrlies Garden

Despite being one of New Zealand's best-known gardens, it is surprising how many Aucklanders have never been here. Beverley McConnell and husband Malcolm turned over the first lump of heavy clay in an empty 1.2 ha paddock sloping down a hillside in 1964. A further 4.8 ha were added in 1980 and a final expansion was 14 hectares of swamp land below the existing gardens.

Accurately described as a 'quintessential New Zealand garden', the appeal lies in that it really mixes things up, both in garden style and in plant choice. Ayrlies takes full advantage of Auckland's benign climate and the plants range from subtropical palm trees through to a group of kahikatea and beds of roses. There are wide lawns, small forests, lily ponds and formal beds; this is a gardener's garden and not for the minimalist landscapist or native plant purist. Ayrlies is a huge version of most New Zealand gardens and it is purely delightfully to turn a corner and be presented with yet another botanic vista and clever plant combination. Added to the all this, the views of the Gulf will come as a surprise.

- 📍 125 Potts Road, Whitford.
- 🕘 Open 9 am to 4 pm Monday to Friday.
- 🌐 www.ayrlies.co.nz
- 💲 Entrance fee.

38. Duders Regional Park

Duders Regional Park occupies the Whakakaiwhara Peninsula and is currently almost entirely farmed with just a few tiny patches of bush. The peninsula has long Maori associations dating back to 1300 when the waka *Tainui* anchored at very end of the Peninsula here while sheltering from a storm, and is remembered in the placename Te Tauranga o Tainui. Whakakaiwhara Pa was strategically located at the very tip of the Peninsula, and terraces, kumara pit and defensive ditch are still visible today. The Duder family purchased the land in 1866, and continued to farm the land up to 1994 when it was sold to the Auckland Regional Council for a park.

The park is not large, but the views are marvellous, out over the Firth of Thames, the Gulf islands of Waiheke, Ponui, Browns and Rangitoto, and to the east the blue tinged Coromandel. From the southern motorway it is a bit torturous to get there but a great place for a peaceful walk for an hour or two.

For the adventurous and the fit there is a very novel way of visiting a number of regional parks along this coast include Duders and this is via the Te Ara Moana Sea Kayak Pathway.

Unique in New Zealand, Te Ara Moana (the sea pathway) is a 51 km kayak trail that links six regional parks on eastern coast of Auckland; Omana, Duder, Waitawa, Tawhitokino, Tapapakanga and Waharau. Sheltered from the prevailing westerly winds, the trail hugs the coastal line and each leg is between 8 km and 14 km. While designed to be done over five days it can be done in two or three days with camping grounds, some only accessible by sea, dotted along the shoreline. A sea kayaking specialist, Auckland Sea Kayak specialises in Te Ara Moana tours. www.aucklandseakayaks.co.nz

---

> From SH 1 travel towards Whitford, and on to Maraetai then follow the coast south to Umupuia Beach. From the southern end of Umupuia Beach turn right into North Road, and the entrance to the park is on the right a short distance down this road.

39. Tawhitokino Bay

It is hard to believe that in a city of over one million people that this little-known bay on the Firth of Thames coast remains relatively obscure. Safe for swimming in all tides, this long sandy beach is fringed by large spreading pohutukawa trees and has an uninterrupted view of the Coromandel Peninsula across the firth. Possibly the 45 minute walk from the car park to the beach via the equally pretty Tuturau Bay is just enough to put people off, but on a lovely summers day or a bright clear winters afternoon this bay is a treat. The beach has also become popular as a clothing optional beach.

> From Kawakawa Bay, follow the coast road for 4 km to Waiti Bay.

Auckland West

40. South Kaipara Head

Auckland tend to turn their backs on the vast Kaipara Harbour which is viewed with distain as muddy, shallow and general unattractive. However, the South Head of the Kaipara Harbour holds some unexpected surprises and makes for an excellent day out.

Waionui Inlet

As far north as you can go on South Head, it takes about 45 minutes to drive from the Parakai turnoff just before Helensville. The distance and the lack of any facilities (other than a few old shady pine trees) deters many visitors and gives Waionui a wonderful feeling of isolation. A vast tidal lagoon ringed by golden sand hills and sheltered from the worst of the westerly winds, this area is one of this country's most important coastal habitats and a destination for birds seasonally migrating between the northern and southern hemispheres. Looking across the lagoon, the high sand hills on the north head are clearly visible. A mixture of habitats, the area includes salt marsh, mangrove forest, tidal sandbanks and dunes so it is not surprising that the Kaipara harbour attracts over 30,000 migratory birds. The sheltered waters of the lagoon are popular with kayakers and at low to mid tide the walking on wide sand flats out to the lagoon entrance is easy.

Lake Rototoa

This little know lake is the largest, deepest and most pristine freshwater lake in the Auckland region. Up to 29 m deep, the large 110 ha dune lake in the rolling farmland of the South Kaipara Head is surrounded by regenerating bush and is home to unique wildlife. Although the name 'dune lake' implies a sandy soil, Lake Rototoa occupies a depression in rock, but like other dune lakes it relies entirely on rain water. Around the shore coastal broadleaf forest, the largest area of native bush on the peninsula, is slowly recovering with around 300 native plants recorded here. Powered boats are not allowed on the lake, so it is ideal for kayaks and swimming. Not well-developed access is limited to the area near the car park.

📍 29 km north of Parakai, turn left into Donaghue Road and entrance to the lake is 300 m on the right.

Te Rau Puriri Regional Park

Established in 2005, Te Rau Puriri Regional Park covers almost 250 ha of rolling hillside down to the Kaipara including a kilometre of coast line of sand and shell beach at Waipiro Bay. While there are patches of regenerating bush in the gullies, the park is largely farmland and a walking track forms a long loop down to the coast and back. In addition to walking tracks there are also horse riding trails. The beach is a lovely spot (best for swimming at high tide), and doesn't attract many visitors so there is a good chance you will have this place all to yourself.

📍 South Head Road 30 km north of Parakai. The park sign is quite small and the off road parking is easy to miss as the entrance is alongside a cattle yard. Going north the turn into the parking area is on a very sharp bend so extra care is needed.

Kaituna Mangrove Forest

Just north of Parakai, a huge tidal inlet along the Puharakeke Creek is the location of the impressive Kaituna mangrove forest. Two small forested islands, Waikau and Motukura rise above the mangroves and far across the harbour is a distant view of Atuanui/Mt Auckland (304 m). From the carpark two short tracks lead down to the water's edge.

📍 Nine kilometres north of Parakai.

Take note that there is no petrol and no stores beyond Parakai, though there is a small café at Shelley Beach on the eastern side of the peninsula. While the road is sealed and in good condition it is hilly and winding, so take it easy and go prepared with a least something to eat and drink.

41. Bethells Beach/Te Henga, O'Neill Bay and Lake Waimanu

These three locations are all in the same area and combined make for a busy, but interesting day out. Only the coastal strip north of the small Waitakere River is part of the Waitakere Regional Park.

The main Te Henga beach is a turbulent wide beach enclosed by dramatic rocky bluffs. Swept by relentless westerly winds unstable sand dunes ensure that the small settlement is well back from the wild beach. On the north side of the beach, the Waitakere River spreads across the sand, the outlet for the Te Henga wetland further up the valley. The largest in the Auckland region, there is no access to the wetland along its southern length, though road to the beach gives numerous views over the swamp. Cliffs at the southern end of the beach are mainly composed of pillow lava. Extreme caution should be taken when swimming here, though a Surf Lifesaving Club patrols the beach in summer. There are no permanent cafes or stores, but in the summer food trucks do operate here.

Just over a ridge north of Te Henga, O'Neill Bay is a wonderful, wild and windy beach that encapsulates the best that the west coast can offer. Erangi Point and Kauwahaia Island at the southern end of the bay offer some protection from the relentless winds which have created a wide bank of sand hills behind the beach. As with all the west coast beaches, swimming is only to be undertaken with great care. This is part of the longer Te Henga Walkway, though beyond O'Neill Bay the track becomes more difficult and more suitable for trampers.

> On the Bethells Road, the track begins on the right over the one way bridge just past Tasman View Road.

Lake Wainamu was created around 6000 years ago when sand driven from the beach up the narrow valley by the continuous wind created an enormous dune that today is around one kilometre long and 200 metres wide. Eventually the dune completely blocked the Wainamu Stream and in the process created long deep lake. The dune is much bigger than it first appears and in a strong westerly wind the sand is whipped across the broad dune, like some desolate desert scene from a movie. Today the dune is more or less stable as the dune stabilisation project behind the beach has cut off the lake as its source of sand. The lake at the edge of the dune is particularly deep making it an ideal swimming spot and children and the young at heart will have great fun sliding down the steep dunes along the stream.

📍 The track from the car park initially follows the stream and then climbs up the steep dune to the lake. Another track encircles the lake which takes about an hour, passing through regenerating bush and while not difficult, it is a bit tricky in places.

42. Totara Waters

When Peter and Jocelyn Coyle purchased one hectare on the water's edge in the upper Waitemata Harbour with little more than a few pine trees in 1999, they had every intention of turning the land into a garden. Equipped with a love of gardening and a good deal of enthusiasm, twenty years later Totara Waters is recognised as one of this country's Gardens of National Significance.

Palms and tropical trees rustle in the breeze, cycads stand upright in the middle of a more formal bed and aloes and succulents send up spikes of multi-hued flowers. Pots and sculptures peek out from the luxuriant foliage, lending structure to the garden. Marooned at the tidal edge since the early 1950s are the remains of the *HMNZ Hawera*. However, under pinning the garden is a passion for bromeliads of every type and colour, and Peter is now hybridising new plants from seed – not the easiest of botanical tasks.

One of the beauties of a subtropical garden is that it has an appeal all year round especially as aloes flower through the winter, however the location is marginal for many subtropical plants as it subject to some pretty nippy winter frosts. In addition to the garden, there is a small plant shop so visitors can take home the best sort of souvenirs, inspiration and a new plant or two.

- 89 Totara Road, Whenuapai.
- Open 10 am to 4 pm, Monday to Saturday.
- 09 416 8272
- www.totarawaters.co.nz

43. Hobson's Gum Hobsonville

In a suburban street in Hobsonville is a massive Sydney red gum, *Angophora costata*, which according to local legend was planted by Governor Hobson when he visited the area in 1840 as a possible site for a new capital for the fledgling colony. However, it is highly unlikely he planted the tree as tree experts say the tree is not that old. One explanation is the over the years the story has mixed up the two Governors, Hobson and Grey. Grey was an avid planter of trees and imported a wide range of Australian species in the 1860s including Sydney red gum. There is, however, no evidence that Grey planted this tree, so the mystery remains.

Governors aside, the tree is impressive with huge multiple trunks and distinctive and highly patterned bark that ranges in colours from pink through red and brown to various shade of grey. Not only is this tree the largest of its species in New Zealand, but no tree matching the size of the Hobsonville tree has yet been found in Australia.

- 5 Williams Road, Hobsonville.

44. Te Ahua Point

Situated between Karekare and Piha beaches, Te Ahua Point is a superb lookout atop towering volcanic cliffs that drop hundreds of metres into a wild sea. To the south the view is along the coast to the dangerous bar that marks the entrance to the Manukau Harbour. The track is well formed and well-marked with a grassy knoll at the turnaround point is a good place for a break, though this area is exposed to strong westerly winds. For those wanting a longer walk the track continues downhill to Karekare Beach.

The dramatic cliffs of Te Ahua Point are the lip of the ancient Waitakere volcano. Erupting about fifteen million years ago, the volcano was active for about six million years and at its greatest extent had a diameter of 50 km. The centre of this gigantic volcano was 20 km to the west, but over a period of five million years the relentless Tasman Sea completely eroded all trace of the volcano above sea level. Further earth movements tilted the eastern rim causing it to rise again above the sea and forming the present Waitakere Ranges.

This is also the location of a haunting love story. Once there was a beautiful chieftainess, Hinerangi, who fell in love with a chieftain from Karekare and moved there to be with him. But then as now, the west coast was notorious for dangerous surf, and one day Hinerangi's husband and two companions were swept off the rocks and drowned while fishing at the southern end of Te Unuhanga o Rangitoto (Mercer Bay). Searching desperately for her husband, Hinerangi climbed to the top of this headland to scan the sea. She refused to leave the spot, and eventually died of a broken heart. Her sad face is now forever outlined in the rocks below the headland on which she sat, which became known as Te Ahua o Hinerangi (the likeness of Hinerangi).

📍 The track begins at the end of Te Ahuahu Road/Log Race Road, which turns left off Piha Road just before the road descends into Piha.

45. Waikumete Cemetery

Waikumete Cemetery, at over 100 hectares, is the largest cemetery in New Zealand and has been the main Auckland cemetery since 1908 but was used for local burials as early as 1886. A vast rolling area of both new and old graves, it has some historic sections notable in their own right. Unidentified passengers from the 1979 Air New Zealand Erebus crash are buried in a site near the main entrance marked by a memorial with the names of those buried here and those not recovered from Antarctica. Another memorial in the form of a granite slab marks the Holocaust memorial next to the Hebrew Prayer House, and buried at the base of the memorial is an urn of ashes taken from the Auschwitz Concentration Camp.

Mausoleums are uncommon in New Zealand cemeteries but Waikumete contains a large number of these, mainly for Dalmatian families from West Auckland, including two fine examples belonging to the Corban and Nobilo winemaking families. In contrast to the elaborate mausoleums are the large unmarked graves of the victims of influenza who collectively have one granite memorial. During the 1918 influenza epidemic over 1600 people died and the bodies were transported from the city to Waikumete by train for mass burial.

- Great North Road, Glen Eden.
- Gates are opened at 7.30 am and closed at 6 pm (winter) and 8.30 pm (summer).

46. Mazuran's Wines

Lincoln Road Henderson was once the stronghold of West Auckland vineyards, but urban sprawl has made the land too expensive to grow grapes and today Mazuran's is the lone survivor. Producing mostly fortified wines, Mazuran's is typical of the many Croatian (better known as Dalmatians or Dallies) wineries that flourished in this area from around 1900. George Mazuran arrived from Croatia and established the winery in 1938 and, like most wineries of the time, mainly produced sherries and ports. Mazuran's became best known for its quality port and has on sale a port for every year since 1942, produced under a label largely unchanged for decades.

Mazuran's claim to be the first New Zealand winery to send wine to an international competition in 1956 and under the counter of the shop lined with wine maturing in oak barrels, is a small glass case crammed with medals won over the year. More awards are stacked in boxes. The small shop is an extension to the garage tucked behind the family home, but grapes are no longer grown behind the house in Lincoln Road, but are brought in from other parts of the country to the winery. Along with the fortified varieties, Mazuran's also make a small selection of popular table wines. Unusual for a New Zealand winery, here cork is still used rather than screw caps.

Yet this is not a winery that looks to the past and, at the 2018 New York Wine and Spirits Competition, the Mazuran's NV Tawny Port Old won a Double Gold Medal for Best Dessert and Best Port.

- 255 Lincoln Road, Henderson.
- Monday to Saturday 9 am to 5 pm, Sunday 11 am to 5 pm.
- 09 838 6945
- www.mazurans.com

47. Babich Winery

Aged just fourteen years old, Josip Babich and his brother Stipan arrived in Auckland from Croatia in 1910 to join three other brothers in the northern gum fields. Within a year the brothers had bought land in west Auckland, and a year later Josip planted his first grapes and, from the first harvest in 1916, wine was sold under the label Babich Brothers that same year. In the intervening 100 years, Babich has now become one of this country's leading wine producers, expanding to include vineyards and wineries in both Hawkes Bay and Marlborough. Still family owned, the Babich family have been stalwarts of the New Zealand industry and their contribution has acknowledged by a number of awards for service to the wine industry.

But home is home, and at Henderson the family are one of just a very small band of winemakers to still grow grapes in this area where once numerous Croatian vineyards flourished. Five hectares of grapes produce chardonnay, with albarino grapes planted for the future. The vineyards are overlooked by a stylish tasting room and cellar door and this is an excellent place for visitors to New Zealand to try a wide range of top New Zealand wines without having to travel to more far flung grape growing regions.

- 15 Babich Road, Henderson.
- Tasting room and cellar door 9 am to 5 pm, Monday to Friday, 10 am to 5 pm Saturday, Closed Sunday.
- 09 833 7859
- www.babichwines.com

48. The Huia to Whatipu Road

Just 10 km long, this road feels like another world even though is barely an hour's drive from downtown Auckland.

Just two kilometres before you reach Huia, take a short side road to Point Lookout with stunning, almost 360-degree view over the Manukau Harbour, the Heads, Huia Bay and the ragged edges that make up the Waitakere Ranges. Just back from the car park a short steep track leads down to the secluded sandy beach of Orphesus Beach.

Beyond Huia the first stop is Karamatura Falls and Valley. Here the Karamatura stream cuts deeply into the old stone of the Waitakere volcano and in process has created sheer bluffs that rise high above beautiful narrow valley. Although heavily milled for timber in the nineteenth century, today the regenerating forest is lush and as varied as anywhere in Auckland. The valley is a popular starting point for many longer tracks in the park and also the easier and much shorter Karamatura Loop track. Although it has steeper section and some steps, the track is in excellent condition and perfect for families. On the highest point of the track is a lookout with panoramic views over the thick bush and the rocky bluffs, and it is easy to spot the large rata trees rising above the surrounding bush. A short distance beyond the loop track are the picturesque Karamatura Falls. Around 15 metres high, a narrow stream of water rushes down a rock face into a small pool perfect for swimming on a hot day.

📍 On the Huia Road, 800 metres past the one-way bridge over the Huia stream.

On the left, 500 m after the seal ends is short 10-minute walk to the Manukau Bar Lookout when a viewing platform looks directly west down the harbour to the notorious Manukau Bay, the scene of New Zealanders worst maritime accident. A lethal combination of ocean swells up to five metres, fierce westerly winds, a tidal variation of around four metres and a sandbank that is constantly changing makes the bar very difficult for sailors to read correctly.

About another kilometre and this time on the right side of the road is Mt Donald McLean Road which leads to the summit of Mt Donald McLean. Rising 389 metres above the sea, the wooden viewing platform on top of the isolated peak of Mt Donald McLean offers unsurpassed views that are hard to beat. To the north are the bush-cloaked ridges and valleys of the Waitakere Ranges; to the west Whatipu and off shore, the churning waters of the Manukau Bar; to the south the sandy slopes below the lighthouse on South Head and beyond that distant Pukekawa. The whole of the Manukau Harbour spreads out to the east while the central city and Rangitoto can be clearly seen in the north east. The short track (fifteen minutes to the top) is an easy gradual climb.

At the end of the road is Whatipu on the broad windswept sands of the North Head of the Manukau. Rising up from the shore the rugged volcanic bush-covered slopes are markedly different to the barren sand country to the south of the harbour entrance. The crashing surf of the wild and treacherous Manukau bar is in direct contrast to the sheltered bays just inside the harbour entrance.

On February 7 1863 the *HMS Orpheus* struck the Manukau bar while trying to enter the harbour. Of the 259 men aboard only 70 survived and this is still New Zealand's worse maritime disaster. The area was once the terminal for a tramway that ran along the coast extracting kauri from the bush inland and then shipping it to Onehunga. Below the cliffs are several large sea caves and a small camping area. Shaped by years of wave action, the caves are now a considerable distance from the sea as the marshy area between the cliffs has built up since 1940. The largest of the caves was once used for dances though sand has now raised the floor level of the cave by five metres. Although substantial, torches are not necessary.

A popular fishing spot, Whatipu is also the beginning of the Gibbons Track, a six-hour loop walk along the cliff tops and returning along the beach.

If you are hungry or thirsty make sure you stop at the café and store at Huia as there are few facilities beyond this point. Drive with caution as the road is narrow, winding and hilly with the last 5 km gravel.

> Take the road through Titirangi to Huia on the northern side of the Manukau Harbour and continue through Huia to Whatipu.

Auckland South

49. Otara Market

In the 1960s, to meet labour shortages, New Zealand encouraged Polynesian migration, mainly from islands that already had some connection to this country. By 1971, over 45,000 people had settled here, the biggest groups from Tonga, Samoa and the Cook Islands and a large number made Otara their home. One aspect of New Zealand life sorely lacking was a weekly market, as New Zealand, despite its European background, had no tradition of street markets. In 1976, Otara established the first open air market and it quickly became a popular meeting place and a unique blend of Polynesian, Maori and Pakeha traditions.

Now more than forty years later, markets have sprung up all around New Zealand and many more markets operate across Auckland both on weekends and during the week, with popular night markets adding a new dimension. Still flourishing, the Saturday Otara market has now added new styles and flavours with more recent Asian immigration to the area. This is the place where families shop for vegetables, fruit and inexpensive clothing, though there are also a handful of craft stalls of varying quality. What Otara has and unlikely to be found else where are food stalls selling tradition Polynesian food such as coconut bread, poke, chop suey, island doughnuts and fried bread.

📍 Car park, behind the Otara Town Centre, Bairds Road, Otara.

50. Rainbow's End Rollercoaster

New Zealand's largest theme park – Rainbow's End opened is 1982 – has a number of wild rides. Wildest of all is the Corkscrew Coaster, New Zealand's only serious roller coaster that was built in 1986. The highest single drop is a heart-stopping 27 metres, followed by a single vertical loop of 12 metres and finally the teeth-rattling double corkscrew. The roller coaster reaches speeds of 60 km/h and takes just 1.08 minutes to cover 400 metres.

If the rollercoaster is not enough, then there is always The Stratosfear, The Invader, The Fearfall and The Power Surge.

📍 2 Clist Crescent, Manukau.
🕐 Open daily 10 am to 5 pm.
🌐 www.rainbowsend.co.nz
💲 Entrance fee.

51. Otuataua Stonefields

While undoubtedly an area of significant historical and archaeological importance, to the untrained eye the Otuataua Stonefields are difficult to make sense of. Settled originally by Te Wai o Hua, and covering 100 hectares, the stonefields highlight the importance of kumara and taro to early Maori.

Despite this country's equitable climate and rich soil, there are few edible native plants; and even those such as fernroot and karaka berries take a huge amount of preparation before they are edible. On arrival from their tropical homeland, the first Polynesian migrants found that only kumara and taro could grow in this cooler climate and even those crops were dramatically restricted by climate. This in turn had a significant impact on where Maori could live. Pre-European Maori populations were largely restricted to the northern part of the country and to coastal areas further south.

Both taro and kumara need a long period of warm sunny weather to mature. One method of maximising the heat required by these delicate tropical plants was to plant the crops very close to rock walls or in a small circle of rocks, thereby taking full advantage of the sun's heat reflected off and held by the rocks. Here at Otuataua, what appear to be merely random stone piles are in fact the remains of carefully constructed walls and mounds designed to grow the best kumara and taro. The site also contains the Otuataua pa, although to the casual visitor this pa is much more difficult to spot compared to those on the volcanic cones.

An easy walk of forty minutes through rocky outcrops and farmland, this stroll is enhanced by the excellent information, certainly helping to interpret what at first glance appears to be a landscape without much form.

📍 From George Bolt Drive (the road to the airport) turn right into Ihumatao Road, right again into Oruarangi Road and finally left into Ihumatao Quarry to the carpark at the end.

52. Ihumatao Fossilised Forest

Along a low line of coastal cliffs and in the expansive tidal flats just beyond the western end of the Auckland International Airport are not one, but two fossilised forests. The first and oldest forest dates back 100,000 years when the climate was cooler and the Manukau Harbour did not even exist. The coastline was far to the west and this area was river valley covered in dense bush. It is likely that this forest succumbed to a change in water levels and the giant kauri trees died and eventually toppled into a peaty swamp. Today the huge stumps and massive tree trunks of kauri trees are clearly visible and easy to see in the muddy sand at low tide and the wood still looks incredibly fresh.

The second forest died 30,000 years ago in very different circumstances when the Maungataketake volcano, just a short distance away, erupted and covered the trees in ash, killing them. The remains of these trees, now fossilised, are in the soft rock cliffs above the high tide mark. If you weren't aware that these were fossils, they would not warrant second glance as they just look like wood that has died a few decades back and not 3000 decades! In some instances the trees were not fossilised, but rotted away leaving tell-tale holes in the cliff.

The forests are best seen at mid to low tides, the fallen kauri trees cover a wide area of the mudflats, while the best examples of the trees destroyed in the volcanic eruption are to the left of the steps leading down from the road.

📍 The end of Renton Road, off Ihumatao Road, Mangere, about five minutes' drive from the airport terminals.

53. Kentish Hotel

Is this New Zealand's oldest pub? That's open to discussion, but it is certainly is a frontrunner and without doubt the Kentish is the oldest hotel in the Auckland region and one of the oldest buildings as well.

In the mid-nineteenth century Waiuku flourished as a portage town providing a vital link between the Manukau Harbour and Onehunga to the important inland waterway of the Waikato River, and a steamer travelled from Waiuku to Onehunga three times a week.

Overlooking the tidal Waiuku Inlet, the Kentish Hotel was built in 1852 and unusually for a wooden pub it has neither changed its name, nor has it been burnt down. Named after his native Kent by the builder and first publican, Edward Constable, the exterior of the pub has changed little. The hotel has been at the heart of Waiuku life since it was built, the Kentish has hosted visiting dignitaries such as the Maori King Te Whero Whero, Sir George Gray, Richard Seddon, Sir Joseph Ward and William Massey.

A popular local spot and now into the second half of its second century, the Kentish is set to be the favourite watering hole for some time yet.

ϙ 5 Queen Street, Waiuku.

54. The Awhitu Peninsula

From the Manukau Head Lighthouse, the Skytower in central Auckland is clearly visible but by road it's a long drive, over 100 km, but well worth the day out.

In contrast to the ancient, rugged and rocky Manukau North Head and the Waitakere Ranges, the Ahwitu peninsula is a geological baby, and is largely composed of consolidated sand under laid by ancient volcanic rock. During numerous ice ages the sea was much lower and at that time the Manukau harbour (and the Waitemata) was a wide tree-covered river valley. Gradually as the climate warmed and the sea rose, the whole basin became one vast bay. Inland eruptions then swept huge quantities of sand and pumice down the Waikato River, which in turn were swept north by the prevailing currents. The same northerly currents dragged black sand from the Taranaki eruptions and together all this material first formed a long sandbar and then gigantic sand hills. Over time the consolidated sand hills supported forest which, since the arrival of humans, has largely vanished.

Sheltered from the westerly wind, Maori settled along the shores of the harbour and as it was easily accessible by sea the area also attracted early European farmers.

One of the few accessible points on the west coast, at Hamiltons Gap, a small stream cuts through the old and very steep dune country that faces the relentless winds off the Tasman Sea. Wild and dramatic, rugged cliffs of golden sandstone which have been shaped by the endless winds rise above the black sand beach. With magnificent vistas north and south, visitors can walk long distances in either direction on the wide sandy beach. There is always a catch and here that snag is the weekend dirt bike riders who race at high speed along the beach. The public toilet fashioned from beach driftwood are very appealing on a number of levels.

Nestled on the sheltered eastern side of the Awhitu Peninsula on the Manukau Harbour, the Awhitu Regional Park is an attractive combination of natural and human history. At the heart of the park is the nineteenth century Brook homestead, typical of the comfortable farm villas of the day and set among fine old trees on a rise above the beach. However, just in front of the homestead is a small roughly built and very modest cottage that initially housed the family until sufficient money was available to build a more substantial home. The area is very tidal and is honestly more attractive closer to high tide, though the tidal flats provide an important feeding ground for birds.

The Manukau Heads Lighthouse is located high on a huge sand dune 244 m above the entrance to the Manukau harbour, and offers stupendous views over the harbour, the Waitakere Ranges and in the distance Auckland city. Just offshore breakers crash over the Manukau bar, scene of New Zealand's worst maritime disaster when in 1863 the *HMS Orpheus*, using outdated charts, ran aground on the bar in clear weather and broke up, resulting in deaths of 189 of the 259 on board. While there is a viewing platform, best views are from the walkway around the historic lighthouse erected in 1874.

In contrast to wild Hamilton's Gap, just inside the entrance are two small bays, Orua Bay and Big Bay, lined with old fashioned baches and very safe for swimming.

HAURAKI GULF ISLANDS

1. Great Barrier Island / Aotea
2. Little Barrier Island / Hauturu
3. Kawau Island
4. Waiheke
5. Rotoroa Island
6. Motutapu Island
7. Motuihe

1. Great Barrier Island/Aotea

The largest and most distant island of the gulf, Great Barrier, or Aotea in Maori, is believed to be the original landing point of the first Polynesian explorers, who named the land Aotearoa, or land of the long white cloud, as from sea the first indication of land is the long low cloud.

Now considered remote, in early times when travel was by sea, the island was readily accessible and has a long history of both Maori and Pakeha occupation. While it is no untouched wilderness, having been ruthlessly stripped of its timber, the island, with a population of around 1000 people, has a relaxed lifestyle, beautiful beaches and some of the best fishing in the country. The western side of the island has several excellent bush-clad harbours, while the east has great beaches. The main settlement is Tryphena in the south of the island (where the ferry terminal is) and while there is no public transport as such, in typical island style getting around the island is easily arranged, though it can be expensive.

All the good beaches are on the eastern side of the island. Medlands, the closest beach to Tryphena, is a beautiful stretch of white sand and has good surf, while Kaitoke is the longest beach on the island. Two other good beaches are Anawa Bay and, in the north, Whangapoua. At the end of Whangapoua beach are the graves of some of the 130 people who lost their lives when the *SS Wairarapa* struck rocks off Miners Head in October 1894.

The fishing both on and under water around Great Barrier is legendary, particularly for snapper and crayfish, and several operators based on the island provide services to suit.

Kaitoke Hot Springs are a pleasant two-hour-return walk to hot springs located in a fork of a stream. The water is quite shallow and is not easy to get a good warm soak despite all attempts to dam the stream. 5 km from Whangaparapara on the Whangaparapara Road.

While patches of kauri remain, the island was heavily logged from 1862 through to 1940 and the use of stringer dams to drive the huge logs down to the sea was common. Built by George Murray in 1926, this is the best-preserved kauri dam in the country and is over 9 m wide and 5 m high. The walk to the dam is about three and a half hours return and can be linked to the Mt Hobson/Windy Canyon Track making it a full-day tramp. The Kaiarara track to the dam is about 5 km from Port Fitzroy.

A spectacular walk through Windy Canyon to the summit of Mt Hobson/Hirakimata takes 30 minutes return to the canyon, and four hours return to the top of the mountain, which at 627 m is the highest point on the island. The volcanic nature of the area is particularly evident, with dramatic outcrops and rocky bluffs as well as the narrow ravine of Windy Canyon itself. From the summit the view of the gulf is exceptional, though be aware that the peak is often shrouded in mist and cloud. The top of mountain is, oddly enough, also the nesting ground of a rare seabird, the black petrel. Signposted from the summit of Whangapoua Hill on Aotea Road between Awana and Okiwi.

> Barrier Airlines, Fly My Sky operate flights to the island from Auckland Domestic Terminal and Barrier Air has limited flights from the North Shore and if you want an adventure there is also Auckland Seaplanes. Sunair operate scheduled flights from Whitianga and Tauranga.
> Sealink runs a regular service for passengers, cars and freight from Wynyard Wharf and the trip takes four and half hours one way.

2. Little Barrier Island/Hauturu

Established as a wildlife reserve in 1895, this island has played a pivotal role in the preservation of some of New Zealand's most endangered wildlife. The island is largely virgin bush with only a small portion of the island ever been cleared and is now completely predator-free. The forest contains hard beech, a cooler-climate tree that usually occurs much further south, and the nikau palms are a subspecies with broader leaves than their mainland counterparts. Rising to 722 m, Hauturu (meaning 'resting place of the wind') is home to over 300 plant species, birds extinct or close to extinction on the mainland (including saddleback, stitchbird, kaka, kakariki, kiwi, black petrel, brown teal, and kokako), 14 species of skink, gecko and tuatara, several species of weta, and both species of native bat.

There is public access to the island but it is a bit of a mission and not cheap, but it is a place that every New Zealander should visit as least once. Numbers of visitors to the island is restricted, often booked out well in advance, and landing on the island is by permit only.

📞 09 425 7812

🌐 For details check the DOC website or phone the Department of Conservation Warkworth area office.

3. Kawau Island

Hardly off the beaten track, Kawau Island is a popular day trip destination for both Aucklanders and visitor alike, but it does have two unusual curiosities.

The island was the site of one of New Zealand's earliest mining ventures and the remains of the Copper mines engine room with its spectacular 20 metre chimney is also one of this country's oldest industrial buildings. Mining began in 1844 and at the peak of production around 300 people lived on the island. However, the copper was difficult to extract with the ore situated below sea level so the mine required continual pumping to avoid flooding. In addition to the mine a smelting works was built in 1849. A combination of insufficient ore and constant flooding forced the whole operation to close in 1852. The remains of the pump house, which housed a steam engine to drive pumps, dates from after the mine closure when in 1854 there was a failed attempt to drain the mine which are directly below the ruins. The photogenic ruins are an easy thirty minute walk from Mansion House.

In 1862 George Grey purchased Kawau Island for 3500 pounds and over the years greatly expanded the house, planted exotic trees and stocked the island with an array of animals. Grey, who had once served as Governor of New Zealand (1845-1853) as well as in Australia and South Africa, was fascinated by the exotic and at Kawau built up an amazing collection of flora and fauna from every corner of the globe. The animals introduced included monkeys, zebras, kookaburras and wallabies. There is still a colony of kookaburras on the island and in 2003, some Parma wallabies from the Kawau Island population were sent back to their native Australia where they were extinct. It is a pity the Australians don't want all their possums back as well.

From seeds and cuttings, Grey propergated a huge variety of plants among which were American and European oaks, bamboos, elms, walnut, Moreton Bay fig, red gum, redwood, coral tree, olive, pomegranates, tea, coffee and a variety of edible nuts.

Like the animals, most of the plants have not survived, but among the trees that are still on the island are two splendid Chilean wine palms. Standing behind the house, these wonderful trees are easily recognizable by their stout trunks, like two enormous elephant legs topped by fronds. They are very slow growing and in their native habitat have been destroyed in large numbers by over-exploitation where they have been relentlessly bled for their sap from which is made a sweet palm syrup. The nuts are also edible, and Grey planted these trees to provide food and shelter for his small troop of monkeys which has long since died out. Today the palms remain, marvellous but monkeyless.

Kawau Cruises run regular ferries (summer and winter timetables) from Sandspit Wharf which take about 30 minutes.
09 425 8006
kawaucruises.co.nz

4. Waiheke

The most populated and easily accessible of all the gulf islands, and once a haven for those looking for the good life, Waiheke is much more cosmopolitan these days with smart cafes, highly regarded wineries and, as it is just a short ferry ride from downtown Auckland, the island attracts a huge number of visitors. Despite all the visitors it does have several unique destinations.

The Bechstein Paderewski Grand Piano, Whittaker's Music Museum.

Polish pianist Ignacy Jan Paderewski (1860-1941) was one of the greatest performers of his age and toured extensively through Europe and North America, and in 1904 included Australia and New Zealand. A rock star of his generation, Paderewski had especially built for him a Bechstein grand piano, which he insisted taking on tour with him as his reputation couldn't risk playing a public concert on a piano not up to standard. Along with the huge piano, his entourage included a piano tuner as well as a robust team of piano movers.

After touring Australia, Paderewski with his piano arrived by ship in Invercargill and worked his way up country until his final concerts in Auckland. Rather than ship the piano back to Europe, and no doubt offered a good price, he sold the piano to local pianist Mr JB McFarlane. The piano stayed in the same family until a grandson decided that the piano should be available for the public to see as well as performed on, and it ended up in the Whittaker collection where it holds pride of place and is regularly used.

Meanwhile Paderewski moved from music to politics, a staunch supporter of a Polish free state, on independence he became Prime Minister of Poland for just one year in 1919.

Retired couple Lloyd and Joan Whittaker have collected New Zealand's largest range of musical instruments, primarily pianos and keyboard instruments but also guitars, harps, squeeze boxes and accordions. Some of the instruments date back hundreds of years and visitors can try their hand at playing them.

The museum remains a musical treasure trove and attracts a good crowd to the monthly Sunday afternoon concerts.

📍 2 Korora Road, Oneroa.

- Open daily 10 am to 4 pm.
- 09 372 5573
- www.musical-museum.org

Waiheke Wineries – Goldwater Estate

The island is now home to over twenty wineries producing, in particular, some excellent Bordeaux blends and providing winery experiences that run from highly sophisticated restaurants and tasting rooms to more rustic and homely affairs.

Goldwater Estate was the first vineyard established on Waiheke in 1978 by Kim and Jeanette Goldwater with the first vintage produced in 1982; and while the focus is still on red, Goldwater now also grows chardonnay and viognier grapes on the island. Additional grapes are brought in from Marlborough and the famous Gimblett Gravels in the Hawkes Bay. Now known as Goldie Estate, the vineyard is also the home of the Goldwater Wine Science Centre, a collaborative venture between the Goldwater Family and the University of Auckland, Goldie Estate aims at combining practical experience with academic development.

- 18 Causeway Road, Surfdale
- Wednesday to Sunday 12 to 4 pm.
- 09 372 7493
- www.goldieestate.co.nz

Stoney Batter

One of the most impressive remains of New Zealand's coastal defence system, this complex was begun in 1942 to protect the northern approaches to Auckland from the Japanese. In reality the batter was not completed until 1948, well after the war was over, and the guns were never fired in defence. While very little exists above ground, the underground rooms are largely intact and surprisingly fresh in appearance. There is a small charge for access to the underground tunnels to support the maintenance of the area.

The area takes its name from distinctive rock formations that are the only remnants of two ancient volcanoes that erupted over eight million years ago. The open and lofty location gives excellent views over the Gulf, and a track leads down to Hooks Bay for those wanting a longer walk.

Stony Batter is at the less-developed eastern end of Waiheke Island and is not easy to get to. While the batter is only a 20-minute walk from the end of the road, getting that far can be tricky as there is no public transport. Cars and bikes can be hired near the ferry wharf. If you are planning to cycle, the road beyond Onetangi is very hilly, with the last 6 km gravel.

After being closed for a number of years, the underground tunnels reopened in December 2020. Access is by tour only on Friday, Saturday, Sunday and some public holidays. For bookings and more information, www. www.stonybattertunnels.nz

---

- Fullers 360 runs a regular ferry to the island from downtown Auckland with some ferries stopping in Devonport.
- 0800 3855377
- www.fullers.co.nz

5. Rotoroa Island

Purchased by the Salvation Army in 1908, Rotoroa was for over 100 years an alcohol and drug rehabilitation centre for men (the women were on nearby Pakatoa Island). Intensely farmed and developed, very little of the island's native vegetation survived with the exception of a few large pohutukawa clinging tenuously to the cliffs. Rotoroa Island today is a very different place and is now a wildlife sanctuary run by the Rotoroa Island Trust, together with the Auckland Zoo and the Department of Conservation. An excellent information centre details the history of the island as an alcoholic and drug treatment refuge under the auspices of the Salvation Army.

Over half the island has been replanted with more than 400,000 native plants, and although most are just a few metres high, common and rare native birds are making a comeback in this predator free environment. Weka were one bird to survive the earlier bush clearances and today large numbers are encountered all over the island. Tieke, kiwi, pateke and a pair of takehe have been reintroduced to Rotoroa, a small gannet colony is being encouraged and New Zealand dotterel nest on the beaches.

Two circuits, one going north and one south are easy walking and offer endless panoramic views over the Gulf, the long rugged hills of the Coromandel Peninsula and nearby Ponui and Waiheke islands. Several beaches are ideal for swimming, the best of which are Ladies Bay and Mens Bay, neither far from the wharf. Two hours is plenty of walking time on the island.

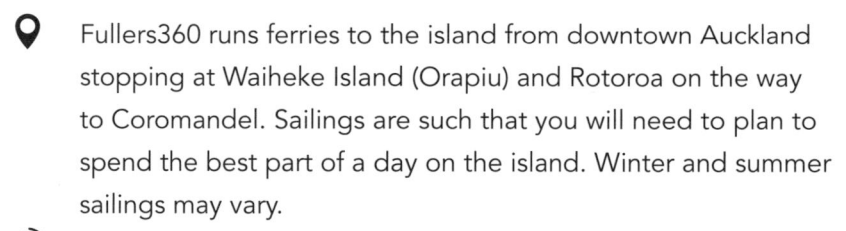

Fullers360 runs ferries to the island from downtown Auckland stopping at Waiheke Island (Orapiu) and Rotoroa on the way to Coromandel. Sailings are such that you will need to plan to spend the best part of a day on the island. Winter and summer sailings may vary.

0800 3855377

www.fullers.co.nz

6. Motutapu Island

Motutapu is in direct contrast to its near neighbour Rangitoto, from which it is separated by a mere few metres. While Rangitoto is less than 700 years old and volcanic in origin, Motutapu comprises sedimentary rock reaching back millions of years. The island has a long history of Maori occupation, and while the eruption of Rangitoto destroyed the villages at the time, it also laid down a layer of ash extremely beneficial for cultivation.

Currently the 1500-ha island is undergoing an intense replanting and predator-removal programme. There are several tracks over the rolling grassy hills with vistas over the gulf (there is very little native bush on the island). At Home Bay on the eastern side of the island is a good swimming beach and it has a wharf and basic camping ground.

> Motutapu is not easily accessible. The most reliable way is to catch the ferry to Rangitoto and then walk to Motutapu, though this is long day out with a lot of walking and you need to catch an early ferry. The other alternative is to plan ahead when Fullers run volunteers directly to the Home Bay for tree planting and related conservation work.
> 0800 3855377
> www.fullers.co.nz

7. Motuihe

This small inner-gulf island of only 179 hectares has a particularly colourful history. Long settled by Maori, it was briefly farmed by John Logan Campbell in the early 1840s but human occupation devasted the native flora and fauna on Motuihe, which was reduced to tiny bush remnants and only the very toughest birds. In 1873, the western part of the island became the quarantine station for Auckland and a small cemetery contains the graves of those who didn't make it through quarantine.

During the First World War it was a prisoner of war camp for Germans captured in Samoa, which was at the time a German colony. The island's most famous prisoner was the dashing Count Felix von Luckner, who engineered a daring escape on Christmas Day and, after a long sea chase, was finally captured near the Kermadec Islands and imprisoned in Lyttelton Harbour.

A naval training base during the Second World War, some buildings remain from this period, and more recently the island is undergoing reforestation and pest clearance for its new role as a bird sanctuary. Volunteers have planted 350,000 native plants and while most of the vegetation is only a few metres tall, 80 per cent of the island now has bush cover. With the removal of predators, the little spotted kiwi, kakariki, tieke and tuatara have all been reintroduced to the island and are flourishing.

Motuihe has two fine sandy beaches, one facing west and the other east which means that one beach will always be sheltered from the wind. The beaches are good swimming in all tides but best mid to high tide. It will take no more than two and a half hours to do the entire walking circuit around the island on good tracks – the signage is a bit erratic, though it doesn't matter too much as you won't get lost.

For such an attractive and accessible island, public transport options to the island have been very erratic. Now Fullers360 run a regular ferry fortnightly in the winter and more often in summer but check the Fullers360 website well in advance of any intended trip.

0800 3855377

www.fullers.co.nz

THAMES AND COROMANDEL

1. Totara Vineyard
2. Hoffman's Pool, Kauaeranga Valley
3. Thames School of Mines and Mineralogical Museum
4. Historic Thames Hotels
5. Bella Street Pumphouse
6. Goldmine Experience
7. Rapaura Water Gardens
8. Square Kauri
9. The 309 Road
10. Coromandel Town
11. Coromandel Seafood
12. Coromandel Coastal Walkway
13. Opito Pa
14. Coromandel Beaches
15. Whitianga Pa
16. The Coroglen Tavern
17. Te Pare Historic Reserve Hahei
18. Paku Peak, Tairua
19. Broken Hills Gold Town
20. Pauanui

This is a loop tour circumventing the Coromandel Peninsula starting at Thames and ending at Whirtoa, just south of Whangamata. This is not the usual north to south listing but is a logical sequence for anyone touring around the peninsula. The Coromandel is very hilly country with a torturous coastline and, while most roads are sealed and in good condition, driving is slow going. The roads are winding and frequently narrow with many one lane bridges, and in the summer months the traffic is very heavy. A long, stretch of the road from Colville to Port Jackson is unsealed and gravel roads are common. Avoid going anywhere in a hurry.

1. Totara Vineyard

Established in 1950 this vineyard is very unusual in that it has always been Chinese owned. Originally a 3-hectare market garden, Joe Ah Chan grew, along with vegetables, Albany Surprise, a popular table grape. Gradually the vineyard expanded as Joe realised there was a market for 'hooch', quietly produced 'out the back'. Things changed when Stanley Young Chan, the father of the current owner, purchased the property. With experience in rice wine and whiskey from China, the quality of the alcoholic beverages improved considerably, and Totara began producing both table and fortified wines of which Totara Café Coffee Liqueur is the most famous. Not great grape growing country, the current winemaker Gilbert Chan sources grapes from elsewhere, but still produces this signature drink on the premises as well a variety of traditional style liqueurs, ports and sherries which are available for tasting. This style of wine is somewhat out of fashion, but keep an open mind and drop in for a taste – you might just be very surprised. Along with locally produced drinks, Totara Vineyard also operates as a regular bottle store.

- 219 Ngati Maru Hwy/SH 25, 4 km south of Thames.
- Open Monday to Thursday 10 am to 6 pm, Friday till 9 pm Saturday and Sunday 10 am to 5.30 pm.
- 07 868 6798

2. Hoffman's Pool, Kauaeranga Valley

It was timber, and not gold, that attracted Europeans to this valley behind Thames, and from 1871 through to 1928 the magnificent kauri forests were milled virtually to extinction. While the scars of the forestry era still remain, the bush has reclaimed much of the land, and the old pack tracks and tramlines now form part of the extensive track system.

Hoffman's Pool combines a nature walk with milling ruins and it is a perfect swimming hole at a point where the Kauaeranga River divides. The pool is deep and clear, there is a rock to jump off, and even better part of the pool has a lovely sandy bottom rather that stones. Across the valley is a view of the rock formation called the Chief's Head, an outcrop that really does look like a head. Along the river is in old stone wall – all that remains of the Thames water supply established in 1874 – and the concrete slab by the pool is one of the piles of the old Kauaeranga Tramline which crossed the river at this point.

📍 Hoffman's Pool is 1.8 km from the Kauaeranga Valley Visitors Centre.

3. Thames School of Mines and Mineralogical Museum

Thames is the largest settlement on the Coromandel and its main street, Pollen Street, still retains a facade that would be familiar to a visitor from 1900 when the town had a population of 18,000. Originally two settlements, Grahamstown in the north and Shortland in the south, Thames flourished in the second half of the nineteenth century in response to the gold mined both locally and on the peninsula. Given its proximity to the mines, Grahamstown dominated early Thames, but after a disastrous flood in 1917, followed by the decline of mining, the retail and service centre of the town moved further south to Shortland.

Mining schools were once common but of the thirty mining schools established throughout New Zealand, only Thames, Coromandel and Reefton have survived. This museum comprises three parts: the school, the mineral collection and a shop. The school, opened in 1886 and closed in 1954, was the largest in the country and the current building has largely survived unaltered, with classrooms looking much as they would have 100 years ago. The Mineralogical Museum was opened in 1900 and has an incredible collection of minerals from both New Zealand and around the world still in their original Edwardian glass cases. The shop has an extensive collection of minerals for sale and entry to the complex is through the shop.

- 101 Cochrane Street, Thames.
- Open Wednesday to Sunday, April to December, 11 am to 3 pm. Daily, January to March, 11 am to 3 pm.
- www.thamesschoolofmines.co.nz
- Entrance fee.

4. Historic Thames Hotels

In 1872 Thames boasted 112 hotels and two breweries providing the boomtown with accommodation, liquor, food and 'other services', but today just three remain.

The Junction Hotel

Built in 1869, it takes its name from its location between the two distinct settlements, Shortland to the south and Grahamstown to the north, the boundary of which was marked by the Karaka Stream. The Junction today would be easily recognised by a time traveller from the gold rush days. The main bar on the corner of Pollen and Pahau Street, with its extensive use of wood, polished floors and historic photos and sketches is both stylish and functional and the atmosphere warm and welcoming.

📍 700 Pollen Street, Thames.

The Brian Boru Hotel

Originally named the Reefers Arms, it was the first pub built by Ned Twohill in 1868. The Twohill family ran the hotel for the next 106 years until 1974 and it is said that the ghost of Florence Twohill who, with her sister Violet, were the hotel's publicans in the 1920s, still lingers in the Brian Boru as she can't bear to leave. The Brian Boru today retains its magnificent Victorian exterior with grand wrap-round wooden verandas presiding over the main street. However, the recent years have not been kind to this fine old hotel and today only one bar along the main street remains open. Cnr Pollen and Richmond Street, Thames.

The Imperial Hotel

In contrast to the The Junction and The Brian Boru, The Imperial Hotel is very different. Established on this site in 1884, the hotel was rebuilt in 1937 in the modern Art Deco style taking full advantage of its corner site. The interior still retains many of its original features and offers comfortable accommodation and good value meals. 474 Pollen Street.

5. Bella Street Pumphouse

Built in 1909 for the Anglo-Continental company for The May Queen goldmine, this pumphouse was, at the time, the largest deep-level mining pump in the southern hemisphere reaching a depth of over 300 m. Very close to the coast, the water table here at Thames is very high and mines had considerable trouble keeping workings dry which severely limited the depth to which they could sink a shaft. This huge pumphouse allowed The May Queen and twenty other surrounding mines to go much deeper. Today the building and concrete foundations seven metres thick are all still in place, along with a huge collection of historic photos and industrial artefacts, and the recreated poppet head behind the pump house.

- 212 Bella Street.
- Open 10 am to 4 pm.
- Entrance fee.

6. Goldmine Experience

Established on the famous Golden Crown mine site, the Goldmine Experience has both a working five-head stamper battery and an underground mine.

Gold was discovered in the area in August 1867 and the name Golden Crown turned out to be so appropriate as this was one of the richest gold strikes in the country, producing over 2,250,000 oz of gold. While the mine closed in 1886, the stamper battery and processing plant continued to service other mines and didn't close until the 1960s. With many of the original buildings still standing, locals realised they had an opportunity to preserve a slice of Thames Historic. A group of ex-goldminers set up the Hauraki Prospectors Association and the Goldmine Experience is still run by volunteers today.

The site is surprisingly extensive and, in addition to the mine and battery, there is an audio-visual and photographic display, steam-powered machines and of course the incredibly noisy stamper battery. Access is by tour only, takes less than an hour and is led by entertaining and knowledgeable former engineers.

- Corner SH 25 and Moanataiari Road, Thames.
- Tours are at 10.30 am and 1 pm.
- 07 868 8514
- www.goldmine-experience.co.nz
- Entrance fee.

7. Rapaura Water Gardens

Established in the early 1960s by Fritz and Josephine Loennig, these gardens are the place to come for quiet relaxation and contemplation. A well-established garden, there is a short walk that links the sculptures and water features set among mature trees and shrubs. In spring, iris, azaleas and rhododendrons are in bloom followed in summer by water lilies, hydrangeas, orchids and begonias. There is also a longer bush walk to a pretty waterfall, 'The Seven Stairs to Heaven', and in summer the cafe is open while accommodation is available all year round.

- 586 Tapu-Coroglen Road, Tapu.
- Open daily 9 am to 5 pm.
- www.rapaurawatergardens.co.nz
- Entrance fee.

8. Square Kauri

A short twenty minute return walk up a lot of steps leads to this huge kauri over 40 m high and more than 1000 years old, and named for the relatively square nature of the trunk.

- On the Tapu-Coroglen Road 9 km from Tapu.

9. The 309 Road

Linking Coromandel town and Whitianga, travelling along this road is a flashback to the early days of travel on the peninsula. Narrow, winding, but not too long (42 km), the road wends its way along river valleys and twists up through the rugged Coromandel Range (summit 306 m). It is not suitable for large vehicles and a 12 km section is a mixture of seal and gravel.

On the Coromandel side of the range are several places of interest, and if you don't fancy driving all the way to Whitianga, these places are in easy reach of Coromandel town.

Four kilometres from the junction with Highway 25 you won't miss Stuart and the Pigs. Here a large friendly group of wild pigs roam alongside the road and are forever on the lookout for a tasty treat. The pigs are not aggressive but are very eager for a tasty snack, so come prepared.

A further 4 km on is the fascinating Waiau Waterworks, a one-hectare garden of water-powered sculptures, a water-driven clock and a pedal-powered pump and, unlike most gardens, this one has plenty of things to play on and is one of Coromandel's popular destinations (entrance fee).

Further up the valley where the road becomes more challenging are the Waiau Falls, a picturesque small waterfall in the bush with a swimming hole.

Half a kilometre on from the falls, and just below the summit, is the Waiau Kauri Grove. Isolated at the head of steep valley, this small grove of massive old kauri luckily escaped the miller's axe, and this rare patch of mature forest is now accessible by an excellent short track. It includes an unusual double trunk tree, which began life as two seedlings that eventually grew together and fused at the base.

10. Coromandel Town

Gold was discovered just north of Coromandel by Charles Ring in 1852, but it was not easy to mine and it was not until much later that technology was developed for extracting the gold-bearing that led to the boom in Coromandel that lasted well into the twentieth century. While most of the buildings in this very touristy town are recent historic lookalikes, the town has several important buildings dating back to the gold-rush era (the Information Centre has an excellent leaflet, complete with map).

In the centre of town is the old Assay House on the corner of Kapanga and Tiki Roads. An Assay House assesses precious metals to independently determine their quality. In this case it determined the quality and weight of a miner's gold prior to the miner selling it, in order to prevent fraudulent dealings. The Assay House is behind the main building which was the old National Bank (built in 1873).

By far the most important building is The Government Buildings and Court House (also built in 1873) which has been beautifully restored. In New Zealand a system of provincial government was set up in 1841 as it was felt that the central government system was too inefficient for so many isolated settlements. However, by the early 1870s, isolation was less of a problem and it was then felt that three levels of government was too many in a country of less than 600,000 people, and the provincial governments were abandoned in 1876. Coromandel was part of the Auckland Province and this building is a very rare survivor from this period.

355 Kapanga Road.

The Coromandel Hotel began life in 1862 when, to take advantage of the business opportunities in the flourishing gold town, the two storied Kikowhakarere Hotel was moved south and renamed the Coromandel Hotel. In the early 1930s the hotel suffered a major fire that destroyed the top floor and only the ground floor was rebuilt, and the hotel today is just a single storey. Affectionately known as the 'top pub', the Coromandel retains all the atmosphere of a good country pub, so if you are looking for a bit of genuine kiwi hospitality away from the 'flash' of Coromandel's trendy main street, then look no further than the Coromandel Hotel.

611 Kapanga Road.

Along the same road (the road changes its name to Ring Road, just past the pub) is the old School of Mines Building. Dating from 1897 it is now known as the Coromandel Mining and Historical Museum.

841 Rings Road.

A little further north on Buffalo Road is the historic Buffalo Cemetery, which takes its name from the ship the *HMS Buffalo*. The first person to be buried here was a seaman on the *Buffalo*, David Wanks, killed while loading kauri spars in January 1838.

11. Coromandel Seafood

Coromandel is home to a small fishing fleet but is now better known for its mussel and oyster farms which generate an annual income of over $75 million and provide 400 local jobs. For the visitor there are two good places to try out these tasty treats.

In the centre of town is the Coromandel Smoking Company which, as the name suggests, focusses on smoked fish and mussels – all of which a locally sourced and smoked on the premises. Available for purchase at any given time are around six types of smoked fish and more than ten varieties of smoked mussels. Even better, you can buy a mix of the mussels which range from plain smoked to very spicy. Rich and flavoursome, they are ideal for cooking or just on their own with your favourite drink, savoured as the sun goes down.

Just five kilometres south of the town is the Coromandel Oyster Company and here you can have your favourite seafood cooked in a rustic garden just a few metres away from the sea. There is a range of casual snacks and meals available including natural oysters and mussels. They also offer seafood chowder, paua patties and a variety of fish including fresh flounder and prawns. It's a lovely spot full of atmosphere and you can even eat your food sitting on an old oyster badge.

12. Coromandel Coastal Walkway

The track, well-formed and medium to easy grade, winds through regenerating bush and has great views over the coastline at the top of the peninsula and out to Great Barrier Island. However, this track links the northern endpoints of the roads of both the east and west coasts and, although only three hours' walk one way, the trip by road is around 120 km (camping grounds either end). You either must walk back the way you came or have someone take a car around to meet you. There are shuttles available, but they are expensive and most rental car companies will not insure their cars on this road.

> This one-way track can either be accessed from Fletchers Bay (27 km from Colville), or from Stony Bay (9 km north of Port Charles).

13. Opito Pa

This magnificent pa occupies the whole of the headland that shelters the southern end of Opito beach. Steep slopes made attack difficult from the north, and sheer cliffs made it impossible from the south. A steep bluff protected the landward side of the pa, which was further enhanced by several defensive ditches. The headland itself has numerous broad terraces and is pitted with rua (for storing kumara) and house sites. The views across the beach and along the coast are spectacular.

> At Kuaotunu take the Black Jack Road first to Otama beach and then to Opito, and follow the road to the very end (parts of this road are winding and gravel).
> The staircase to the pa is a short walk along the beach.

14. Coromandel Beaches

For many, Coromandel is epitomised by visions of an azure sea breaking on to the sparkling white sand on a lonely beach backed by huge shady pohutukawa. The reality, however, is that this popular holiday destination for both New Zealand and international visitors is often crowded, and spots like the famous Cathedral Cove and Hot Water Beach are just as packed as Takapuna Beach or Oriental Parade. The good news is that it only takes a short walk to reach some very idyllic spots and while you may not have the beach all to yourself, you will be far away from the noisy crowds. These seven beaches all on the eastern side of the Coromandel peninsula are easy to get to beauty spots that won't disappoint. A word of warning – isolation has its price. The facilities at these beaches are basic and mostly just a simple toilet and few if any have surf lifesaving patrols, even in the middle of summer. The eastern side of the peninsula is often exposed to heavy swells directly off the open ocean and can be dangerous for swimming. The beaches are listed north to south.

Waikawau Bay

A wonderful sweep of untouched beach, this bay is 40 km north of Coromandel town (a good stretch of this road is dusty gravel). There is huge DOC camping ground which has basic facilities and can get pretty crowded at the peak of the holiday season.

New Chums Beach

A twenty-minute walk from the northern end of Whangapoua beach is a long stretch of white sandy beach lapped by clear water. The beach is backed by handsome native bush and over-hung with old pohutukawa trees which provide plenty of shade.

Otama Beach

In comparison with tree-lined New Chums, Otama Beach is totally open and backed by high sand dunes covered only in grasses. With only a few houses at the southern end, the dunes are now a nature reserve protecting the whole length of the beach from further development. The beach looks out over the Mercury Islands and the best access is from the northern end at the bottom of the Black Jack Hill. There is a basic camping ground at Otama with water, but no toilets.

📍 To reach Otama from Kauotunu take the Black Jack Road for 5 km - the road is narrow, unsealed and winding.

Shakespeare Cliff and Lonely Bay

Located between Cook's Beach and Flaxmill Bay, this headland has extensive views over the bay, and a plaque commemorates James Cook's visit in November 1769. Cook fancied he saw a likeness to an orator reciting Shakespeare outlined in the cliff and named it after the bard. A steep track leads down to the quiet, pohutukawa-lined Lonely Bay, one of Coromandel's loveliest small beaches which is very safe for swimming.

📍 Purangi Road, Cooks Beach or catch the Whitianga Ferry and walk 1.5km to the reserve.

Sailors Grave and Otara Beach

Sailors Grave is a small sand cove and it really does have a sailor's grave. In May 1842 William Samson from the ship *HMS Tortoise* was killed while loading kauri spars. His lonely grave is now maintained by the New Zealand Navy. Just a short 20-minute walk over a headland to the north is Otara Bay, another less visited lovely sandy beach.

📍 Four kilometres north of Tairua on SH 25 turn right into Sailors Grave Road and drive down to the beach.

Opoutere Beach

A ten-minute walk from the road seems to be too much for most people. One of the few undeveloped beaches on the Coromandel, Opoutere is a taste of what this coast was like before the baches took over. This is such a long beach that, even on a busy day, it is just a matter of strolling along the shore until you find the spot you like. There is no shade along this beach, and it can be quite exposed on a hot summer's day. Towards the mouth of the river is the Wharekawa Harbour Sandspit Wildlife Refuge, an important breeding ground for several endangered birds including the New Zealand Dotterel, and the nesting grounds are roped off during the spring and summer. (Leave the dog at home).

📍 To get to the beach, the turnoff to Opoutere is 10 km north of Whangamata and the beach access a further 5km from the turnoff.

Waimama Bay

From the northern end of Whiritoa Beach, this tiny cove is reached by an easy track over a headland which takes about twenty minutes to walk. Flanked by rocks at either end of the beach, this small stretch of white sand has large spreading pohutukawa trees, ideal for lounging in the shade on a hot day. The beach drops steeply into the water here and the surf can be surprisingly powerful so take extra care swimming. At the southern end of the beach at low tide are bath-sized rock pools ideal for cooling off while the waves crash against the rocks below.

📍 Whiritoa Beach is 14 km south of Whangamata.

15. Whitianga Pa

Whitianga is a contraction of Te Whitianga-a-Kupe, 'Kupe's crossing place'; as the name suggests, Kupe explored the area around 1000 AD. While tradition has it that his people settled here and built the pa, the area has been more closely associated with Ngati Hei. Hei was the captain of Te Arawa waka. He settled here, and what is now called Mercury Bay is known in Maori as Te Whanganui a Hei, 'the great harbour of Hei'.

However, when Captain James Cook visited the area in November 1769 the pa had fallen into disuse, the blackened stumps of the palisades a sign that the pa had been burnt. Local Maori told Cook that about thirty years earlier the pa had fallen to an attack by Ngati Rangi, an iwi from the Tauranga area. Even though the pa was in ruins, Cook was impressed by the defences, especially the very deep defensive ditches which would originally have been topped by a bank and crowned by stout palisading. Cook commented:

'A little with[in] the entrance of the river on the East side is a high point or peninsula jutting out into the River on which are the remains of one of their Fortified towns, the Situation is such that the best Engineer in Europe could not have choose'd a better for a small number of men to defend themselves against a greater, it is strong by nature and made more so by Art.'

Even today the pa is very impressive and surprisingly large. The main defensive ditch remains, though substantially diminished in size, and is now part of the track to Back Bay. Like all headland pa, Whitianga relied heavily on the steep cliffs water for defence. An unusual feature of the pa is the shallow holes in a flat slab of rock in the middle of the pa: the best guess is that the hole supported poles for some type of platform, possibly a watchtower.

📍 Take the ferry from Whitianga township over to Ferry Landing. The pa is immediately to the right of the landing.

16. The Coroglen Tavern

A hotel was originally built down by the river in 1879 when Coroglen was known by the glamourous name of Gumtown, reflecting the reliance on kauri gum rather than gold or timber. Like so many Coromandel towns, the population declined and the gum diggers were long gone by the time the town changed its name to Coroglen in 1922 (after a famous racehorse). Burnt down and moved several times, the current pub dates from 1946.

Justifiably one of New Zealand's iconic pubs, the Coroglen skilfully combines the rustic with the modern and is famous as a summer music venue. Whether you want to grab a good coffee, a cold beer or good country food, this a great place to kick back and relax in the very best of New Zealand style or just settle down and watch the world go by from the front veranda.

📍 On SH 25, 17 km south of Whitianga.

17. Te Pare Historic Reserve Hahei

A stronghold of Ngati Hei, who arrived in the area on the waka Te Arawa in 1350, this reserve includes two pa sites: Hereheretaura Pa on the headland and Hahei Pa on the high ridge to the right. Hereheretaura Pa must be one of the most beautifully situated pa in the country, with broad terraces occupying a rocky headland, the sea on three sides and with a magnificent outlook over Mercury Bay and Hahei beach.

Hahei Pa is quite different and is less accessible but easily recognised by the north-facing terraces that fan out down the hillside, though there are no visible signs of defence earthworks. Hereheretaura, on the other hand, has both a ditch and steep banks to protect the pa from attack.

📍 The track to the pa site begins either at the end of Pa Road or leads up from the southern end of the beach.

18. Paku Peak, Tairua

Discovered by Kupe around 1000 AD, the Coromandel coast has a long history of Maori settlement. They were originally attracted to the area by the now extinct moa and the abundant kai moana. Ngati Hei settled here and Paku, once an island, was the ideal position for a major fortified pa.

Below the old pa site is an ancient pohutukawa tree. Tradition tells of a chief who left his wife to go off to battle and, when her husband did not return his wife, consumed with grief, climbed into the tree and there she died. Thereafter the tree was named Pikiariki or 'the climb of the chieftainess'.

Originally a Ngati Hei stronghold, Tairua succumbed to Ngati Maru invaders in the seventeenth century. Their tenure was not to last as Ngapuhi, heavily armed with muskets, swept down the coast in the 1820s. Ngati Maru escaped inland to take refuge with their Tainui relatives, where most settled permanently and the pa was never reoccupied.

The only known artefact linking Aotearoa to Eastern Polynesia, a fish lure, was found in the sand dune behind Tairua beach in 1964. The lure is made from black-lipped pearl oyster shell. These oysters are not found in New Zealand and so, given the location of the find, this must have been brought to the area by an immigrant from Eastern Polynesia.

European Tairua began life as a timber-milling town, shipping out vast quantities of kauri and other native timber from the small port on the Tairua River. Today, visitors are attracted by the fine sweep of surf beach that faces out to Slipper Island and Shoe Island and beyond them, the Aldermen Islands, well known for their excellent fishing.

A short rocky scramble leads to the top of the volcanic peak and the rewards are dramatic coastal and inland views.

> From the Tairua shopping centre off SH 2, turn into Manaia Road, then left into Paku Drive and follow the road to the carpark just below the summit.

19. Broken Hills Gold Town

Gold was first discovered here in 1893 and, as was typical of goldfields, a small town sprang up overnight. In the 1930s the gold ran out and today Broken Hills is a maze of short walks that lead to fascinating ruins. Not far from the car park are the substantial ruins of the battery built in 1899. A longer track follows the old water race that supplied water to the battery, and this features a number of short tunnels. Further up the hill are old mine shafts and the impressive Collins Drive. This tunnel, over 500 metres long, was dug not to find gold but as a short cut through some particularly steep and difficult terrain. A torch is necessary for the Collins Drive and there are some great lookout points from this track as well.

However, it is the old gaol that is really appealing. Dug out of rock, the tiny, dark and damp cell looks like something from the dungeon of a scary castle, and scarier still are the hordes of cave weta quietly shuffling on the stony ceiling. Although very small, you will need a torch and be prepared for a big surprise.

This is a great place to bring children to explore and there is also a camping ground beside the river.

○ Take Morrisons Road opposite the Pauanui turnoff on SH 25 and after 1 km turn left into Puketui Road and follow to the carpark at the end of this road.

20. Pauanui

Pauanui is completely different from most coastal settlements which have grown from a cluster of self-built baches to busy townships in a haphazard manner without the benefit of planning or design. Pauanui, however, was built from scratch in the early 1970s and, while parts of the town may look a bit like a Lockwood museum and the Waterways area is well known for some of the most extravagant seaside houses in the country, it has protected public access to the water with wide reserves, along with excellent cycleways and footpaths. A regular ferry operates between Pauanui and Tairua, a short distance across the Tairua river estuary, but a long way by road.

Right in the centre of the town is a landing strip where light aircraft take off and land just metres above the beach. At the southern end of the beach, Mt Pauanui is a short but steep climb to the top (387 m) and the reward is fantastic views north over Pauanui and Tairua.

BAY OF PLENTY

1. Martha Mine, Waihi
2. Victoria Battery and Museum
3. Waitewheta Tramway
4. Waihi Beach – Orokawa and Homunga Bays Walk
5. Haiku Park, Katikati
6. The Cider Factorie, Te Puna
7. Te Puna Quarry Park
8. Macrocarpa Tree, Bethlehem
9. Patrick's Pie/Gold Star Bakery Bethlehem
10. The Elms Mission House
11. Central Tauranga
12. Gate Pa
13. The Historic Village
14. Yatton Park
15. The Rising Tide and the Mount Brewing Co, Mt Maunganui
16. Classic Flyers Museum
17. The Lion and Tusk – Museum of the Rhodesian Services Association
18. Mayor Island
19. McLarens Falls Park
20. Kaiate Falls
21. Karangaumu Pa, Papamoa Hills Regional Park, Te Puke
22. Maketu
23. White Island
24. Moutohora/Whale Island
25. Matahina Dam
26. Kaputerangi/Toi's Pa, Whakatane
27. Whakatane River and Historical Walk
28. Ohope Scenic Reserve – Fairbrother Loop Walk
29. Ohiwa Oyster Farm
30. Burial Tree/Hukutaia Domain, Opotiki
31. Hiona St Stephen's Church, Opotiki
32. Royal Hotel, Opotiki
33. Shalfoon's Store and the De Luxe Theatre – Opotiki Museum
34. Tirohanga Dunes Trail

1. Martha Mine, Waihi

In 1878 gold was discovered at Martha Hill behind what is now Waihi town, and work quickly began on establishing a mine. By 1882 a stamper was in operation and the huge Victoria Battery at Waikino was constructed in 1897. The Cornish pump house (a short walk from the Waihi Information Centre) was built in 1904 and finally closed in the 1930s. It is often mistaken for the ruins of an old church. Waihi was the centre of a bitter six-month strike in 1912 that resulted in the death of miner Fred Evans, one of only two deaths during industrial disputes in New Zealand. The Martha Mine was finally closed in 1952 and by that time had produced 174,160 kg of gold and 1,193,180 kg of silver.

During the 1980s, with gold prices rising, the Martha Mine was reopened, though this time as an open-cast mine. In 2006 the massive concrete pump house was moved 270 metres as the ground on the original site had become unstable. The Martha mine website has a good series of photos showing the move (www.marthamine.co.nz). There are two viewing platform, one on the western side of the pit, the other by the pumphouse.

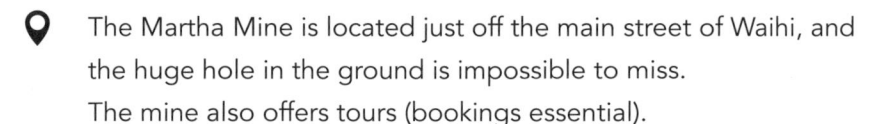

The Martha Mine is located just off the main street of Waihi, and the huge hole in the ground is impossible to miss.

The mine also offers tours (bookings essential).

07 863 9880

www.marthamine.co.nz

2. Victoria Battery and Museum

One of New Zealand's largest industrial sites is today reduced to substantial concrete foundations with scattered rusting machinery which was either too large or valueless to cart away.

Operating from 1897 to 1954, the Victoria Battery had 200 stampers – the largest such operation anywhere in the world – and processed around

800 tonnes of ore a day. Working 24 hours a day, the stampers were only turned off from midnight Saturday to mid-Sunday. Such was the noise that the stampers could be heard at Waihi eight kilometres away and, with little regard for health and safety, those working near the stampers became stone deaf.

The ore came from the Martha Mine at Waihi by rail with fourteen trips a day of forty wagons each loaded with a tonne of ore. The battery used huge amounts of timber to process the ore and eventually resorted to direct crushing once the timber ran out.

The only building remaining on the site is the Transformer House built when a hydro power station was constructed in 1913. This building is now a museum which is open Wednesdays and Sundays (precise hours seem to be erratic so it might pay to phone ahead if you want to visit the museum).

Throughout the extensive site are excellent information boards with detailed historical photos showing the original complex.

> You can drive to the site via a narrow road off Waitawheta Road (by the waterfall) on SH 2 but it is much easier to park opposite the Waikino Hotel and walk across the footbridge.

3. Waitewheta Tramway

Karangahake Gorge has become such a popular destination that during the busy holiday periods it is difficult to find a park, so this less known walkway is a good alternative if you want a more relaxed day out.

Following an old logging tramway used between 1898 and 1928 to extract kauri, almost 14 km of the bush track is still intact. Naturally this track has a gentle gradient, but there is one major river crossing as the bridge is long gone, though the piles still remain. The track leads through a spectacular river gorge with rocky bush-clad bluffs, and near the beginning of the track there are some great swimming holes. The whole track can take up to seven hours return, but a more manageable walk up to the replica logging boggie takes just one hour.

📍 Turn right into Waitawheta Road 12 km east of Paeroa off SH 2 and follow the rather torturous road signs to the carpark at the end of Franklin Road.

4. Waihi Beach – Orokawa and Homunga Bays Walk

The first stretch of this well-formed track is a forty minute walk to Orokawa over bush-cloaked headlands with great views along the coast and out to Mayor Island. This track is easy walking and ideal for all ages. Orokawa Bay is lined with old pohutukawa trees overhanging a long stretch of untouched beach, just perfect for picnicking, but the surf here can be rough and there are no lifeguards, so take care when swimming – there are also occasional stingrays in the shallow waters.

At Homunga Bay a small stream drops off a steep bluff onto the beach, creating an ideal shower to rinse off after a swim. While most visitors just do the return trip to Orokawa Bay, the coastal stretch from Orokawa Bay to Homunga Bay is far more attractive and with fewer people. The best way to do this walk is to start from the northern end, but that requires a cooperative person to drop you off at the start. This means you walk down a steep hill to Homunga Bay then follow the coast, a pleasant and relatively easy two-hour walk. Failing that, this is a four-hour return walk.

📍 The northern end of the track to Homunga Bay is at the very end of Ngatitangata Road FromWaihi. Take SH 25 towards Whangamata and, after 1.2 km, turn right into Barry Street, which becomes Golden Bay Road and then Ngatitangata Road, a distance of 9 km. The southern end of the track begins at the northern end of Waihi Beach and can be a little tricky to reach right on high tide.

5. Haiku Park, Katikati

Haiku is a seventeen syllable poem and consists of five, seven and five syllables arranged in three lines. The world's shortest form of poetry, it was established as great literary form in Japan and is used to express profound truths in the simplest natural images.

Here in a small park in Katikati, the locals have been particularly innovative and rather than just establish yet another walk by a river, there is the Haiku walk. On rocks and stones along the riverbank are haiku poems from both local and international sources. This poetry is particularly suited to such a natural environment and at various points the haiku is directly related to the view in front of you. So when you are travelling on the busy SH2, stop for a while and contemplate the larger issues of life in this small park behind the shops.

📍 SH 2 Katikati, the easiest entrance is next to the Hammer Hardware in the main shopping centre.

6. The Cider Factorie, Te Puna

Entering the Cider Factorie through an avocado orchard, first thoughts immediately turn to 'is avocado cider, or even avocado flavoured cider, possible?' Concerns are immediately allayed once you set into the packing-shed style building, which is stylishly fitted out as a tasting room, eatery and cellar for this innovative cider brewery.

Producing three ranges including traditional and sparkling, the brewer has his finger firmly on New Zealand's most popular flavours. Despite New Zealand's long tradition of growing apples, cider has until recently occupied the fringes of local alcoholic tastes. Now New Zealand cider is internationally recognised as producing flavours that appeal to a whole new generation of drinks.

Here the feijoa cider leads the charge as the feijoa flavor has in recent years become as kiwi as ANZAC biscuits and pavlova, and sparkling feijoa cider is the perfect drink either at lunch or for a late afternoon tipple.

Cider aside, the location on a ridge above Tauranga harbour offers surprising views both north and south, and a thoughtful menu makes lunch on the wide sunny terrace just perfect. A local secret, the Cider Factory is a short detour off busy SH 2, just north of Tauranga.

📍 50 Oikimoke Road, Te Puna.
🕐 Open 11 am to 5 pm Wednesday to Sunday.
📞 07 552 4558
🌐 theciderfactorie.co.nz

7. Te Puna Quarry Park

What do you do with an old quarry in your neighbourhood? Well, lots, if you are the locals at Te Puna, just north of Tauranga. With an abandoned quarry on their doorsteps, residents banded together to form the Te Puna Quarry Park and set about creating a whimsical and delightful garden.

Leaving some of the infrastructure and machinery intact, the society has overlaid the quarry with gardens and artwork that not even the meanest and hardest heart will fail to enjoy. From the old storybook-like digger that children can play on in the car park through to heritage roses, there is plenty here for every age group. Over thirty pieces of artwork are spread around the gardens including a stylized sculpture of Hineura stone, pottery and a fabulous mosaic family grouping, complete with a small dog. Children in the know head straight for the outdoor percussion area, where young and old can bang and crash to their hearts content on a variety of 'instruments' without the fear of disturbing the neighbours.

The more formal plantings are on the lower area near the car park and include a contemplative oriental garden, heritage roses, vireya rhododendrons, bromeliads, succulents, South African plants and even a small kauri grove, while from the higher terraces there are excellent views over the Bay of Plenty.

📍 108 Te Puna Road, well signed posted off SH 2 at Te Puna just north of Tauranga.
🕐 Open daily 7 am to 7 pm.
🌐 www.quarrypark.org.nz

8. Macrocarpa Tree, Bethlehem

Sitting within a group of three macrocarpa (Cupressus macrocarpa), it is a bit difficult at first to spot which is the tallest tree, but concentrate and the true size of this tree becomes apparent. Towering over 50 metres, this is not just the tallest macrocarpa in New Zealand but in the world (though to be fair there is not much competition from trees in its native California). There the species is confined to just two small areas on the central coast and, exposed to the salt-laden air, the trees are little more than hedge height.

Planted in 1928 by Gordon Cummings, the trees at Bethlehem were part of a longer shelter belt as macrocarpa were extensively planted at that time to provide quick growing protection for orchards and animals in open paddocks. With close competition these trees grew tall and straight in comparison to the solid spreading shape of trees grown in the open.

📍 The tree is on private property at 168 Moffat Road, Bethlehem and is easily seen from the road.

9. Patrick's Pie/Gold Star Bakery Bethlehem

New Zealand has a long tradition of pie making and an enthusiastic tradition of eating them. Over the last twenty years the number of immigrant bakers, especially from Asia, has grown enormously and the range of pies now available is incredible. In 2003, Cambodian refugee Pat Lam from Bethlehem, won first place in the Bakels New Zealand Supreme Pie Award and then again in 2004, 2009, 2010, 2016 and 2018. In addition Pat has won so many prizes for his pies that certificates almost paper the walls in all of his three bakeries at Bethlehem and Tauriko in Tauranga and also in Rotorua.

📍 19 Bethlehem Road, Tauranga.
🕐 Open daily 8.00 am to 4.30 pm.

10. The Elms Mission House

Superbly sited on a bluff above the harbour, the Mission House was built in 1847 and is regarded as New Zealand's finest Georgian building. Unlike other missions, which were prefabricated elsewhere, this house was built of kauri on the Te Papa site. The house is virtually unaltered, including the beautiful curved staircase to the dormer bedrooms. The house contains some of the original furniture including a 'campaign' table from the 1820s, which is designed to come apart and be transported from place to place.

What also makes this mission special is that many of the mission outbuildings are still on site. The tiny freestanding library built in 1839 was the first permanent building at Te Papa mission, and still contains 1000 of the original books. Easily missed in the extensive grounds are the belfry dating from 1843 and a fencible cottage originally from Onehunga. The entrance to the mission is from behind the house, although the most attractive view of the house is from the other side. Recently a heritage garden has been established on recently acquired corner site with a focus on traditional Maori and Colonial period food gardening.

📍 15 Mission Street, Tauranga.
🕐 Open daily 11 am to 3 pm.
📞 07 577 9772
🌐 www.theelms.org.nz

11. Central Tauranga

With the stunning beaches of Mt Maunganui just a few kilometres away few visitors make central Tauranga their prime destination. Downtown Tauranga is a curious place and undergoing a transformation, but transforming to what is unclear. Shopping has been gutted by the rise of suburban malls and empty shops are everywhere. At the same time, the central city is increasingly becoming the place to eat or a night out. Mixed in with the food places are a number of appealing attractions, a scattering of historic buildings and a waterfront undergoing a revival. The following places can all be reached in a leisurely two hour walk around the city, though naturally this will take much longer if you decide to linger.

Robbins Park as a starting point is mostly significant in that the parking here is relatively easy and is close to The Elms Mission House.

Robbins Park

A small formal garden on a bluff overlooking the harbour with an exceptional rose garden, fountain, a tropical house and an ivy-covered Italianate colonnade.

📍 Cliff Road.

Monmouth Redoubt

In 1864 soldiers of the the 43rd Monmouth Light Infantry took over the old pa site Taumatakahawai on a high bluff above the harbour and created a redoubt which later became the headquarters of the Armed Constabulary.

◉ Cliff Road.

Te Awanui waka

Taking its name from the original name of Tauranga harbour, *Te Awanui* was created by master carver Tuti Tukaokao in 1973. Constructed from a single 300-year-old kauri tree, the waka is over 14 metres long and is housed in Te Urunga, a shelter that combines both traditional and contemporary styles.

◉ Cnr McLean Street and the Strand.

Te Kahui Matariki

In early June the constellation Matariki (Pleiades) rises above the horizon and heralds the southern New Year. These seven poupou by Tauranga carver James Tapiata each represent a star. The main carving, Kahui Matariki, is dressed in prestigious dogskin cloak and faces the mountain Mauao as a sign of respect.

◉ Cnr Dive Crescent and The Strand.

Bobby's Fish Market

Fishing boats land their catch literally metres from one of Tauranga's best secrets. Rain or shine this place is always busy whether you want to buy the freshest fish in town or a tasty meal to eat on the waterfront. Their mussel fritters are a speciality.

◉ Dive Crescent.

Tidal Steps

Sometimes the simplest ideas are the best. A set of broad concrete steps give access to the water, appealing to youngsters of all ages, and especially appealing is a narrow platform where the most energetic can dive and bomb all they like.

◉ Waterfront, The Strand.

Hairy Maclary Statues

Only opened in 2015, many of the figures are already worn smooth by the thousands of children clambering over their favourite story book character and his troublesome friends. While the cat at top of the pole grabs the attention, look out for Slinky Malinki hiding out on the edge of the group.

◉ Waterfront, The Strand.

Jazz Festival Historical Photos

Tauranga is famous for hosting the National Jazz Festival every Easter and this display of photos features highlights since the first festival in 1962.

◉ The Strand, near Wharf Street.

The Strand Restaurants.

Long the heart of Tauranga, this strip of eateries along the waterfront disguises some of the city's oldest buildings, but in all honesty, no one comes here for the architecture. The perfect place for the indecisive, restaurants, cafes and bistros line a long section of The Strand on Tauranga's waterfront. Nowhere else in New Zealand quite matches Tauranga's Strand for variety, choice and relaxed dining, especially appealing on a warm summers evening when diners pack the outdoor tables.

📍 The Strand.

Old Post Office

Legend has it that the original Tauranga Post Office was designed and destined for Gisborne which at the time was known as Turanga. Built completely in the wrong town, Turanga subsequently changed its name to Gisborne to avoid any further mix ups. True or not, this fine building in grand imperial baroque style opened in 1910 after the older wooden building burnt down in 1902. The stylish building now houses an equally stylish bistro and bar with a wide terrace along the front of the building ideal for lunch and summer dining. Holding pride of place is a dramatic (and somewhat dangerous looking) Russian coffee machine built in the early 1970s.

📍 41 Harrington Street.

Our Place

If eating at the Strand doesn't appeal head up to Our Place, a combination of speciality retail and casual eating in a complex entirely constructed of shipping containers.

📍 91 Willow Street.

Mosaics

Not content with mere coloured and patterned paving, Tauranga Council commissioned numerous artists to create tiled mosaics throughout the central city. Depicting a wide range of subjects, here you literally have art at your feet.

Devonport Street

At the top of Devonport Street are three of Tauranga's best known and longest established casual eateries that offer tasty food at excellent prices. They are in no particularly order: Turkish to Go, Queen Sushi and the Devonport Chinese Restaurant.

Brain Watkins House

First reaction is that someone has spelt Brian incorrectly, but Brain is the surname of the well-established Tauranga family who built this house in 1881 and whose family occupied it for the next 100 years. Gifted to the city in 1979 by Elva Brain Watkins, what makes this house unique is that it contains the family's furniture and possessions accumulated over 100 years. Walking through the house it like stepping into someone else's life.

Memorial Gates, Wharepai Domain

Last stop on this walk are a fine pair of memorial gates erected in 1921 to the dead of World War One. Just inside of the gates is an equally impressive statue to someone few people have even heard of, the Rev Canon Charles Jordan. Surely not intended as joke, why there are two small cannons in front of the statue is a mystery. Known to be argumentative, feisty and strong willed, the cannons possible reflect his personality.

📍 91 Cameron Road.

12. Gate Pa

During the conflict in the Waikato, Maori sympathisers in the Tauranga area supported the Tainui war effort by providing supplies through the port and with food from their farms and gardens. When rumours of Maori reinforcements from the East Coast on their way to the Waikato reached Governor Grey, he decided to finally cut off supplies by sending troops to Tauranga.

Realising that war was imminent, Rawiri Puhirake, rangatira of the Tauranga based iwi, Ngaiterangi, instructed Henare Taratoa to draw up a list of rules that the combatants were to follow – a list that the Maori fighters religiously adhered to in the fighting. Issued 28 on March 1864, this extraordinary document read as follows:

To the Colonel,

Friend, – Salutations to you. The end of that. Friend, do you give heed to our laws for regulating the fight.

Rule 1. If wounded or captured whole, and butt of the musket or hilt of the sword be turned to me, he will be saved.

Rule 2. If any Pakeha, being a soldier by name, shall be travelling unarmed and meets me, he will be captured, and handed over to the direction of the law.

Rule 3. The soldier who flees, being carried away by his fears, and goes to the house of the priest with his gun (even though carrying arms) will be saved. I will not go there.

Rule 4. The unarmed Pakehas, women and children, will be spared.

The end.

These are binding laws for Tauranga.

By Terea Puimanuka
Wi Kotiro
Pine Amopu
Kereti
Pateriki.
Or rather by all the Catholics at Tauranga

With the rules established, Rawiri then proceeded to construct a fortified pa at Pukehinahina, about 5 km from the Te Papa mission where the British had set up camp. Designed by Pene Taka, this pa had traditional Maori elements of defence such as palisades and ditches, but significantly adapted them to take into account long-range rifles and, more importantly, cannon fire. This sophisticated design was later attributed to both the defeat and the high number of British casualties suffered in the attack. Consisting of two redoubts, the main pa occupied the top of the small hill, while a smaller redoubt was located 20 metres away. Between the two was a deep ditch which was to accommodate 600 warriors.

On 21 April General Sir Duncan Cameron finally arrived at Tauranga with over 600 troops and heavy artillery. He was joined a short time later by 430 naval personnel, and by 28 April Cameron had almost 2000 men under his command. Opposing him were fewer than 250 Maori defenders.

The attack began on the morning of 29 April with a bombardment of the pa by mortars, howitzers, naval cannon and Armstrong guns, which continued through to the middle of day and resumed a short time later, finally ending at 3 pm. With such substantial firepower against a fort of earth and timber, the British had every reason to feel confident when the advance assault party of 300 men attacked the pa at 4 pm.

What happened next is not entirely certain, but one thing is clear: the defenders had suffered few casualties during the bombardment as they had been safe deep underground in the superbly designed pa. In addition, a flagpole had been placed at the back of the pa and not in the centre, causing the British to aim for the pole, only to have the shells overshoot the main redoubt. Storming deep into the pa, the attacking force was met by withering crossfire, only made worse when General Cameron mistakenly believed that the pa had been taken and ordered a further 300 reinforcements into the small space.

With many of the officers killed or wounded the British panicked and retreated from the pa and were then caught in the open by further crossfire from the smaller redoubt. By the end of the day the British had suffered 100 casualties, compared to an estimated 25 Maori casualties. However, the Maori defenders realised that the pa was impossible to defend against such overwhelming odds and by dawn the next day the pa was deserted.

The battle was a disaster for the British and the blame rightly fell on General Cameron, though official accounts smoothed over the defeat. However, revenge was not long coming and on 21 June the British inflicted a heavy defeat on Ngaiterangi at Te Ranga, about 6 km from Gate Pa. During the battle both Rawiri Puhirake and Henare Taratoa were killed, resulting in a final surrender in July. Following the surrender came the inevitable confiscation of Ngaiterangi land by the government, who in turn sold the land to settlers.

Several stories of Maori chivalry are connected to the battle. Maori adhered to the guidelines drawn up by Henare Taratoa, and during the night after the battle Henare is said to have crossed through British lines to bring water to the British wounded. In 1900 Heni Pore made the claim that she had given water to the fatally wounded Colonel Booth during the same night.

Rawiri Puhirake, who died and was buried at Te Ranga, was later reburied in the Tauranga cemetery next to his foe Colonel Booth.

Today Gate Pa Domain, a small attractive park, occupies the site of the battle and a carved gateway leads to a short walk with excellent storyboards outlining the details of the battle. The main pa was on the high point where St George's Anglican church now stands along with a small memorial to the dead from both sides of the conflict.

The name 'Gate Pa' is derived from a gate in the boundary fence to let in supplies; and the main road through Tauranga, Cameron Road, is named after the leader of the British troops.

Gate Pa Domain, Corner Cameron and Church Streets.

13. The Historic Village

On a pleasant autumn Sunday afternoon, the car park is empty, no one walks the empty streets, and nothing is open in Tauranga's Historic Village. Neat and tidy, it feels like strolling through a movie set. You begin to wonder if there is about to be a shootout, but you are the only one who doesn't know about it. Opened in 1977, at first the village was a huge attraction and even won a tourism award in the same year. Visited once or twice, few people returned and, located at some distance from the central city, the village has struggled ever since. Possibly it is busier during the week, but if you want to feel like a film star on an empty movie set, come on a Sunday afternoon.

17th Avenue West, Tauranga.

14. Yatton Park

Yatton Park sits on a bluff overlooking an estuary thick with mangroves in suburban Tauranga. Purchased in 1864 by John Chadwick, a keen horticulturalist, he called his property Yatton and set about building a house and importing over 100 trees from around the world. In 1884, Yatton was sold to Lucy Mansel, a keen gardener who extended the garden even further. Sold in 1918 and again 1919, the house burnt down and many of the pines were milled for timber.

In the early 1950s local MP George Walsh convinced the government to purchase the land for a park, but the land became neglected and overgrown and it wasn't until 1970 that Yatton was developed into the superb public park it is today.

The combination of the benign climate and the densely planted trees has produced many trees that are the tallest in the country particularly pine trees including chir, hoop, Norfolk Island and Bunya pine. The Bhutan cypress at 37 metres is the tallest in the world.

Along with the exceptional trees are more formal flower gardens, a water feature and a children's playground, making Yatton Park a great place for a botanical stroll or a family picnic.

Yatton Park, Fraser Street, Greerton.

15. The Rising Tide and the Mount Brewing Co, Mt Maunganui

When the sun goes down over Mt Maunganui's industrial area, businesses close for the day, the workers go home, and the streets are empty … except for one bright spot – The Rising Tide.

Industrial chic in style, The Rising Tide is located in a large open warehouse which also houses the Mount Brewing Co. Running along the sunny north side of the building is a huge outside deck and a stage for live music on the weekend. Behind the bar is a long wall studded with thirty-nine taps offering The Mount Brewery's handcrafted beers, along with rotating guest beers, ciders, wines and even gin on tap. Their Dark N Stormy Cider won a place in the New World 30 Top Beers and Cider Awards in 2019. For those who can't make up their minds, on offer is a tasting paddle of five drinks of your choice. The food is casual, mainly dumplings and burgers, and ideal for an inexpensive night out, though the quality is variable.

Away from the Mount Brewing Co., the tourist-packed main street it is easy to get to and more importantly easy to park, making the Rising Tide a big local favourite.

- 107 Newton Road, Mt Maunganui.
- Open daily 11 am to 10 pm Sunday to Thursday and to 11 pm Friday and Saturday.
- 07 575 2739
- www.therisingtidemt.com

16. Classic Flyers Museum

New Zealand has a surprising number of aviation museums, a reflection of our isolation in the the South Pacific and that the country is long and narrow (2080 km from North Cape to Bluff), making air travel an attractive way of getting around. Few museums, however, are located at a working airport and even fewer have so many older planes that actually fly.

Opened in a purpose-built hanger in 2005 by local aviation enthusiasts, the museum now displays over thirty aircraft in three hangers and outside, including one hanger dedicated to restoration. When you see what these engineers work on, the word 'dedication' takes on a whole new meaning. One very appealing aspect of this collection is that you can go inside the old Catalina Flying Boat and sit in the cockpit of a fighter plane; and it's not just the kids who want to sit in the cockpit. Along with the aircraft are excellent static displays including an old NAC check-in counter, a children's playground retail shop and a popular cafe.

The museum offers flights in an glider, a WWII Boeing Stearman and, in summer, scenic flights over the Bay of Plenty and Waikato in a classic DC3 (see the website for details).

- 8 Jean Batten Dr, Mount Maunganui.
- Museum: Daily 9 am to 4 pm.
  Avgas Café: 7 am to 4 pm, Friday night only bar and casual meals from 4 pm.
- 07 572 4000
- www.classicflyersnz.com

17. The Lion and Tusk – Museum of the Rhodesian Services Association

Tucked away in Mt Maunganui's industrial area is one of New Zealand's most intriguing museums. One for the military buffs or those of Rhodesian/Zimbabwean descent, this collection mostly consists of material covering the period from 1890 to 1980, the pre-independence armed forces of Rhodesia/Zimbabwe. It would be easy to just dismiss this a den of militaristic crackpots, but that would do this small museum a great disservice. For a start it is amazing how much material has ended up in New Zealand, especially considering that the collection (established in 2000) has relied on donations from individuals and families who have settled in New Zealand. Moreover, it is very well displayed, with uniforms on life sized dummies, good descriptions, a war memorial and a library holding over 1000 books. The museum is home to four original Roll of Honour memorials from Zimbabwe.

📍 10/14 Portside Drive, Mt Maunganui.
🕐 Open daily 9 am to 3 pm.
🌐 www.thelionandtusk.org
📞 07 572 0348
💲 Entrance fee.

18. Mayor Island

Lying off the Bay of Plenty coast this rhyolite volcanic cone has a special appeal of its own. Dormant rather that extinct this volcano has, on average, erupted every 3000 years over a period of 130,000 years. It is very similar in shape to the more active White Island further east, with most of the island comprising of a large caldera containing two small lakes appropriately, but unimaginatively, named Black and Green. In pre-European times the island supported a significant Maori population which traded in obsidian or tuhua (and hence the island's Maori name), a rare volcanic glass with a sharp edge that was a highly valued commodity in a stone-age culture. Several major pa sites are still visible. Captain Cook sighted the island on November 3 1769, naming it Mayor to commemorate that the date was also Lord Mayor's Day in London – he also named islands further north The Aldermen. With the coming of iron tools the island population fell substantially and, as the island was unsuitable for farming, it has been virtually untouched for over 200 years. At one stage the New Zealand Navy considered digging a short canal to one of the lakes to build a secret offshore harbour which would have been just so James Bond, but no doubt some sensible bureaucrat killed that fabulous idea. Today it also contains a superb pohutukawa forest and recent clearance of pests has led to a recovery of native bird life including bellbirds. A walk around the island will take around six hours and there is a good swimming spot in Sou'East Bay where the boat lands. The waters around the island are renowned for the excellent fishing and the area holds the record for the largest Mako shark, 481 kg and the Tiger shark, 429 kg.

There is limited camping and cabin accommodation on the island.

- Blue Ocean Charters run boat trips run to the island during the summer but as there is no regularly timetable, you need to plan ahead. The 35 km trip takes about three hours.
- 0 800 224 278
- www.blueocean.co.nz

19. McLarens Falls Park

McLaren Falls is justifiably one of Tauranga's most popular recreation areas, though it is often ignored by visitors to the area, unable to tear themselves away from the Bay's magnificent beaches.

The heart of the 190-hectare park is Lake McLaren, a long, narrow waterway surrounded by forest, park and farmland. Offering bush walks, lakeside strolls, trout fishing, camping and kayaking, the park has one of New Zealand's outstanding collections of trees. A short loop walk combines bush, a picturesque waterfall and, at night, glow worms.

Those with an engineering bent can walk or cycle along a long canal to the heights above the Ruahihi Power Station, opened on September 19, 1981. The canal collapsed the following day, and it wasn't until 1983 that the station was recommissioned.

- The park is well signposted 1 km off SH 29.

20. Kaiate Falls

Falling in a series of pretty cascades and deep rock pools, the Kaiate stream tumbles down a steep gully thick with native trees and dense with ferns and shrubs. A leisurely loop walk will take at most forty minutes, but there a lot of steps here and below the main waterfall the rocks can be wet and slippery so wear decent shoes. Unfortunately, the water is polluted which is really disappointing as the marvelous rock pools would be a perfect place to cool off on a summer's day in a very lovely spot.

📍 Kaiate Falls Road, Off Waitao Road, Welcome Bay.

21. Karangaumu Pa, Papamoa Hills Regional Park, Te Puke

One of eight pa sites in the Papamoa Hills Regional Park, Karangaumu is very impressive. Located on a high vantage point (224 metres), the pa, also known in earlier times as Te Ihu O Ruarangi, covers the entire top of the hill with a narrow ridge being the only access to the pa. The ancient ramparts, defensive ditches and terraces are all clearly visible. Established around 1500 AD, the strategic advantage of this pa is immediately obvious, even to the untrained military eye. Watchful lookouts would have missed nothing from this ancient fortress – the whole bay is clearly visible, north to Coromandel, south to Ngongotaha, out to sea to White Island and far inland. It's a steady but not hard climb up to the pa along a very good track. Recently the pine forest was completely cleared from the lower slopes and replaced by 145,000 native trees, though these are yet to grow to any height.

📍 5 km east of Te Puke on SH 2 turn left into Poplar Lane and drive 800 metres to the car park.

22 Maketu

From Waihi Beach running right through to Opotiki is 140 km of coastline, mostly white sandy beaches, just broken occasionally by small headlands. One of those headlands is Maketu. The original landing place of the Arawa waka, Maketu is still today part of Arawa territory of Ngati Whakaue, and not far from the mouth of the estuary is a large monument commemorating the arrival of the waka in 1340. The historic Maketu marae, with its superb carved house Whakaue, was built in 1928 and lies alongside the lagoon.

During European settlement, Maketu become a busy port and an important mission station. The Anglican church of St Thomas was built in 1869 and the Catholic St Peter's in 1888. This last church is highly unusual in that it is built entirely with screws and not nails so it could be easily dismantled. Why the Catholics thought they might have to move their church remains a mystery.

Today Maketu is like stepping back in time. Having avoided large scale development common elsewhere in the bay, this is a settlement of modest homes, old fashioned baches, and a strong sense of community. The sandspit running 3.5 km west from the narrow harbour entrance is one of the longest stretches of preserved dune in the bay and an important conservation area. Overlooking the spit, estuary and coast is the Maketu Beachside café with a view to die for.

Just over the hill from the main township and below a steep bluff is Newdicks Beach. Free from development and sheltered from the prevailing wind, this is one of the loveliest beaches on this coast. The narrow bumpy track to the beach is through private land and there is a small charge for vehicles.

Maketu is also home to the famous Maketu Pies, and their smoked fish pie is one of the most popular choices.

On SH 2, 3 km from the junction with SH 33 turn into Wilsons Road North and drive to the 6.5 km to the end.

23. White Island

White Island is one of New Zealand's most active volcanoes and New Zealand's only marine volcano, with approximately one third of the mountain above sea level. The volcano is unusual in that the water in the crater is derived from rainwater and condensed steam, as the volcano is actually sealed from the surrounding sea water, with the vent below sea level. The steam from the crater is sometimes visible from the mainland depending on the level of water in the lake.

Know to Maori as Whakaari (to be made visible) and named White by Captain Cook in 1769, it was purchased by a Danish sea captain, Philip Tapsell, in the late 1830s. In 1913 a Canadian company, The White Island Sulphur Co. of Vancouver, set up on the island to extract sulphur, but this ended in disaster in 1914 when a lahar killed all the men working there and destroyed the buildings. The ruins visible today are the remains of a factory built in 1923 and closed in 1933. As one of the world's most accessible marine volcanoes, trips to the island, which included a two-hour walk right inside the crater, were very popular. On the 9th December 2019, the volcano suddenly erupted killing 22 people and injuring a further 26. Tours to the island have been suspended for the foreseeable future.

A combination of the warm Auckland current and the proximity of the volcano makes the waters around White Island several degrees warmer than the surrounding ocean. This attracts a wide variety of species of fish, including subtropical species only found much further north, in huge numbers to this one location. The aquatic volcanic landscape and the water's clarity allows for visibility up to 30 m, making this a great spot to go diving.

The Eastern Bay of Plenty is famed for superb fishing in uncrowded waters. While the range of fish to be caught is wide, including snapper, kingfish, terakihi, trevally and marlin, the area is particularly notable for catches of yellow-fin tuna which run from early December through to April (though this is unpredictable).

📍 Aerial trips over the island are operated from Whakatane and Rotorua airports and several fishing and diving operators are based in Whakatane.

24. Moutohora/Whale Island

Set aside as a reserve in 1965, over the years wild goats, cats, rats and rabbits have all been eradicated from this tiny island of 1.5 sq km. With the land pests gone an extensive planting programme has re-established the bush and today the island supports a varied bird population including penguins and dotterels, along with fur seals, dolphins and visiting whales from which the island takes is name. The boat trip is just 20 minutes from Whakatane and visitor numbers are strictly controlled.

🌐 Moutohora Island Sanctuary tours, www.moutohora.co.nz

25. Matahina Dam

Construction on the Matahina dam on the Rangitaiki River began in 1959, but it wasn't until 1967 that the power station began operation. The largest earth dam in the North Island, Matahina towered 85 m above the riverbed, but the location was geologically unsound and prone to earthquakes. In the twenty years from 1967 to 1987, the dam slid one metre down downstream and a further 150 mm during the 1987 Edgecumbe earthquake, though it has since been strengthened. What is particularly impressive is the extensive stonework that covers the broad face of the dam, consisting of careful placed boulders of a uniform size.

Lake Matahina behind the dam has filled a deep gorge and is now a popular spot for kayaking and fishing. Steep bush clad hills and sheer cliffs rise from the water and the cliff face is famous for its eerie echo while further up the lake a small island is a popular destination.

📍 60 km south of Whakatane on the Galatea Road to Murupara.

26. Kaputerangi/Toi's Pa, Whakatane

Toi was one of Polynesia's greatest voyagers, not only exploring the coastline of New Zealand, but repeatedly crossing back and forward across the South Pacific. According to legend, the original inhabitants of this area were known as Kakahoroa, descendants of Tiwakawaka, the grandson of Maui the great voyager and fisherman. When Toi arrived, his people intermarried with these earlier people and all the numerous descendants of Toi were then known as Te Tini o Toi, the multitude of Toi.

Kaputerangi is also the place where kumara came to Aotearoa. Tradition tells that one morning Te Kurawhakaata, the daughter of the chief Tamakihikurangi, was walking along the river when she came across two strangers lying on the shore and clearly exhausted. These two brothers, Taukata and Hoaki, had journeyed from Hawaiki in a waka called Nga Tai-a-Kupe, and Kurawhakaata took the tired and hungry men back to Kaputerangi for food. However, when the meal of fern root, mamaku and cabbage tree was placed before them, they were, despite their hunger, very unimpressed.

Taukata asked for water and from his pocket took some dried root, which he crushed and stirred with the water into a paste. He then offered the mash to the people of the pa, who were so impressed with the flavour that they clamoured to know what the food was and how they could get more. Explaining that this was kumara and could be obtained from their homeland, the people of the pa, who at that time had lost the art of building ocean-going waka, set about building a large waka with the help of the two brothers. From a great totara tree emerged the waka *Te Aratawhao*, and it was this waka that journeyed to Hawaiki and brought back the kumara to Aotearoa.

The views from the summit are endless in all directions and, with the steep drop on the river side of the pa, the site was eminently defendable. The track is in excellent condition, with some stepped sections, and at the very beginning the walk crosses the top of Wairere Falls.

📍 The walk begins from the carpark on Seaview Road in Whakatane; if walking up from the town centre, take the long flight of stairs in Canning Place behind Pohaturoa Rock.

27. Whakatane River and Historical Walk

Toroa, the captain of the famous waka *Mataatua*, was given specific instructions by his father Irakewa before leaving Hawaiki to look for three distinctive landmarks: a cave, a waterfall and a tall rock; and when he found all three, then that would mark the place to settle. These instructions are evidence that Maori voyaging to New Zealand was not hapzard, but well planned with return voyages and extraordinary navigational skills without instruments or mathematics. Today, more than 800 years later, these three landmarks still remain within the central business area of Whakatane and are linked by an easy walk.

The first landmark is Muriwai's Cave (partially collapsed), where Irakewa's daughter lived. This cave was considered highly tapu until the tapu was lifted in 1963. The second is Wairere Falls, and while this is not so spectacular, it is nonetheless a very attractive waterfall, considering it is right in the middle of town. The final landmark is Pohaturoa Rock, which has at the base a highly tapu cave where tohunga performed sacred ceremonies.

Start the walk by the Visitor Centre and follow the river towards the sea, past the busy Whakatane wharf and on to the landing place of the *Mataatua*, marked by a replica of this famous waka. From here continue to the heads and the bronze statue of Wairaka overlooking the narrow entrance to the river. Follow the road back to town, taking in Toroa's three landmarks – Muriwai's Cave, Wairere Falls and Pohaturoa's Rock in the very centre of the business area.

When the waka *Mataatua*, captained by Toroa, arrived and moored in the estuary of the river, the men climbed up to Kaputerangi, leaving the women and children behind on the Mataatua. A swift outgoing tide put the waka in danger of being carried out to sea but, in a breach of tradition, Toroa's daughter Wairaka saved the day by picking up a paddle and exclaiming 'E! Kia Whakatane au i ahau' ('let me act like a man'), and with the other women she brought the waka back to safety. This action is the origin of the name of both the river and the town.

📍 Start the walk at the Visitor Centre in Kakahoroa Quay, Whakatane and the entire stroll will take about one hour.

28. Ohope Scenic Reserve – Fairbrother Loop Walk

The usual image of the pohutukawa is of a gnarled old tree overhanging a beach or high on a cliff face. Pohutukawa is also a tree of the coastal forest and at the Fairbrother Reserve in Ohope the growth habit of the trees is much more upright, less spreading. They compete for light with other trees to reach some surprising heights. This loop walk is through such a forest, dense with tall pohutukawa from saplings through to ancient trees. There is no lookout point along this loop track, though the sea is occasionally glimpsed through the trees.

📍 The reserve is at the northern entrance to Ohope on the corner of Pohutukawa Avenue and Ohope Road.

Cape Reinga. (Northland #1)

Te Werahi beach, Cape Reinga. (Northland #1)

Te Paki sandhills. (Northland #3)

Kaikohe Hill. (Northland #19)

Kaikohe Hill. (Northland #19)

Hokianga Harbour. (Northland #20)

Busby Head, Whangarei Heads. (Northland #32)

Moreton Bay fig, Pahi. (Northland #29)

Maungaraho Rock. (Northland #27)

Trekka, Packard Motor Museum. (Northland #35)

Whangarei Quarry Gardens.
(Northland #34)

Whangarei Quarry Gardens.
(Northland #34)

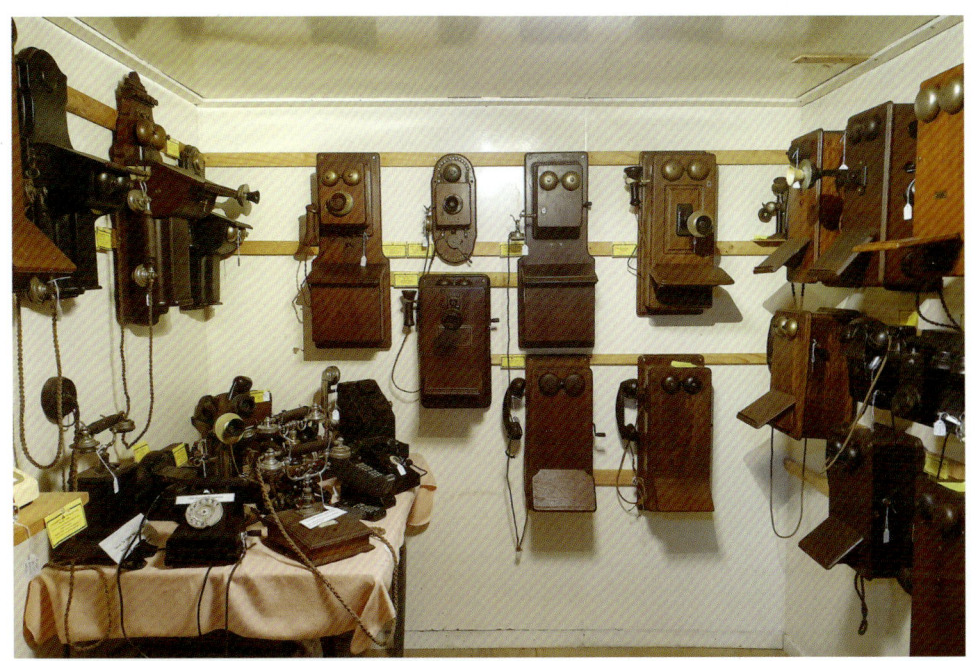

Packhard Motor Museum. (Northland #35)

Marsden Point Oil Refinery. (Northland #36)

Utopia Café, Kaiwaka. (Northland #40)

The Bechstein Paderewski Grand Piano, Whittaker's Music Museum. (Hauraki Gulf Islands #4)

Motuihe. (Hauraki Gulf Islands #7)

Brick Bay Winery, Snells Beach. (Auckland #1)

Cement works, Warkworth. (Auckland #3)

Under the Auckland Harbour Bridge. (Auckland #10)

1YA Radio Station. (Auckland #13)

Parnell Pool, Parnell. (Auckland #22)

The Pah, Hillsborough. (Auckland #29)

Melanesian Mission, Mission Bay. (Auckland #24)

Auckland Potters studio, Onehunga. (Auckland #31)

Fo Guang Shan Temple, Flat Bush. (Auckland #36)

Ayrlies Garden, Whitford. (Auckland #37)

Mazuran's wines, Henderson. (Auckland #46)

Totara Vineyard. (Thames and Coromandel #1)

The Coromandel Smoking Company. (Thames and Coromandel #11)

Paku Peak, Tairua. (Thames and Coromandel #18)

morning cloud
reclaiming the hills
from early light

Ernest Berry
NZ

Haiku Park, Katikati. (Bay of Plenty #5)

Hairy Maclary Statues, The Strand.
(Bay of Plenty #11)

Gate Pa, Gate Pa Domain.
(Bay of Plenty #12)

The Historic Village, Tauranga.
(Bay of Plenty #13)

Classic Flyers Museum, Mount
Maunganui. (Bay of Plenty #16)

Pine Man, Tokoroa. (Waikato, Hauraki Plains and the King Country #16)

Vivian Falls, Kohanga. (Waikato, Hauraki Plains and the King Country #18)

HMS Pioneer Gun Turrets – Mercer and Ngaruawahia. (Waikato, Hauraki Plains and the King Country #20)

DEKA Sign, Huntly. (Waikato, Hauraki Plains and the King Country #21)

Maori Parliament Building, Ngaruawahia. (Waikato, Hauraki Plains and the King Country #24)

Hamilton Model Engineers Miniature Railway, Minogue Park, Hamilton. (Waikato, Hauraki Plains and the King Country #25)

Classics Museum, Dinsdale. (Waikato, Hauraki Plains and the King Country #27)

Good George, Somerset Street, Frankton. (Waikato, Hauraki Plains and the King Country #30)

Duck Island Ice Cream, Hamilton East. (Waikato, Hauraki Plains and the King Country #33)

Cosmonaut sleeping bag, Te Awamutu Space Centre. (Waikato, Hauraki Plains and the King Country #41)

Karam and John Haddad Menswear, Otorohanga. (Waikato, Hauraki Plains and the King Country #44)

Marakopa Beach. (Waikato, Hauraki Plains and the King Country #45)

Marakopa Falls. (Waikato, Hauraki Plains and the King Country #45)

The Mokau Mine, Mokau. (Waikato, Hauraki Plains and the King Country #46)

Footbaths, Kuirau Park. (Rotorua #3)

Tarawera Falls. (Rotorua #8)

The Bridge Hot Pool, Wai-o-tapu. (Rotorua #13)

Ohaaki Power Station. (Taupo and the Central Plateau #3)

Wairakei Steamfields. (Taupo and the Central Plateau #4)

Team Carrot Park. (Taupo and the Central Plateau #15)

Tolaga Bay Wharf, East Cape Highway. (East Cape, Gisborne and Te Urewera #1)

Christ Church, Raukokore. (East Cape, Gisborne and Te Urewera #1)

Manutuke Marae. (East Cape, Gisborne and Te Urewera #8)

Rere Rockslide. (East Cape, Gisborne and Te Urewera #10)

Rere Falls. (East Cape, Gisborne and Te Urewera #10)

Gaiety Theatre, East End Café and Saloon Bar. (Hawkes Bay #4)

Pania of the Reef. (Hawkes Bay #10)

Otatara Pa Historic Reserve. (Hawkes Bay #13)

Napier Prison. (Hawkes Bay #12)

Pekapeka Wetlands. (Hawkes Bay #22)

The public toilets, Ongaonga. (Hawkes Bay #23)

Birdwoods Gallery. (Hawkes Bay #18)

Norsewood. (Hawkes Bay #24)

29. Ohiwa Oyster Farm

Ohiwa Harbour is very tidal, with over 70 per cent of the seabed exposed at low tide, and is one of the most important refuges for wading and migratory birds including the godwit, which flies non-stop from the Arctic each spring. Established in 1967 as part of a government initiative to encourage aquaculture, this farm is the most southern fishery to grow Pacific oysters and the main beds can be viewed from the road. There is a small shop which sells fresh and cooked oysters as well as a range of fresh fish along with burgers and meals which can be enjoyed at a few rustic tables overlooking the tidal harbour.

- 111 Wainui Road, 5 km south of Ohope Beach.
- Open daily 9.30 am to 6.30 pm.

30. Burial Tree/Hukutaia Domain, Opotiki

Known as the Hukutaia Domain, this small reserve of lowland rainforest just out of Opotiki was established in 1918 primarily to protect Taketakerau, an ancient burial tree. The large sprawling puriri tree was used for centuries by the local Upokorehe hapu to conceal the bones of the notable dead from desecration by enemies, a common practice among early Maori. After the tree was damaged in a storm the remains were buried elsewhere. Thought to be over 2000 years old, this huge old tree is still impressive and highly tapu. In addition to Taketakerau, the Domain contains one of the most extensive collections of native trees and shrubs in the country. From 1933 to 1970 local amateur botanist Norman Potts travelled throughout New Zealand to gather plants that were then planted in the Domain and after his death the work was continued by March Heginbotham from 1970 to 1990. For years a bit neglected, the reserve is now much improved with good signage, excellent information boards and good tracks. The actual reserve is small and any walk will take no longer than thirty minutes.

📍 From Opotiki take the road to Whakatane and just over the Waioeka River bridge turn left into Woodlands Road, and the reserve is on the left 7 km down this road.

31. Hiona St Stephen's Church, Opotiki

Throughout the 1860s Maori resistance to the pressures of European settlement grew, and many backed the new religious and political movement Hauhausim, led by charismatic leader Te Kooti. The Reverend Volkner, a missionary based at Hiona, regularly reported to the authorities the movement of Hauhau in the area and was, not surprisingly, regarded by local Maori as a government spy. After visiting Auckland, Volkner insisted on returning to the area despite warnings that he was in danger, and in March 1865 he was killed by Hauhau in the church in a very grisly manner. However, as it often the case the Maori and settler versions vary considerably. To the settlers the death of Volkner confirmed the savagery of the Hauhau and the need for protection. Maori versions contend that Volkner was hanged as a government spy and that the manner of his death was much exaggerated by settlers keen to have government troops stationed in the district – which is precisely what happened. In reaction to Volkner's death, the government sent forces to the Opotiki area, where fighting continued off and on until the final surrender of Te Kooti at Waiotahi in 1889. Volkner is buried at the back of the church.

📍 128 Church Street. Owing to vandalism the church is only open when someone is in attendance (check with the Opotiki i-SITE).

32. Royal Hotel, Opotiki

Built in 1879 entirely of native timber, the Royal Hotel was once the home of Fannie Rose Howie. Of Ngati Porou descent, Fannie Porter/Poata was born into a prominent East Coast family in January 1868, eldest of eleven children. She received her initial music education at home and at Mrs Sheppard Ladies' School Napier, but after a public concert in Gisborne she moved to Australia in 1891 to study music not long after marrying John Howie. After returning briefly to New Zealand, Fannie went on to study music in England and in 1901 gave her first performance to much acclaim performing under the name Te Rangi Pai. Between 1901 and 1905 Fannie successfully toured Britain, though she did have a reputation for being somewhat temperamental and unpredictable. After the death of her mother and youngest brother she returned home in 1905, and several times toured New Zealand until ill health forced her to retire in 1907. It was then that she composed the song that was to make her famous, the Maori lullaby Hine-e-hine. Her health continued to deteriorate, and Fannie was living at the Royal where she died on 20 May 1916 in a room directly above the main entrance. Fannie was buried at Maungaroa under a pohutukawa tree. Today, a gentle presence believed to be the spirit of Fannie is still felt in the hotel.

The exterior of the hotel has changed very little in the last 100 years and now offers budget accommodation along with a family restaurant and bar.

- Cnr King and Church Street, Opotiki.
- 027 555 0935
- www.theroyalopotiki.co.nz

33. Shalfoon's Store and the De Luxe Theatre – Opotiki Museum

In the 1890s two Lebanese cousins, George and Stephen, arrived in Opotiki and began selling clothing from packhorses along the coast especially to isolated Maori communities. Establishing a depot in the town, gradually this expanded into a general store selling all manner of goods from hardware to groceries. By 1915 the business had expanded into four stores and included a translating business as by this time George was fluent in Maori and English. Business continued to flourish and in 1926 the family built the De Luxe Theatre right next door to the main shop, which is still operational today and is one of New Zealand's oldest picture theatres. George's son Epi became a well-known band leader of the Melody Boys in the 1930s and 40s. The store finally closed in 2000 and along with the theatre is now part of the Opotiki Museum.

- 123 Church Street.
- Open Tuesday to Saturday 10 am to 4 pm.
- 07 315 5193

34. Tirohanga Dunes Trail

Running 10 km from Memorial Park in Opotiki to the beginning of the Motu trail at Tirohanga, this walk and cycleway is one of the best planned trails in the country. Winding through restored dunes and along the beach, the track is a very easy grade (the highest point is 15 m) and is carefully shielded from the busy road just a short distance away. Views abound over the Bay of Plenty, out to White Island and East Cape and with ample opportunities to access the sandy beach along the way.

- Memorial Park, North end of St John Street, Opotiki.

WAIKATO, HAURAKI PLAINS AND THE KING COUNTRY

1. Whakatiwai Regional Park
2. Kaiaua Fish and Chip Shop
3. The Cheese Barn, Matatoki
4. The Big Lemon and Paeroa Bottle
5. Te Aroha
6. Waiorongomai Valley
7. Wairere Falls
8. Morrinsville Cows
9. Te Miro Mountain Bike Park
10. Firth Tower
11. Okoroire Hotel and Hot Springs
12. Blue Springs and Waihou River
13. Railway Station Water Tower, Tiru
14. Over the Moon Cheese, Putaruru
15. The Chainsaw Collection - Putaruru Timber Museum
16. Pine Man, Tokoroa
17. Pokeno Ice Creams
18. Vivian Falls, Kohanga
19. Port Waikato
20. *HMS Pioneer* Gun Turrets - Mercer and Ngaruawahia
21. DEKA Sign, Huntly
22. Lake Puketirini, Huntly
23. Taupiri Mountain
24. Maori Parliament Building, Ngaruawahia
25. Hamilton Model Engineers Miniature Railway, Minogue Park, Hamilton
26. Frankton Junction Railway House Factory
27. Classics Museum
28. Taitua Arboretum
29. The Church of Jesus Christ of the Latter-day Saints (Mormon Temple)

30. Good George, Somerset Street, Frankton
31. Ice Age Mini-golf
32. It's Astounding! Riff Raff Statue
33. Duck Island Ice Cream
34. Punnet, Tamahere
35. New Zealand's Tallest Native Tree
36. Matakitaki Pa, Pirongia
37. Alexandra Redoubt, Pirongia
38. Vilagrad and Three Brothers Winery
39. Battle of Hingakaka, Lake Ngaroto
40. Uenuku Te Awamutu Museum
41. Te Awamutu Space Centre
42. Kakepuku
43. Kawhia
44. Karam and John Haddad Menswear, Otorohanga
45. The Road from Waitomo to Mokau via Markopa
46. The Mokau Mine
47. Madonna Falls
48. Pureora Forest The Buried Forest Centre of the North Island Totara Walk Poukani
49. Omaru Falls
50. Mapara Scenic Reserve

1. Whakatiwai Regional Park

If you are not a keen geologist or geographer, it might be best to stop reading. At first glance, this regional park appears to have very little to offer and honestly at second glance it still just looks like farmland and a bit of bush on the higher slope, but the area is internationally recognised for its unique geography. This undeveloped park of 324 hectares stretches from the coastline up to the low ridges of the Hunua ranges and protects a unique landscape, the Whakatiwai gravel fields. Over the last 4000 years, these fields were built up by gravel washed down streams and rivers from the Hunua Ranges and then pushed into long low ridges running parallel to the coast by southerly currents and tides. The lighter material was washed further south, mixed with sand and shell to become the Chenier plains at Miranda. The ridges and attendant hollows of the park run along the coastline for nearly six kilometres and extend one kilometre inland. Because farming and road developments have altered much of the area, the park was established to protect the remaining area.

There you have it, now you know, and up to you to go and see it.

📍 Access to the park is on the East Coast Road, three kilometre north of Kaiaua.

2. Kaiaua Fish and Chip Shop

Nestled on the shores of the Firth of Thames, the fish and chips at the Kaiaua Fisheries have an almost cult status. Wherever possible the shop uses fresh fish and the customers can usually chose between hoki, snapper, terakihi, flounder, gurnard and lemon fish. Coated in their own special batter, the fish is then deep-fried in beef lard; they did try cooking in oil but had so many complaints from customers that they decided to move back to fat!

Aware that they have a long and good reputation, the staff, some of whom have worked here for over twenty years, know that when it comes to food, reputations come and go with the sea breeze, and it therefore essential to maintain consistently good service and food. Although there is a small restaurant, the favourite option for most people is still fish and chips wrapped in paper and enjoyed either on the terrace or at the picnic tables on the grass out front with the view across the Firth to the Coromandel Ranges.

📍 East Coast Road, Kaiaua.
🕐 Open daily 9 am to 8.30 pm.

3. The Cheese Barn, Matatoki

Tucked just off SH 26, it would be easy to miss this small cheese factory even if you came this way – which not many people do in the first place – and that would be a great shame. It's not a big or flash place, but what is lacks in size, it makes up for in atmosphere, and of course, top class cheeses, but then the cheese maker Kelvin Haigh has plenty of experience. Established in 1994, the awards for the cheeses started coming in 1998 and haven't stopped since, with the cumin seed Gouda scooping the Champion of Champions Award at the 2018 New Zealand Cheese Awards. Sourcing local and organic milk, the Cheese Barn make BioGro certified organic products including cheeses and yoghurts that are unhomogenised, gluten free and contain no artificial additives, growth hormones, chemical sprays or antibiotics. Best know for Gouda style cheeses, The Cheese Barn also produces blue, halloumi, mozzarella, feta, brie, camembert, quark and cottage cheese.

If the cheeses weren't enough reason to stop, the small café has excellent food and coffee in a garden setting with expansive views to the west over the Hauraki Plains.

📍 Wainui Road, Matatoki, SH 26, Thames.

4. The Big Lemon and Paeroa Bottle

In the beginning was the Big Bottle, long before the Big Carrot, the Big Crayfish, or the Big Trout. Just to confuse things, Paeroa now has two big bottles, but the original bottle erected in 1969 is on the southern end of the town by the Ohinemuru River bridge so don't go stopping and taking pictures of the wrong bottle!

Lemon and Paeroa, more commonly just L&P, was created in 1904 using water from a local spring and was originally known by the reverse name Paeroa and Lemon. The promotional phrase 'World famous in New

Zealand since ages ago' has now become part of everyday New Zealand language and has certainly put Paeroa on the map.

📍 Corner of SH 2 and SH 26.

5. Te Aroha

The literal translation of Te Aroha is 'love'; however, for those expecting a tale of romance and passion, the 'love' in this case is quite different. Te Mamoe was the son of an Arawa chief living at Maketu. On an expedition west of the Kaimai ranges, Te Mamoe became hopelessly lost in the vast swamp that once covered the Hauraki Plains. Climbing to the highest peak in the ranges, he became homesick when he saw Maketu shining in the distance. As an expression of the love he felt for his home, he named the mountain 'the love of Te Mamoe'. Te Mamoe left behind his mauri, or spirit, and this caused a spring to well up from the heart of the mountain and emerge in the foothills as hot springs – which later became famous for their therapeutic properties. A pool of clear water in a cliff on the mountain was known as 'the mirror of Mamoe' and attracted newly married couples to make a wish.

Covered in dense bush the mountain became a refuge for local people when they were attacked by Ngapuhi in 1821 and later during the New Zealand Wars, wounded Maori warriors came here to recuperate in the healing waters of the springs.

Once the railway line reached Te Aroha in 1886, the small settlement rapidly developed as a spa town, with bath houses, hotels, boarding houses and a fine public domain. As spa towns fell out of fashion, Te Aroha's prosperity declined.

In more recent years Te Aroha has successfully renovated its Edwardian Domain and the historic buildings. Modern hot pools with family appeal complement the old buildings including the 1898 Cadman Bath House, which now houses the local museum, and the renovated No. 2 Bath House. The annual 'Day in the Domain' festival celebrates Te Aroha's heritage as a spa town. At the back of the Domain is Mokena, the only hot soda water geyser in the world. Erupting every forty minutes to a height of around 4 m, the soda water is reputed to have medicinal values and a drinking fountain nearby provides an opportunity to taste the unusual water. Across the road from the Domain is the historic Grand Tavern, built in 1902, which once stood opposite the now demolished Hot Springs Hotel, the largest wooden hotel in New Zealand.

Long closed, the railway is a now part of an extensive 173 km cycle track, which stretches to the Firth of Thames to the north, Waihi in the east and in the near future, south to Matamata. To celebrate, Te Aroha has several fantasy bike racks, an attraction in their own right.

A track to the top of the mountain begins at the rear of the Domain by the Mokena geyser and is approximately two and a half hours one way. There are no two ways about it: the walk to the top is unrelentingly steep and you need a good level of fitness to climb the 952 metres to the summit. Near the top the vegetation becomes distinctly subalpine. The track, however, is clear to follow, in reasonable condition and, as Te Mamoe found, the views from the summit are spectacular: on a good day, Ruapehu and Taranaki can be glimpsed on the southern horizon.

If the summit is beyond your reach, the trip to Whakapipi is a very good second option. While it's a solid climb to 350 metres, the track is well formed, zigzagging through the bush to the lookout that has excellent views over the town below and the Hauraki Plains beyond. Of course, a reward for both is a good soak in the hot pools.

If retail therapy is more you style, Te Aroha has a treat: Williams Furniture and Hardware, where time has stood still (in a good way) since the store was established in 1955. If you can't find it in Williams, you don't need it.

Across the other side of the river is the very odd Howarth Memorial Wetland. This substantial wetland is mainly planted with exotics, with a few natives added in more recent years. The plantings are eccentric to say the least: a grove of ash trees is laid out in straight lines, there are odd clumps of feijoa, then a line of cherry trees, and large swamp cypress everywhere. Water birds now flock to the area, and it used to be the town dump so, however strange the plantings, it is much better than it ever was.

6. Waiorongomai Valley

Ghost towns are always appealing, but Waiorongomai is not so much ghost – more completely vanished.

Gold was discovered here in 1881 and, for the next forty years, the southern slopes of Te Aroha Mountain were the scene of feverish activity with stamper batteries, a tramway, pack trails and inclines. A small town sprang up on the flats at the foot of the Waiorongamai Valley, but the gold yields were light and by the 1930s, the mines had ceased operation and the population drifted away, so today not a trace of the town remains.

The old trails and tramway now form a series of excellent tracks of all grades zigzagging up the mountainside right to the summit. You need to be fit to get to the top, but two of the lower level tracks form a loop that is an easy walk for all ages, and what is especially appealing is that not all of the old tracks and equipment has been hauled away. Here you will find a short tunnel, old rail tracks, gold mines, mining equipment and the bottom of the dramatic Butlers Incline, an engineering feat designed to bring gold-bearing ore down a very steep hillside. Adding to the appeal is the fantastic signage all along the tracks, which is both informative and enjoyable as they feature historical photos, newspaper clippings and diagrams. Especially useful is the map at the start of the walk, which shows how all the tracks linked the mines, inclines and batteries.

◉ End of Waiorongamai Loop Road, 5 km south of Te Aroha on the Te Aroha-Gordon Road.

7. Wairere Falls

Set in attractive native bush, these falls drop 153 metres in two stages over the Okauia Fault, making them the tallest falls in the North Island. The walk to the lower lookout takes around forty-five minutes, and to the top of the falls a further forty-five minutes, and is through very handsome bush following the stream. The stream itself has been subject to dramatic floods and the valley is full of huge boulders scoured by the power of the water. The falls are at the head of a long narrow valley and in very strong westerly winds water from the falls is blown forcibly upwards back into the bush with the power of a high-pressure hose, an experience that is not to be missed.

This idyllic valley was the scene of a tragic and brutal killing in 1836. Young Tarore lived with her father Ngakuku in a pa near Waharoa and after being taught to read by local missionaries, she was given a book, *Te Rongopai a Ruka, the Gospel of Luke*. Tarore, just twelve years old, set off with her father along with a group of Maori Christians for Tauranga when they stopped for the night near the falls. Here the small band was attacked by Arawa warriors who, seeking utu for an Arawa man murdered at Waharoa, killed Tarore, took out her heart and stole her gospel.

Rather than continue a cycle of revenge killings, Ngakuku told his followers not to seek utu; instead he said, 'There lies my child. She has been murdered as payment for your bad conduct, but do not rise to seek a payment for her. God will do that. Let this be the finishing of the war with Rotorua. Now let peace be made'. Ngakuku's forgiveness and the words of the stolen gospel brought peace between the two belligerent iwi. Tarore is buried in a small cemetery near Waharoa.

⚲ The track to the falls starts at the end of Goodwin Road off Te Aroha-Okauia Road about 20 km south of Te Aroha.

8. Morrinsville Cows

A cow town is a cow town, and there is no escaping the fact that Morrinsville thrives on dairy farming and owes its prosperity to the humble milking cow. Travelling from Hamilton to Morrinsville, visitors are welcomed to the town by the huge statue of the Frisian cow standing 6.5 metres tall and now acknowledged as the 'mama' cow to Morrinsville's more artistic 'Herd of Cows'. Spread throughout the small town are over fifty cow statues all painted by different artists. As corny as it might sound, these brightly painted cows are a delight and will not fail to raise a smile in a town that seriously lacks any other attractions (apart from the historic Nottingham Castle Hotel). In short it is a simple and clever idea that really works and if you have young ones with you, grab a map from the local i-SITE and see how many colourful cows you can find.

9. Te Miro Mountain Bike Park

Te Miro Forest is a combination of native bush and exotic plantations above the Te Miro Reservoir which supplies water for Morrinsville just to the north. In more recent years it has been developed as a premier mountain bike park by a gang of enthusiastic volunteers under the auspices of the Te Miro Mountain Bike Club. A maze of tracks weaves up the hillsides, through the forest and caters for every rider from the easy learner level to the extreme, more suited to experienced riders.

Between the small carpark and the reservoir is a large grass area with shady trees, just the spot to stretch out after a hard and sweaty ride.

The track around the reservoir is also popular with walkers and those taking their dogs for a stroll, but be aware those some of those mountain bikers can travel very fast.

Tucked in a low range of hills equidistant from Cambridge, Morrinsville and Matamata, the park is not so easy to find, but it is well worth the effort.

📍 Waterworks Road, Te Miro.

10. Firth Tower

Josiah Clifton Firth liked towers and they were highly fashionable in the late nineteenth century. His house on the slopes of Mt Eden featured a substantial tower and on his 10,000-ha Matamata Estate he decided to build a tower in the innovative building material of the day, concrete. The tower has the appearance of a defensive fortification, with walls 46 cm thick and loopholes for rifles, but the area faced no military threat when construction began on the tower in 1880. Essentially a large and expensive folly, the 20-m tower offers good views over the local countryside.

The museum is very well presented and has excellent displays of local history, both in the tower and in the other historical buildings moved onto the site.

- 266 Tower Road, 4 km east of Matamata.
- Open Monday 9 am to 3 pm, Tuesday, Wednesday closed, Thursday, Friday 9 am to 3 pm, Saturday, Sunday 10 am to 4 pm.
- 0 7888 8369
- www.firthtower.co.nz
- Entrance fee.

11. Okoroire Hotel and Hot Springs

Long known to Maori for their healing properties, the Okoroire hot springs also began attracting Europeans when the road from Tirau to Rotorua was completed in 1883. The Okoroire Hotel opened a year later catering for tourists and travellers who visited the springs on the way to Rotorua and Taupo. The first licencee Mrs Isaacs set about developing the hotel grounds which cover 76 acres, with the construction of four baths and planting many of the fine old trees that remain today.

Although the hotel has been altered over time, both the exterior and interior are largely original. The long accommodation wing of the hotel, with its original sash windows and long veranda running the full length of the single storey building, is typically Victorian. The central part of the hotel also retains its Victorian charm, though the entrance was altered in the 1920s. Inside the hotel is a delight, renovated where possible and tastefully restored elsewhere and all reflecting an era of grace and elegance. The hotel is still situated in the original grounds and, in addition to the pools, there is now a nine-hole golf course and a large picnic ground.

However, don't come expecting hydro slides, private spa pools or a fancy café, as the hot pools, like the hotel, are Victorian in style and character. Set into the steep bush-covered slope are three small soaking pools, a tranquil haven alongside the rushing waters of the Waihou River. One of the pools retains a sandy bottom through which warm water wells up into the pool. The only facilities are a small changing shed.

The entry to the pools is via the hotel reception where you pay and are given access to the gate.

📍 18 Somerville Road, Okoroire.
📞 07 883 4876
🌐 www.okohotel.co.nz

12. Blue Springs and Waihou River

To those familiar with the sluggish dirty brown Waihou River as it flows out to sea by Thames, then the headwaters, will be nothing short of a shock. The Waihou River begins as the most stunningly pure water, which has filtered down from the Kaimai Ranges. Remaining underground for up to fifty years, the water that emerges from the ground at the Blue spring is crystal clear, a brilliant blue/green colour and a cool 11°C all year round. The stream itself supports an incredible array of aquatic plants that drift languidly in the transparent water while trout, very easy to spot, swim effortlessly in the swift current.

📍 One entrance to the springs is on SH 28 between Putaruru and SH 5 to Rotorua and the other is 4 km down Leslie Road which turns off SH 28 to the right just beyond the bridge crossing the Waihou River.

13. Railway Station Water Tower, Tirau

In the early years of rail, what the great lumbering steam trains needed was water, and lots of it. Along the entire length of the railway network were hundreds of water towers, mostly constructed of wood on simple iron frames. As diesel replaced steam, the water towers became redundant and were either gradually pulled down or fell down. In Tirau the water tower still stands, which is in itself is unusual, but also unique is that this tower is handsomely constructed of brick with a concrete water tank.

Originally known as Oxford (the pub is still called the Oxford Hotel), Tirau was earmarked as a major city for the Waikato, but the land was bought by the Rose family who hoped to make a fortune on land sales and the city plans were dropped. The railway line reached Oxford in early 1886 and the station consisted of a goods shed, small passenger station and the water tower. While trains still thunder through the town, the station has long gone and today only the historic water tower remains.

📍 Prospect Ave, Tirau.

14. Over the Moon Cheese, Putaruru

Within just a few decades, New Zealand has gone from a country where a great five kilo block of cheddar cheese reigned supreme, to a nation that produces superb boutique cheeses to match our great wines. Near the top of the new breed of cheese makers is Sue Arthur. Like so many New Zealanders who travelled in the 1970s, Sue questioned why a nation of dairy farmers didn't make even some of the varieties seen on her travels, especially in Europe. However, the opportunity to make cheese didn't materialise until the early 2000s and Putaruru was chosen to take advantage of the thousands of cars that stream past each day on SH1. Today the wall of the small store is jammed packed with awards.

All cheeses are made on the Putaruru premises and most from locally sourced milk. Along with cheese production and a deli, Over the Moon now trains new cheesemakers in the New Zealand Cheese School. Best known for OMG Brie, Over the Moon has bucked tradition and produces an intriguing range of cheeses from blends of goat, cow and sheep which results in smooth multi-flavoured cheeses. It's not cheap, but now it is the time to treat yourself to the best New Zealand cheese, so don't drive past. There is also now an Over the Moon Deli in Cambridge.

- 33 Tirau Street, (SH 1), Putaruru.
- Open 9.30 am to 5 pm Monday to Friday, 10 am to 4 pm Saturday and Sunday
- 07 883 8238
- www.overthemoondairy.co.nz

15. The Chainsaw Collection - Putaruru Timber Museum

In such a country originally abundant with timber, the early logging industry made a massive contribution to the development of colonial New Zealand, a contribution which has largely been forgotten. This is the only museum wholly dedicated to the timber industry and is on the site of the original Tuck and Watkins sawmill, while right next door a pine nursery was established in 1926 for the NZ Perpetual Forests. The original timber mill is now the main museum building. The displays are extensive, covering every aspect of timber and related industries and, while well laid out, not all exhibits are well labelled. For those interested in industrial heritage, this museum is impossible to resist.

Particularly impressive is the vast collection of chainsaws. Chainsaws became widely used in the 1930s and were massive machines, several metres long and operated by two men. Even though heavy and awkward, they were a vast improvement on the double ended hand saws then in use. The Putaruru museum features the entire range from these early whoppers to the light and highly portable modern chain saw.

- SH 1, 2 km south of Putaruru.
- Open 10 am to 4 pm Tuesday to Saturday.
- 07 8837621
- www.nztimbermuseum.co.nz
- Entrance fee.

16. Pine Man, Tokoroa

Tokoroa is a timber town, and not just any timber – specifically radiata pine – so a giant statue of a timber worker carved from pine is a fitting symbol of this south Waikato town. The pine wood used in this enormous carving was not just any old pine, but came from the summit of the ancient pa of Pohaturoa, 30 km south of Tokaroa. Cut in 2000, the trees were airlifted off the peak by helicopter to waiting trucks and transported to Tokoroa the trees were milled to a uniform size and then tanalised. Glued together to create a huge block of wood, once thoroughly dried, artist Peter Dooley set to work to carve The Timber Worker. Now affectionately known as Pine Man, the statue was erected right alongside SH 1 in March 2004. Square jawed, resolutely gazing upwards and with a chainsaw firmly clutched in one hand, the statue is a tribute to hardworking forestry workers everywhere.

17. Pokeno Ice Creams

Pokeno was always the place to stop for a break on a trip to or from Auckland before the motorway bypassed the town completely. However, those in the know still skip the more commercial and far less interesting rest stops and take the short detour into Pokeno. If you need to ask why, then you really are a visitor. While the village offers a range of food, Pokeno is famous for just one thing: its huge ice creams. When it comes to ice cream size does matter and big is good.

Two small food outlets — side by side and neither of them flash — both offer an incredible range of flavours under the iconic Tip Top brand and, given their intimate proximity to each, compete on price and size. There really is not difference which one you go to, what really matters is taking the time to stop for a 'Pokeno ice cream'.

In truth there are two reasons to stop, the second is the Pokeno Bacon, a family run business since 1977, famous for its excellent pork products and fantastic sausages.

The ice cream stores are easy to find with crowds on the footpath happily licking enormous ice creams, and the butchery is right next door.

📍 Great South Road, Pokeno, two minutes off SH 1.

18. Vivian Falls, Kohanga

Looking for a small adventure? Hidden in the Harker Reserve, these pretty falls are little known outside the local district and attract few visitors. The reserve itself is in two parts and the waterfalls are in a small separate patch of bush to the west of the main reserve. Unlike most public reserves, the Harker Reserve is a 25 ha area of bush protected by the Harker family under a Queen Elizabeth covenant to which further areas including the waterfall have been added.

The falls drop 12 metres in a single drop into a jumble of limestone rocks in a deep gully surrounded by old nikau palms and regenerating bush. It's not so far to walk from the road, but the track can be slippery when wet, especially the last section down a small flight of stone steps. Known in Maori as Te Wai heke a Maoa, excellent information boards tell the story of the warrior Maoa and his connection with the waterfall.

Returning to the top, you can then walk the road to the main reserve if you can in the mood for a longer walk.

Not so easy to find and not well sign posted you will need to locate the falls on a map before you go.

> From Kaipo Flats Road, turn into Miller Road and continue to the sign 'Walking Track to Harker Reserve (no vehicles beyond this point)' There is a small car park there with no facilities. You can hear the waterfall, but just walk a couple of minutes along the road where the track drops off to the left.

19. Port Waikato

Although not so far from Auckland (an hour's drive), Port Waikato feels like a place time forgot, so best not to come expecting cafes and beach umbrellas. Below the bridge over the Waikato River near Tuakau, the river begins to fan out into a wide delta of low islands and multiple streams, but near the mouth of the river reforms into wide shallow lagoon, protected from the open Tasman Sea by a wide spit of sand dunes. Huddled along the southern shore of the lagoon and behind the sand dunes is the small beachside settlement of Port Waikato.

It is hard to believe that this was once a lively port originally called Putataka (still the name of the high hill above the town). Established as a base during the New Zealand Wars, it was from here that gunboats moved upriver to bombard Maori pa with devasting effect.

Caesar Roose championed the river as a major shipping link between Auckland and the Waikato towns along the river, but the rail link was more efficient, and the shipping gradually faded away. One of the Roose's barges still lies on the west bank of the river, just south of Mercer and is clearly visible from the road.

Today a quiet seaside town of around 1000 people, Port Waikato is best known for its surf at Sunset Beach with its fine black sand, exposed to the turbulent sea and the prevailing westerly wind. The mostly small old-fashioned baches hunker down away from the wind in the broad flat behind the dunes and high hills. A very pleasant picnic spot, Coburn Reserve borders the lagoon, and its shade trees, picnic tables and grassy dells are well sheltered the westerly wind. The town's only store was built in 1893, but now looks more like a small 1950s fibrolite bach than a Victorian shop.

20. *HMS Pioneer* Gun Turrets - Mercer and Ngaruawahia

During the British attack on the Waikato during the New Zealand Wars in the 1860s gunboats were used to bombard river pa, against which the Maori had no real defence. Several pa were abandoned as Maori quickly recognised that they could not fight the iron clad boats as they moved slowly up river. Tucked away in what is left of Mercer's main street is the gun turret of the *HMS Pioneer*, used by British forces against Maori in the Waikato. First used as the town's gaol, the turret later became a war memorial. A smaller gun turret from the same boat is located on The Point in Ngaruawahia.

The *HMS Pioneer* was paddle driven and built in July 1862 for the New Zealand Colonial Government. It took active part in the attack on Rangiriri Pa under the command of Sir William Wiseman in November 1963. Three years later in 1866 the *Pioneer* was wrecked on the Manukau bar and the two turrets are all that are left.

📍 Mercer Gun Turret, 7 Roose Road, Mercer.
Ngaruawahia Gun Turret, The Point, Broadway Street, Ngaruawahia.

21. DEKA Sign, Huntly

No one knows what the name DEKA meant or even it if was supposed to be a single word or an acronym as the signage had small coloured triangles separating the letters. Rumours even circulated that the name had Satanic links. The major mass market retailer during the 1980s and 1990s, DEKA struggled to adjust to modern retailing and finally closed all its stores in 2001. The owner of the Huntly store continued business as an independent retailer, but as he was rather fond to the tall sign, decided not to pull it down. Now faded and tired, much like the town in which it stands, locals have become irrationally attached to the sign and rallied to save it when in 2013 plans were made to pull it down.

📍 48 Main Street, just off SH 1.

22. Lake Puketirini, Huntly

Not many New Zealand towns have to cope with a disused opencast coal mine, but Huntly has coal mines to spare. What's more, Huntly has plenty of lakes to spare was well, with six shallow lakes all within 10 km of the town. However, when the old Weavers Opencast Mine closed in 1993, it was decided to create a deep lake suitable for swimming and boating. A lake, Rotoiti, did exist on the site prior to the area being designated for coal mining in 1929, but the new lake is much larger (54 ha) and considerably deeper at 64 metres. A small creek, the Puketirini Stream was diverted into the pit which took eleven years to fill, and around the lake over 30,000 trees and shrubs were planted. In December 2006 Solid Energy handed over the lake and surrounding land, 104 ha in total to the Waikato District Council.

From the air the dark blue water of Lake Puketirini is in startling contrast to the muddy brown waters of the adjoining Lake Waahi which is only 5 m at its deepest point. Now popular with local swimmers, a walkway runs around the perimeter of the lake linking several large grassy picnic areas. The old Huntly Railway station has also been moved to the lake's edge.

Clearly this is an idea catching on as the old East Mine has been purchased by a local couple Jennifer and Murray Allen who plan to turn the former coal pit into a wetland and lake.

📍 Rotowaro Road, 1.5 km off SH 1.

23. Taupiri Mountain

Ko Waikato te awa Ko Taupiri te maunga Ko Te Wherowhero te tangata.

(Waikato is the river Taupiri is the mountain Te Wherowhero is the man.)

The importance of Taupiri to the Tainui people cannot be overstated. The name means 'beloved' or 'the close-clinging lover'. In legend, Taupiri is the wife of the great Pirongia, and the smaller peaks Kakepuku and Te Kawa near Te Awamutu are their children. In some versions of Maui hauling up his great fish, it is Taupiri that is the first point of the fish to break the surface.

A pa crowned the lower hill below the summit, and once was the home of the great chief Te Patu. At war with Ngati Raukawa, who were gradually encroaching on their territory, and after scoring a decisive victory on the bank opposite Taupiri, Te Patu agreed to a request that he meet with the defeated rangatira Ngatokowaru. The two men met just below the pa and as they greeted each other with a hongi, Ngatokowaru fatally stabbed Te Putu in the neck with a dagger made from the barb of a stingray.

Furious at the death of the chief, Te Putu's son Tawhiakiterangi sought revenge. But before setting out to attack his enemies, he met with a powerful tohunga near Waahi to acquire extra powers. The Waikato war party set off upriver, and when they came near Taupiri, a ghost canoe joined the flotilla. Although this waka was invisible, the chanting of the warriors and the splash of the paddles could be easily heard. The Waikato fleet followed the wake of the ghost waka upriver to meet the enemy. So powerful was the magic entrusted to Tawhiakiterangi that when they arrived they found the people of Ngati Raukawa lying on the ground and so helpless that Tawhiakiterangi's warriors were able to kill them with just the stems of toetoe.

Te Putu's mana was so great that his spilt blood made the area below Taupiri so tapu that the pa was abandoned and never reoccupied. European travellers later remarked that when approaching Taupiri they had to cross to the other side of the river to avoid touching tapu ground.

Te Wherowhero, who later became the first Maori King, had a pa at Taupiri, but this was abandoned during the Ngapuhi raids in 1826 and never fully reoccupied. After the land confiscations in 1864 when Waikato Maori could return to their homes, the people were dismayed to see that a road had been built around the foot of Taupiri. The construction of a railway line and later even a quarry further desecrated the tapu ground.

Today a small meeting house sits on the banks of the Mangawara River below the mountain. The lower slopes are the principal burying grounds of Tainui, and all the Maori kings and queens are buried here.

Though the Taupiri mountain is highly sacred to Tainui, they have allowed access to the summit. There are two tracks forming a loop, and both are marked by small wooden gateways. The first is just by the carpark and is the steeper and rougher of the two tracks. The second entrance is about 500 metres along the gravel road: this is not so rough and has a gentler grade, though it will take longer to get to the top. From the summit on a crisp sunny winter's day, snow-capped Ruapehu is clearly visible far to the south, while below, the Waikato River wends its way through fertile farmland.

The cemetery is not a tourist attraction and casual visitors are requested to respect this area and not walk among the graves.

📍 SH 1 just north of Taupiri township. The track to the summit, begins at the end of Watts Grove, Taupiri.

24. Maori Parliament Building, Ngaruawahia

The years before the Treaty of Waitangi were generally a period of cordial relations between Maori and European settlers and Maori were enthusiastic adopters of European technology. Maori encouraged European settlers, often gifting and selling land so that they could trade more easily and during the bitter Musket Wars, European settlers were seen as offering some sort of protection to local Maori.

After the Treaty, the situation changed rapidly. What Maori had not anticipated and quickly alarmed them was the sheer numbers of settlers who began arriving and showed no signs of stopping. When four ships bringing settlers arrived in Wellington, a local chief asked if all the tribe of England had come to New Zealand.

Far sighted Maori leaders understood the need to hold on to their land and others saw that political solutions were also necessary in this rapidly changing environment. The Kingitanga movement was one such solution and what could be better than to emulate the greatest power in the world at the time by setting up their own royalty. At the heart of the Kingitanga movement was Maori unity driven by a desire to halt the loss of land while the British saw the establishment of a Maori King very close to treason.

The initiative came from Waikato tribes and was only partially supported even in the North Island and many iwi including Te Arawa and Ngapuhi allied themselves with the government. Initially reluctant, the rangatira of Ngati Mahuta was crowned at Ngaruawahia in June 1858 and became King Potatau Te Wherowhero or most often as just Potatau.

Severely set back by the New Zealand wars and disillusioned by minimal representation in the national parliament, in 1891 the Kingitanga movement set up its own parliament and eventually settled on Ngaruawahia to construct a purpose-built parliament house.

Completed in 1919, the building is an extraordinary fusion of Maori and European architectural styles, designed by Hamilton architects Warren and Blechynde. Drawing primarily on the Art and Craft style, the stucco and concrete construction is crowned by striking carvings by Te Motu Heta over the porch and gables and has a richly decorated interior. It was also one of the first major Maori buildings in an urban area. Politically it saw little use as internal divisions undermined the original purpose of the building with Turangawaewae Marae becoming the main focus of the Kingitanga movement; eventually it became the permanent home of the Tainui Maori Trust Board.

📍 2 Eyre Street, Ngaruawahia.

25. Hamilton Model Engineers Miniature Railway, Minogue Park, Hamilton

When it comes to miniature railways in New Zealand, of which there are many, the Hamilton Model Engineers based in Minogue Park, are in a class their own. Established as long ago as 1931, the Engineers have had several 'homes' before moving to a large area in Minogue Park in 1983. This is no mere circuit, but two separate tracks that wind though field and bush over 1.6 km and include six bridges and three tunnels. Operating five different engines, the highlight is the full working model of a stream train which, with a trail of smoke and a clatter of wheels, pulls delighted adults and happy children around the track.

In addition to the miniature trains, the old Frankton Junction Signal Box is also located in the park.

📍 End of Tui Avenue, Forest Lake, Hamilton.
🕐 Open Sundays only 10.30 am to noon, 12.30 pm to 3.00 pm.

🌐 www.hme.co.nz

$ Entry is free but there is a fee for the rides.

26. Frankton Junction Railway House Factory

Manufactured in kitset form at a factory in Frankton, Hamilton, railway houses were transported all over the country to provide accommodation for railway workers often in isolated areas. The Railways Department was the first major housing scheme in the country and had provided housing since the 1880. However, in the early 1920s, the Department consolidated building at Frankton Junctions and the cottages, regarded today as a typical railway house, were built during this time. Architecturally designed and based on the American bungalow style fashionable at the time, the houses came in several designs, but all the key elements were standardised, the entire house pre-cut, packaged and railed to their final destination, where they took 2 -3 weeks to build. Opened in 1923 and producing 400 houses a year, the operation was too successful and by 1926 the department had a stockpile of house packages they couldn't use. By 1928 just fifty houses were built, and the factory closed in 1929 after producing over 1300 houses.

The only 'house factory' in the southern hemisphere in the 1920s and now a Category 1 Historic Place, the distinctive saw-tooth building design allowed for both a large floor space and maximum natural light.

Many of these simple wooden houses have long gone or been altered beyond recognition, but numerous examples remain - there is even a small cluster in Kingsland, Central Auckland. Once considered inferior, today an original railway house is a treasured gem of domestic New Zealand architecture. Just around the corner on Rifle Range Road are several excellent original examples of the railway houses produced in the factory.

📍 Railside Place, off Rifle Range Road, Frankton.

27. Classics Museum

When it comes to collecting, cars are a firm favourite, but for most car collectors, space and money keeps a firm reign on ambitions, not to mention the influence of a less enthusiastic and sensible partner. If there is a car collection that has it just right, this must be a strong contender. In this purpose-built museum in Hamilton, over sixty vehicles (mainly cars) are superbly displayed along with equally impressive collections of motoring memorabilia.

It's a familiar story when it comes to cars and, like his collection, Tom Andrews' story is a 'classic'.

Hamilton born and bred, Tom's passion for cars began early and gradually, like Topsy, his collection of cars kept outgrowing whatever shed he built. Eventually, on land alongside the railway line, Tom built the ultimate 'shed', though even this huge hangar-like building doesn't accommodate his entire collection and the cars on the ground floor rotate on a regularly basis. Most of the vehicles are American and British, but the Italians, French and Germans are not forgotten and while there are exceptional and rare cars, there are plenty of examples of popular models that were once the family car. Every car is in impeccable condition, though not all are roadworthy. The collection is enhanced by a huge range of petrol signs, oil cans, bonnet mascots and car badges.

For some, even more appealing is the Jukebox Diner, a licensed American style diner, which has become a firm local favourite for breakfast and lunch.

- 📍 11 Railside Place, off Rifle Range Road, Dinsdale.
- 🕒 Open 7 am to 5 pm Monday to Friday, 8 am to 5 pm Saturday and Sunday.
- 📞 07 957 2230
- 🌐 www.classicsmuseum.co.nz
- $ Entrance fee

28. Taitua Arboretum

Fond of trees, John and Bunny Mortimer began planting trees on their farm west of Hamilton in 1972. With little plan or even much thought, the primary idea was to provide a habitat for wildlife. Never intending to create an arboretum, both Bunny and John purchased trees that interested them and each just planted them where they liked.

It is the haphazard nature of this collection and the planting that makes the Taitua Arboretum so loved by Hamiltonians, including those who are not even that interested in trees. Paths wander almost without direction and everywhere there are gentle surprises with hidden glades, shady ponds, an unexpected piece of sculpture, stately groves and even a cow paddock or two. The plants are a mixture of natives and exotics and the human touch is evident at every turn. Few trees are labeled so you don't even have to read anything, though there are various 'collections' marked out on a map, (although in reality they are not so obvious on the ground). This place is just perfect for a nice walk.

Covering over 20 hectares, the arboretum has more than 1500 different trees. Birds, including lots of feral chooks are everywhere. Their book *Trees for the New Zealand Countryside* is widely recognised as a gardening classic. In 1997, the Mortimers gifted the land to the Hamilton City Council, which was at first very reluctant to take it on, but now with 60,000 visitors a year, it is this city's hidden gem.

The arboretum is on Taitua Road, but this road is split into two sections, which are a long way apart. Dogs are welcome on a leash.

📍 The main entrance is on Taitua Road off Howden Road, Templeview.

🕐 Open daily 8 am to half an hour before dusk.

29. The Church of Jesus Christ of the Latter-day Saints (Mormon Temple)

'Knock, knock!', 'Who's there?' Mormons!!

New Zealand has long been a missionary outpost for the Church of Christ of the Latter-Day Saints, better known as Mormons, but today most towns have a church, and Mormonism is now generally considered a mainstream church. What might come as a surprise to most is that this temple situated west of Hamilton is not only the largest Mormon church in the southern hemisphere, but it was also the first, opened in April 1958. The style of the church, the library (formerly a high school) and the original village are particularly American in their design and layout and once sat rather uncomfortably in the rural New Zealand landscape. However, extensive new subdivisions in the area have softened the American style.

The Church offers tours of the temple from the Visitor's Centre so if you have never been inside a Mormon temple and are curious, this is not a bad place to start. Sitting on top of a hill the church is particularly prominent at night when the church is floodlit and easily seen from Hamilton. It is also very famous locally for its Christmas lights.

📍 509 Tuhikaramea Road, Temple View, Hamilton
📞 07 846 2750
🌐 www.churchofjesuschrist.org

30. Good George, Somerset Street, Frankton

Within a few short years, boutique beers have made a huge impact on the beer market and one of the most stellar newcomers is Hamilton-based brewery and eatery Good George. What started as a good idea among a group of friends became reality in 2011 when the first establishment opened in the old St George's Church in Somerset Street, Frankton, a down-at-heel industrial suburb of Hamilton. Now Good George has ten outlets (including Auckland, Tauranga and Rotorua) and produces over one million litres of beer plus a range of innovative ciders. Right from the beginning the Good George company was determined to be more than beer and Somerset Street promotes good food, friendly service and a relaxed atmosphere.

All Good George beer and cider is brewed at Somerset Street with beer tanks both inside and outside the old church, and even right in the bar. Essential to the success of the company is that it has remained focused on a core range of excellent quality batch-brewed beer, to which it has added a small range of awarded winning ciders with Doris Plum and Scarlett Peach leading the pack. Another great feature are the 'squealer' beer bottles, which are resealable and refillable (only at some locations).

The Somerset Street Dining Hall in the old church has a funky atmosphere combining ecclesiastical architecture, industrial design with a beer garden style, all surrounded by stainless steel vats of brewing beer.

📍 32A Somerset Street, Frankton, Hamilton.
🕒 Open 11.30 till late Monday and Tuesday, 11.00 am till late Wednesday to Sunday.
📞 07 847 3223
🌐 www.goodgeorge.co.nz

31. Ice Age Mini-golf

It's a gloomy winter Waikato day, the heavy fog is unlikely to lift until after 1pm and the kids are restless. What are you going to do? Ice Age! The temperature has topped 30°C, the kids are still sunburnt from their trip to Raglan. What are you going to do? Ice Age! Its spring and it has been raining for a week and the playground and park are a sea of mud. What are you going to do? Ice Age! You finally have that date with the girl from school, but you are shy and sitting around having a chat is going to be super awkward. What are you going to do? Ice Age!

Most mini golf courses are outside and of course weather dependent, but Ice Age is inside on the first floor of Centre Place, which as the name suggests is right in the middle of town. The 18-hole course is spread over three separate rooms and is not too challenging. A dinosaur theme dominates the first room, but it is second room that has the most appeal. Here the Ice Age theme is a bit thin, but this doesn't matter as it is an eerie glow-in-the-dark room with fluro golf balls that make this room special. Then it's back to the Ice Age in the third room with hairy rhinoceros and a giant woolly mammoth. What is there not to like? Helpful hint: it is cheaper to buy tickets online.

Level 1, Centre Place, Victoria Street.
Open daily 10 am to 9 pm and 10 pm Friday and Saturday.
07 834 0578
www.lilliputt.co.nz

32. It's Astounding! Riff Raff Statue

Hamilton is often considered a good solid farming city, so it's a bit hard to believe that Hamilton inspired the slock horror musical and movie *The Rocky Horror Picture Show*, but yes it did. True!

Richard O'Brien, creator of *The Rocky Horror Picture Show*, worked as a barber on the ground floor of the Embassy Theatre in Hamilton's Victoria Street from 1959 to 1964. The Embassy, one of Hamilton's oldest theatres, had by that time become rather rundown and tired, specialised in running B-grade double feature horror movies. The barbershop was right at the entrance and no doubt the low-grade movies were a welcome relief from trimming and snipping the hair of Hamilton's men folk. Eventually spawning *The Rocky Horror Picture Show*, the stage show premiered in 1973 and two years later the film, now a popular classic, took Rocky Horror to a much wider audience. O'Brien played the character Riff Raff in both the show and the film. There is hardly a babyboomer in New Zealand who can't dance and sing Time Warp.

The theatre has now been pulled down but in 2004 a life size statue of Riff Raff was erected in a small square on the site of the theatre.

📍 Victoria Street, 100 m north of the museum.

33. Duck Island Ice Cream

You don't need to look that hard to find Duck Island as you will easily spot the queue out the door and the crowds of people outside on the footpath munching on ice creams.

Opened in 2015, Duck Island Ice Cream quickly became a phenomenon, and from the first outlet in Hamilton East, they have opened two more, one in central Hamilton and the other in Auckland, though the ice cream is also stocked in various supermarkets.

Duck Island's success is based on two simple premises, quality and variety of flavours. Sourcing organic milk and cream along with the freshest seasonal ingredients, the ice creams have a rich, velvety texture and a clean, sharp taste. They also offer coconut milk based ice creams that are dairy free and vegan, along with varieties that are gluten free.

Flavours rotate constantly, and while they do border on the crazy, (carrot and cardamom, banana, lemongrass and coconut, cinnamon smoked apple pie) they don't bother with the purely sensational such as cauliflower or curry ice cream. If you are at one of their scoop shops and you find an unusual flavour you really love, then you better have a second helping.

📍 300a Grey Street, Hamilton East.
🕐 Open daily 11 am to 7 pm Sunday to Wednesday, 11 am to 10 pm Thursday to Saturday.
🌐 duckislandicecream.co.nz

34. Punnet, Tamahere

'Pick Your Own', is a great New Zealand tradition and is especially popular when it comes to field-ripened strawberries. Punnet, a family run business at Tamahere between Cambridge and Hamilton, takes the PYO experience up a notch. Surrounded by strawberry fields is a delightful café and specialty gift shop, along with grand children's playground. The café and shop have been constructed with recycled materials and the result is not some old shed, but a surprising stylish and immensely appealing rustic building. Excellent food and coffee complete the experience. As well as gift items, the store stocks food specialties from local suppliers.

Children love the PYO experience and parents love the café with its wide windows out to the playground so they can relax with a coffee and a tasty treat and keep an eye on their little ones. Strawberry picking season runs from November to the February, depending on the kindness of the weather.

Punnet should really be called 'Chip', a word peculiar to the north of North Island as a container for holding berries, particularly strawberries.

- 372 Newell Road, Tamahere.
- Open daily 8 am to 3 pm.
- 07 838 1901
- www.punnet.co.nz

35. New Zealand's Tallest Native Tree

You'll need to be fit and up for a long hike if you want to see New Zealand's tallest native tree. At 66.6 metres, this kahikatea stands more than 15 metres taller than Tane Mahuta which most New Zealanders think of as our tallest tree. By their very nature kahikatea are tall trees and growing in dense groves, the trees are drawn up to the light making them taller still. For all their height, kahikatea are slender trees in comparison to totara and kauri.

Located deep within the rugged 13,500 ha Pirongia Forest Park, it's a six-hour return trip to see this exceptional tree. The track begins at the Kaniwhaniwha car park and follows the Nikau and Bell Track beyond the Kaniwhaniwha Caves, from where the track becomes rougher and muddier. At the swing bridge over the Blue Bull Stream, do not cross the bridge but continue upstream for a further ten minutes to the tree.

📍 Kaniwhaniwha Reserve, 600 Limeworks Road, Karamu, 19 km south west of Whatawhata.

36. Matakitaki Pa, Pirongia

On the northern outskirts of Pirongia stand the remains of Matakitaki pa, which in February 1822 witnessed one of the greatest battles of the Musket Wars.

After raiding the Tamaki isthmus, Hongi Hika turned towards the Waikato iwi, whom he accused of giving refuge to Ngati Whatua and Ngati Paoa survivors. Gathering a great war party of around 3000 men, Hongi crossed the Manukau, paddled up the Waiuku River and, after dragging their waka overland, led his fleet up the Waikato River.

As Waikato fled south in front of the advancing Ngapuhi, their chiefs decided to make a stand at Matakitaki. This superbly defended pa was built on a headland where the Mangapiko Stream entered the Waipa River. It was protected by the water and the steep bluffs on the riverside, and also by several rows of ditches and palisading on the land side. Crammed full of refugees, Matakitaki sheltered as many as 10,000 people, a situation that had a major impact on the course of the battle.

Waikato warriors under Te Wherowhero seized the advantage and launched a surprise attack on the invaders, killing around 150 men and, more importantly, capturing ninety muskets. The victory was shortlived as Ngapuhi surrounded the pa and, with muskets, picked off any inside the pa who dared to shout insults from the parapets. Now under attack, the people inside the crowded pa grew alarmed. The unease turning to panic when Waikato warriors fired the captured guns inside the pa, causing the people to think that Ngapuhi had broken through the palisades. Total confusion reigned inside the pa packed with people, and hundreds were trampled to death in the ditches while trying to escape. Meanwhile Te Wherowhero tried to hold the position, but the situation in the pa was impossible and he was forced to withdraw to the south.

The battle left 1500 dead and many hundreds more taken prisoner. Following this overwhelming defeat, Waikato iwi abandoned traditional weapons and began to arm themselves with muskets.

It is a short easy walk across farmland to the pa — though originally it was much bigger and extended out to the main road. The main features remaining are the deep defensive ditches on the landward side. Don't forget to close the farm gates behind you.

📍 The pa is located on SH 35 at the northern end of Pirongia township.

37. Alexandra Redoubt, Pirongia

After the fall of Rangiriri, the King Tawhiao's position at Ngaruawahia was impossible to defend and slowly the Maori were forced ever further south. Moving deeper into Waikato territory, the British troops found the Maori settlements along the river empty, while Maori gathered at the heavily defended Paterangi pa. However, as with Meremere and anxious to avoid the losses of Rangiriri, the British troops outflanked Paterangi and moved south to Rangiaowhia, which fell with little fighting.

The final battle came at Orakau, though by this time the Maori defenders numbered just 300 against 1200 well-armed British troops. After bitter fighting, the pa fell with 160 Maori dead and just 17 British killed. While this engagement effectively ended the fighting in the Waikato, tensions continued, with the Maori simmering with resentment in what is now known as the King Country.

Pirongia, then called Alexandra, was a frontier town and in 1868 a redoubt was built in anticipation of further hostilities. Four years later a larger and more sophisticated redoubt was built on a low rise; the Anglican church of St Saviour was moved from the site to accommodate the fortifications. This is the best-preserved redoubt in the Waikato. It forms a square with arrowhead-like parapets in each corner all encircled by a deep trench. The redoubt was less than 2 kilometres from Whatiwhatihoe, the headquarters of Tawhiao, just over the aukati or confiscation line.

📍 From the southern end of the main street in Pirongia (Franklin Street), turn into Bellot Street and the redoubt is on the left.

38. Vilagrad and Three Brothers Winery

Vilagrad is Waikato's oldest and currently only winery, and a story of hard work and determination. Ivan Milicich left his small Dalmatian village of Podgora in 1893 and immigrated to New Zealand where he spent a backbreaking ten years working the gumfields and saving to help his brother emigrate. In 1906 he had brought a small farm near Ngahinepouri and began growing grapes, though it wasn't until 1922 that he obtained a license to make and sell wine under the Vilagrad label.

Four generations on, today the three great-grandsons of Ivan still continue his wine making tradition. The winery produces wine under two labels, Vilagrad from grapes grown on the home property and Three Brothers from grapes from New Zealand's premier grape growing areas. More recently cider has been added to the mix. Made from locally grown pink lady apples, the cider is drier than other sweeter New Zealand ciders and is slightly sparkling. Not forgotten are the old-style ports and sherries made from vineyards planted by Ivan 100 years ago; the ports have a dedicated following and are often sold out.

Mention Vilagrad to locals and they will immediately say 'Sunday Lunch'. A long-standing Waikato tradition, Vilagrad hosts a sumptuous Sunday lunch with roast pork in the Croatian style a speciality, and you definitely need to book. Vilagrad also caters for weddings, social functions and offer accommodation.

- 702 Rukuhia Road, Ohaupo.
- Cellar door open 9 am to 3 pm Monday to Friday, 12 pm to 4 pm Sunday. Restaurant is only open Sundays.
- 07 825 2893
- www.vilagradwines.co.nz

39. Battle of Hingakaka, Lake Ngaroto

Lake Ngaroto is a small wetland lake not far south of Hamilton – and yet on its shores was fought the Battle of Hingakaka, said to be the largest battle ever fought in this country. The dates of the battle vary between 1790, 1803 and 1807.

Tensions had been growing between coastal Tainui, closely allied with Taranaki, and their inland relatives Ngati Maniapoto and Waikato, allied with Hauraki. The issue finally came to a head over the uneven distribution of the fish harvest. Ngati Toa chief Pikauterangi, based at Marokopa, gathered together a huge war party of between 7000 and 10,000, crossed into Ngati Maniapoto territory and invaded the Waipa district.

Wahanui, a Maniapoto chief, sent out the call to his Waikato allies and gathered together a force of around 1600 to 3000. They decided to confront the invaders on a narrow ridge overlooking Lake Ngaroto. Pikauterangi and his warriors took up positions at the foot of the ridge and made the first attack, but clever tactics on the part of the defenders confused the invaders. The decisive point of the battle came when Pikauterangi was killed. Retreating towards the lake, the invaders were further ambushed, then in full panic were trapped in the swamp around the lake. Attempting to escape through the unfamiliar terrain or by swimming across the lake, thousands died. The name Hingakaka means 'fall of the kaka', as so many chiefs died that it was compared to a hunt for kaka (a native parrot).

In the past it was traditional to carry into battle powerful tribal talismans to assist in the fighting. In 1906 the sacred carving Te Uenuku was found hidden in the swamp at Lake Ngaroto; it is believed that it was carried into the Battle of Hingakaka and was quickly hidden by the fleeing warriors. This highly unusual carving embodies the spirit of the war god Te Uenuku, who appears in the form of a rainbow. Te Uenuku is made of totara and may date back as far as 1400; the style is similar to Eastern Polynesian and Hawaiian carvings.

Lake Ngaroto was also known for its island pa, and the remains of these can be seen today.

The walk around the lake is flat and easy, and for the most part, vegetation obscures the view of the lake. Two island pa sites can be seen on the eastern side of the lake, but the level of the lake is considerably lower than in the past and these pa are now little more than small hillocks on the shore. The track can be very wet in places. The battle itself took place on a ridge south of the lake, and Bank Road, which leads to the lake, crosses the actual battlefield.

📍 From the main street of Te Awamutu (Alexandra Street), head north 2 km and turn right into Paterangi Road. After 4 km turn into Bank Road; the lake is at the end of this road.

40. Uenuku Te Awamutu Museum

This small but professionally curated museum has one outstanding exhibit, Uenuku, God of the Rainbow. This highly unusual and incredibly stylish carving, Uenuku is a god who appears as a rainbow and whose spirit was brought to this country on the Tainui canoe in the form of a stone.

Believed to have been carved around 1400, Uenuku is distinctly eastern Polynesian in style and is a very rare carving from this period. A great taonga of the Tainui people, the Uenuku carving has an exceptionally powerful life force and should be treated with the utmost respect.

The museum used to have a small but excellent exhibition on Tim and Neil Finn who hail from Te Awamutu, but it unfortunately has been put in storage.

📍 135 Roche Street, Te Awamutu.
🕐 Open 10 am to 4 pm Monday to Friday, 10 am to 2 pm Saturday and public holidays, closed Sunday.
🌐 www.tamuseum.org.nz
$ Koha/donation.

41. Te Awamutu Space Centre

The old Kihikihi St Andrew's Presbyterian Church Hall is not really where you would expect to find a space centre and the amateur spaceship model out front doesn't really help. However, the world is full of surprises, and Te Awamutu Space Centre is one of those surprises. The collection of space artefacts is small, but this is New Zealand's only and largest such collection and includes real gems such as the cosmonaut sleeping bag, Russian space food and American astronaut suit, all of which have been into space. However, it more than just a collection of memorabilia and it is the interactive activities that really hold the visitor's attention along with the live video and data feeds including one of the sun.

There is also the Lego space exhibition, a small shop selling space related books and gifts. If it's a telescope you are after Dave has a good range for sale and he really knows what he is talking about. Hugely popular with local school groups, the centre is only open to the public on weekends, but if you have any interest in space, the stars and the universe, this is a compulsory stop for you.

And why Kihikihi? It's simple really, local Dave Owen wanted to do something for his home town so he set up the Space Centre in 2009.

📍 Corner of Whitmore and Lyon Street/SH 3, Kihikihi, 4 kilometres south of Te Awamutu.
🕐 Open by appointment.
📞 07 870 1966
🌐 www.spacecentre.nz

42. Kakepuku

Impossible to miss, Kakepuku dominates the landscape south of Te Awamutu and the name is a contraction of 'Kakepuku te aroaro o Kahu', 'the swollen stomach of Kahu'. The mountain was named by Rakataura, a tohunga on the voyaging waka Tainui, and honours the pregnant stomach of his wife Kahu.

There are five pa in the reserve area protecting the mountain, settled in around 1550: Hikurangi, Tokatoka, Torewera, Omango, Arikiturere. In pre-European times most of the bush had been cleared from the mountain, but by the 1860s all the pa on the mountain were abandoned and the bush began to return.

The bush has completely returned and is now quite mature and the view from the top (449 m), though partly obscured by trees, is well worth the trip. The most obvious pa site is on the summit, which is ringed by wide terraces. The track also passes through another pa site just as you reach the lip of the old crater, though the remains here are a little hard to detect.

The track to the top is hard work, all uphill but in good condition.

📍 From Te Awamutu turn off SH 3 into Fraser Street which becomes Puniu Road and then Pokuru Road, travel 6.5 km and turn left into Te Mawhai Road. After 1 km turn right into Kakepuku Mountain Road; the carpark is on the right.

43. Kawhia

This large tidal harbour has a long and important Maori history beginning with the arrival of two important waka, Tainui and Aotea. The harbour was named by Turi, the captain of the Aotea, who then went on to settle in Patea. Kawhia is the final resting place of the Tainui waka, which is behind the historic Auaukiterangi marae, marked by two stones one at either end of the waka and over 20 metres apart. Hoturoa, the captain of the Tainui, is featured on the tekoteko (the figure at the top of the front gable) of the meeting house. Just along the beach from the marae this tree, Tangi Te Korowhiti, marks the spot where the Tainui waka tied up. The tree is tapu and should be treated with respect so do not climb on it or swing off the branches.

Now a quiet backwater that is as yet unspoilt by modern development, Kawhia has a relaxed, unhurried atmosphere that is in direct contrast to busy Raglan to the north and a world away from the east coast beaches such as Whangamata and Ohope Beach. Not so well known as Hot Water Beach on the Coromandel Peninsula is the Te Puia Springs. Accessible for two hours either side of low tide these hot water springs that are situated directly out from the main track to the beach from the car park. This beach is exposed to the westerly wind so bring a substantial digging tool to make a protective wall around your very own hot pool in the sand.

In the small museum in the same building as the Information Office is a racing whale boat built of kauri in the 1880s, the only craft of its kind in New Zealand. Longer and narrower than actual whale boats, these were popular racing boats in the nineteenth century. On New Year's Day crews from communities around the harbour race replicas of whale boats, competing for the appropriately named Whale Boat Racing Cup, in the only race of this type in the country. Kawhia is the home of the very popular Kai Fest. This annual festival of Maori food and culture is held in Omimiti Park on the weekend closest to Waitangi Day and attracts over 10,000 people. As well as traditional food such as hangi, puha, paua, kanga wai and mussels, there is also Maori craft, art, kapahaka and music.

44. Karam and John Haddad Menswear, Otorohanga

Are you a man who hates shopping for clothes or is there a man in your life who hates clothes shopping? Then Haddad's in Otorohanga is the place for you. Opened in 1965, brothers John and Karam Haddad have plenty of experience with reluctant shoppers. They are certainly not pushy, but they have experience with back country farmers who shop for clothes once a year and understand that the patience level for many male shoppers is thirty minutes max. With their Lebanese trader heritage, they also understand a bargain and the store is packed with good quality branded clothing at sharp prices.

The Haddad connection to Otorohanga goes back to 1928 when Michael Haddad (the father of the two brothers) opened a fruit shop which later expanded into a milk bar next door; the parapet above the store is proudly crowned 'Haddad Building 1935'.

The large shop is overflowing with stock, much of it stacked in cardboard boxes or packed tight on racks and the atmosphere is friendly and relaxed. You can trust these two guys to tell you the truth whether something looks good or fits right. Not relying on fancy marketing, sharp displays or online sales, Haddads relies on word of mouth and returning customers; on a Saturday it's hard to move in the shop.

There is no other store in New Zealand like Haddads, so if you are travelling through Otorohanga you just have to stop, even if all you need are socks or undies.

- 65 Maniapoto Street/SH 3, Otorohanga.
- Open Monday to Friday 8.30 am to 5 pm, Saturday 9 am to 1 pm. Sunday closed.

45. The Road from Waitomo to Mokau via Marakopa

Huge numbers of tourists flock to the Waitomo Caves every year, but few venture much further. Traversing rugged hill, this 110 km road passes through empty New Zealand backcountry with some gems to visit along the way. The road is sealed with the exception of a short stretch just south of Marakopa but is frequently narrow and winding so take you time, after all you are on a road trip, not a road race. There is a camping ground at Marakopa and a pub at Awakino but not much else so much sure you have enough petrol and a snack. If you only want to go to Marakopa the distance is 48 km.

Highlights include the following:

Only two kilometres from the Waitomo caves and next to the Aranui Cave is the Ruakuri Walkway. The short thirty minute walk along the Waitomo River is crammed with fantastic limestone outcrops, caves, and a huge natural tunnel. The unspoilt bush features luxurious growth, in particular ferns, mosses and lichens. The area has glow-worms at night but don't forget your torch. The track is well formed and clear even if the signage is a bit confusing.

Just a short distance from the road (ten minutes walk) the Mangapohue natural bridges are two natural arches up to 17 metres high, one on top of the other, cut through limestone by the Mangapohue stream. The wonderful walk to the bridges passes through the steep cliffs of an limestone gorge, overhung with native trees and at night has glow-worms. A torch is necessary if a night walk is planned. Just beyond the caves are the fossils of giant oysters 20 million years old clearly visible in the exposed rocks.

Further along the road on the right is the Piripiri Cave, unusual in that the cave is both easily accessible and free. A few minutes' walk from the road, a short flight of steps leads to a platform which allows you to view this large cavern and its delicate environment. It can be quite slippery in the constant damp so you need decent shoes and you will also need a torch.

Especially impressive after rain the Marakopa River powerfully cascades 30 metres over a limestone bluff creating a spectacular waterfall. The spray from the waterfall has created bush lush with ferns and mosses that thrive on the permanent damp. The falls are only a short fifteen minute walk from the road and at the end of the road is Marakopa Beach, a small settlement of tiny baches. This is not a beach for brushing up on your tan, but a place to go fishing, for a walk on the wild beach facing the Tasman Sea or just lazing around and reading a book.

Twenty-eight kilometres south of Marakopa is the turnoff to Waikawau Tunnel Beach (there is a school at Waikawau). One of few accessible parts of the coastline along this road, the highlight is a short tunnel driven through the soft sandstone cliffs at the mouth of the Te Marama Stream. Only three men built this tunnel in 1911 with only shovels and picks so cattle could be driven to the beach and then on barges in the relative shelter of Ngarupupu Point. Beautifully built with a high pitched ceiling, the neat pick marks are still visible along the entire length of the tunnel. At high tide the beach is mostly underwater and, as always on the west coast, swim with great care.

Just before Awakino, the road crosses the Awakino river and rejoins SH 3. Both the Awakino and Mokau rivers are famous for their whitebait. The young of the smelt family, whitebait come to the river between mid-August and mid-November, and with the fish come the whitebaiters to their favourite places along the river, with their time-honoured fishing techniques. Most famously, whitebait is made into fritters.

The Mokau river was once an important link inland for both Maori and Pakeha. Mokau was the home of the author June Opie, whose book *Over My Dead Body*, telling of her battle with polio, sold over 100,000 copies in New Zealand and became an international bestseller. There is a June Opie display at the local Tainui Museum (open daily 10 am to 4 pm).

46. The Mokau Mine

In the middle of the road in the middle of Mokau opposite the museum is a German mine found at the mouth of the Mokau River in December

1942. But why did the Germans want to mine the Mokau River mouth? Did the Germans know something no one else knew or was is quite possibly something was lost in translation? Apparently, locals tell of a German gentleman who turned up in Mokau well after the war clutching a map of New Zealand and on this map were just marked three places, Auckland, Wellington and Mokau. Another story is that the mine was New Zealand made and just made to look like a German mine to keep the New Zealand public alert. And what about the other rumour that a Japanese mine was also found, but the discovery was hushed up by the Government of the day. The official line is that this mine, along with two others, just drifted across the Tasman from where the Germans had been laying mines on the Australian coast, but who will ever know the truth of the Mokau Mine which local school children today nickname 'Da Bomb'.

📍 Corner of Rerenga Street and SH 3.

47. Madonna Falls

New Zealand has very few roadside shrines, but these sacred falls are an exception. In 1980 the water from the falls was pronounced to have special healing powers and the falls were declared sacred and named by local Maori as Te Whaea o te Rere/ Our Lady of the Waterfall. A special contraption has been set up making it easier to collect the healing waters.

📍 25 km south of Te Kuiti on SH 4.

48. Pureora Forest

This forest located between Te Kuiti and Mangakino is frequently overlooked, but has some of the most magnificent native trees in the country.

Over 1800 years ago a cataclysmic eruption blew out the western side of Lake Taupo more than 70 kilometres away. Even at this distance the force of the blast was so strong that it decimated the entire forest in the area, knocking over huge trees, and then burying them under a deep layer of ash and pumice. The eruption deposited a thick layer of nutrient rich ash, that acted like a super booster plant food, making these trees (along with those in the Whirinaki forest east of Taupo) especially large.

Logging was finally halted in the early 1980s and the area is currently a mixture of forest park and commercial forest, giving some interesting contrasts between pristine native bush and clear-felled pine forest. It is also worth noting that the roads in the forest are a combination of forestry and narrow metalled roads, some little better than tracks and rough in parts. Along with the usual bush walks there are four curiosities worth a detour in the forest

Pureora Forest Tower

The short flat track leads to a 12-metre tower which gives both an excellent view over the forest treetops and the opportunity to enjoy the sound and sight of forest birds, especially kaka. Particularly impressive are the huge rimu which loom high above the small tower.

This area is where the conservationists made their stand in 1978 by securing themselves high in the trees selected to be felled. At the time the policy was one of selective logging, in which a proportion of mature trees were felled and then removed along the access road which is now the track. It is easy in a more conservation-minded age to label the loggers as greedy and insensitive to the environment, but in many areas, milling was the only source of work and cessation of felling meant a loss of valuable jobs in an area where no other employment was available.

Excellent information boards and a handful of historic logging machinery add to the trip.

From SH 30 between Bennydale and Mangakino, turn into Barryville Road. Drive 2km and turn left into Pikiariki Road and continue another 2.5km to the carpark

Centre of the North Island

Quite frankly there's not much to see here either apart from a gigantic rimu right next to a plaque marking the geographical centre of the North Island, but standing on the plaque and thinking 'this is the middle of the North Island' is a sort of un, if pointless thing to do. Let's face it, we don't always have to have a good reason for everything we do.

📍 Two kilometres on from the track to Mt Pureora, turn right into Waimanoa Road. The entrance to the track is a further 3 km along this road.

Totara Walk

The Totara Walk takes less than thirty minutes but contains some magnificent trees such as totara, maire, rimu and tawa. The height of some of these trees has to be seen to be believed – they are huge. These stunning trees will make you understand why those protestors fought so hard to save this forest.

📍 From SH 30 between Bennydale and Mangakino, turn into Barryville Road. Drive 2.5 km and the walk is well marked on the left.

Poukani

While everyone flocks to the largest Tane Mahuta, the largest kauri (which by the way is nowhere near the tallest tree in New Zealand), Poukani, the tallest totara tree only attracts a handful of visitors and it isn't fair. This massive tree, over 42 metres tall and 1800 years old, is very impressive, though rather a bit lost and hard to see properly in the thick bush. The walk to the tree takes about one hour return.

📍 The entrance to the track is 10 kilometres from the Barryville Road turnoff towards Mangakino on SH 30.

49. Omaru Falls

Rarely visited, these falls are located just off the main highway south of Te Kuiti. Here the Mapiu Stream plunges 50 metres over a hard basalt lip into a rocky pool, and after heavy rain the falls are spectacular. The track is not very clear but it is flat all the way and follows the stream through farmland and regenerating bush that include several huge kahikatea trees. Eventually the track crosses the stream over a rickety swing bridge to a viewing platform high above the falls, which gives the visitor an excellent view, though there is no access to the pool below the falls.

📍 30 km south of Te Kuiti on SH 4 turn into Omaru Road. The falls are 500 m down this road. There is a small sign and it is easy to miss.

50. Mapara Scenic Reserve

Good news stories about the survival of our unique native birds are relatively rare and usually involve isolated, offshore islands. Mapara is one of the last strongholds of the rare kokako and this reserve is the most accessible for those who want to hear or see this elusive and handsome bird.

Like so many of our native species, kokako are very vulnerable to imported predators, but with persistent trapping of nasty killers between 1978 and 1995, the kokako numbers in the reserve rocketed from a low of five pairs to around 100 breeding pairs, and now Mapara has provided numerous birds to populate other reserves around the North Island.

Kokako hold a very special place in Maori myths, especially in relation to the demigod Maui. In the legend of Maui and the sun, when Maui traps the sun in his net in order to slow its crossing from east to west, it is the kokako who bring water in its long wattles to the struggling and thirsty Maui. To reward the bird for its great kindness, Maui gave the kokako long nimble legs so it could more easily hop through the trees to find food.

The loop track in the reserve leads through the territories of several birds so the chance of hearing these birds is very high, but you will need to be very patient to actually see a bird. The best chance is the period two hours after dawn, so you must get up very early, especially in summer.

📍 Travel 26 km south of Te Kuiti on SH 4 and turn left into Kopaki Road and then, after 2 km, turn right into Mapara South Road. The reserve is 5.5 km down this gravel road. The reserve is not sign posted from SH 4 so you have to keep an sharp lookout for Kopaki Road.

ROTORUA

1. Mamaku Blue
2. Mt Ngongotaha
3. Kuirau Park
4. Princes Gate Hotel
5. Maori Rock Art, Lake Tarawera
6. Tree of Hinehopu
7. Te Koutu Pa, Lake Okataina
8. Tarawera Falls
9. Waikiti Valley Thermal Pools
10. Rainbow Mountain/ Maungakaramea
11. Kerosine Creek
12. Wai-o-tapu Boardwalk Mud Pools
13. The Bridge Hot Pool, Wai-o-tapu
14. Kaingaroa Forest

1. Mamaku Blue

If you didn't think blueberries were the secret elixer to what ever ailed you before you visited, you will surely think that after a visit to Mamaku Blue. Apparently blueberries can sort out nearly every health problem from aging and bad eyesight to preventing just about every sort of cancer. Leaving all the health benefits aside, what will surprise anyone who visits here is all the forms and varieties blueberry food takes. Believed to be the first and only blueberry experience of its kind in the world, Mamaku Blue has available a dazzling array of blueberry product. There is wine, chutney, jelly, jam, icecreams, juice, chocolate, liquers, sauces, sweets, toiletries, vinegar, not to mention just plain blueberry fruit in season. Flourishing in the cool climate of the Mamaku Plateau, over 7 hectares are planted out in blueberries and tours are available by appointment, but from the cafe there is a good view out over the rows of blueberries if that is enough to satisfy your curiosity. In autumn the bushes turn a vivid bright red while in spring the blossom are clusters of bell-like flowers faintly blushed with pink. If blueberries aren't enough, then they also have a small range of produce based on the very old fashion fruit, the English Gooseberry.

- Mamaku Blue, Maraeroa Road (off SH 5) at Mamaku.
- 07 332 5840
- www.mamakublue.co.nz

2. Mt Ngongotaha

While today Ngongotaha is better known for the luge and gondola, it is a mountain of great mana and once a major stronghold of the patupaiarehe or the fairy people who were also known as iwi atua, 'the godlike tribe'. Patupaiarehe shunned human contact and were known for their trouble-making, and very seldom showed any kindness to humans. The tribe of patupaiarehe who occupied the mountain were known as Ngati Rua and numbered over a thousand living close to the summit, which was then known as Te Tuahu a Te Atua (the altar of the god).

Many different legends surround these mysterious people. Some versions have them normal size with light hair and skin, which indicates to some that an ancient Caucasoid race once inhabited these islands. Around Whanganui the tradition is that they were very tall – well over 6 foot. Most versions though describe the patupaiarehe as small and slim, often with red or lighter hair and light-coloured skin. Maori with red hair are often said to be the offspring of a liaison with the patupaiarehe. They only moved at night as light would kill them, and they lived in the deep forest on rugged mountains. Their main strongholds were Moehau, Pirongia, Urewera, the Waitakere ranges and Ngongataha in the North Island and the peaks of the Banks Peninsula, Takitimu Mountains and the headwaters of the Arahaura River in the South Island. Usually invisible they were rarely seen but were often heard talking and playing music on dark misty nights. Adept at music, weaving and carving they only lived on raw foods, were never tattooed and, while they usually resented any intrusion into their domains, they could also show kindness. The name Ngongataha means 'to drink from calabash' and relates to the story of the explorer Ihenga who became thirsty while climbing the mountain and was given water by a patupaiarehe woman. Another story tells that the patupairehe were eventually driven from the mountain by Maori setting fire to bracken on the lower slopes and they never returned. Or did they ... listen carefully on a dark misty night and you might just hear soft voices or fairy music from the mountain.

A road goes to the top but a better way of reaching the summit is via a good track that begins through fine virgin forest and then gradually climbs to the summit through the dense bush much favoured by the patupaiarehe. The grade on the Jubilee track to the top is steady rather than steep and if that seems a bit daunting then there is an excellent loop track near the entrance. Near the top it joins Mountain Road for the short section to the summit. The summit is bush-covered and there are no views.

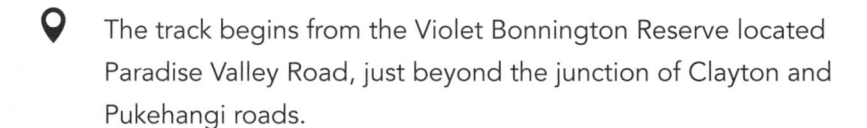

📍 The track begins from the Violet Bonnington Reserve located Paradise Valley Road, just beyond the junction of Clayton and Pukehangi roads.

3. Kuirau Park

A stroll in this large central park is a treat in Rotorua where not too much is free. Thermal activity is concentrated in the north-eastern section of the park, but this varies considerably from year to year and season to season. One large pool is crossed by a board walk which makes for eerie atmosphere photo in the dense drifting steam. After heavy rain, especially in winter, the park is spectacular and almost disappears in the dense clouds of warm steam.

The park has a dark mythical past and takes its name from Kuiarau, who lived here with her husband Tamahika. As Kuiarau was bathing in a hot pool she was seized by a taniwha lurking below the surface, who then dragged Kuiarau down to his lair. However, Kuiarau fought back and the gods who witnessed her struggle with the taniwha, made the water boil and thereby destroyed the taniwha together with the helpless Kaiarau, who is now remembered in the name of the park (though slightly altered to Kuirau).

At the southern end of the park are two small foot baths, making this the perfect spot to end a busy day walking around the city. Shallow with raised seating, the footbaths are like sitting around a large table and just the place to engage in friendly conversation with fellow visitors and locals. One pool is covered while the other is in the open. This is spot is also ideal for small children with a large playground nearby.

📍 Corner of Lake Road and Ranolf Street.

4. Princes Gate Hotel

This grand Victorian hotel appears to be part of the very fabric of Rotorua, but things are not always what they seem, and this hotel has definitely had two very distinct lives. Working class in origin, the hotel catered for thirsty miners in the goldfields of Waihi as the New Central

Hotel. In 1908, the Ohinemuri electorate, which included Waihi, voted to go dry and the hotel was closed the following year. As was common at the time, wooden buildings were often moved and reused, and in 1917 the New Central was dismantled and railed in pieces to Rotorua. Like a giant model, each piece of the hotel was labeled and numbered and by 1921 was rebuilt and renamed the Princes Gate. The name reflected the hotel's prestigious position directly opposite the elaborate wooden arch that commemorates the visit to Rotorua by the Duke and Duchess of York in 1901. The old New Central Hotel at Waihi had an incredible seventy-five rooms, many of which would have been tiny single rooms, but the new hotel had just thirty-four spacious rooms.

Exuding a wonderful old-world charm, the hotel features huge leadlight windows, wooden panelling, elegant chandeliers, a grand staircase and period furniture. The wrap-round Victorian verandas upstairs are for guests only and are just the perfect place to watch the busy goings on in the street below and in the Government Gardens opposite. The Duke's Bar and Restaurant successfully combine yesteryear elegance with modern style and are perfectly complimented by the north facing garden bar. High Tea on the ground floor terrace at street level is particularly popular.

📍 1057 Arawa Street.
📞 07 348 1179
🌐 www.princesgate.co.nz

5. Maori Rock Art, Lake Tarawera

This large lake of beautiful clear water lies at the foot of Mt Tarawera, and was substantially altered by the 1886 eruption. Nine days prior to the eruption a mysterious waka was seen on the lake by a party of tourists returning from the Pink and White Terraces, but as the boat came closer, the waka suddenly disappeared. Believed by many to be a waka wairua (spirit canoe) come to warn of the approaching doom, it is said that a reappearance of the waka will signal the next eruption.

The eruption itself was said to be caused by the powerful spirit Tamaohoi. The great Arawa tohunga Ngatoroirangi was travelling over the mountain when he clashed with Tamaohoi, who resented Ngatoroirangi crossing his land without permission. In the fight that ensured, Ngatoroirangi's magic was much greater and he managed to trap Tamaohoi deep underground inside Tarawera. Finally in 1886, Tamaohoi burst out of his underground prison in the form of a violent volcanic eruption that brought disaster to the area around the mountain.

To the right of the carpark is a short walk to the Wairoa Stream, the outlet for the Green Lake, and to the left another short walk leads to Maori rock drawings. Rock art is very rare in the North Island, but it is not certain whether rock drawing was rare in the first place or the art has not survived in the humid conditions in comparison with the drier conditions of the South Island. These drawings were originally covered by the 1886 eruption but were rediscovered in 1904. Executed in korowai or red ochre, the drawings are at first indistinct but, on closer inspection, the drawing of waka full of people, including standing figures, becomes increasingly clear. This perhaps is a drawing of the waka wairua.

---

9 Turn off SH 30 on to Tarawera Road and go to the very end.

6. Tree of Hinehopu

Linking Lakes Rotoiti and Rotoehu, this track is known both as Hinohopu's Track or Hongi's Track. Both names reflect the importance of this trail in the history of the Arawa people of Rotorua. Halfway along the track (and accessible by the busy road) is the famous matai tree under where as a baby Hinehopu was hidden from enemies by her mother in the seventeenth century. It was also under this tree that she met her husband Pikiao, and many of the iwi Ngaiti Pikiao trace their lineage directly back to this couple.

It was also along this track that Ngapuhi warriors, led by Hongi Hika, launched their attack on Rotorua; the track is also called Hongi's Track. Seeking revenge for earlier deaths, in 1823 Hongi Hika arrived in the Bay of Plenty and led a large war party towards Rotorua, only to discover that the Arawa people had all decamped to Mokoia Island and, for extra protection, had ensured that all waka were secured on the island. Not discouraged, Hongi travelled up the Pongakawa River to Lake Rotoehu and then dragged his waka along this track to Lake Rotoiti. Hongi's warriors were well armed with guns and the Arawa people, now trapped on Mokoia Island, were overwhelmed, defeated and many were slaughtered.

The track is easy walking through handsome bush of rewarewa matai, rimu and tawa and takes about one hour one way.

📍 The most convenient place to start is at Korokitewao Bay at the eastern end of Lake Rotoiti as there is very little parking at the Rotoehu end.

7. Te Koutu Pa, Lake Okataina

The full name of Okataina is 'Te moana i kataina a Te Rangitakaroro' or 'the ocean where Te Rangitakaroro laughed' and refers to an incident that occurred around 300 years ago. The chief Te Rangitakaroro was sitting on a rock on the shore of the lake with a number of warriors when one remarked that the lake was like an ocean, a comment that the chief found so funny that his laughter echoed around the lake.

Te Koutu Pa was the most important of the numerous settlements around the lake and was occupied by a number of iwi before Ngati Tarawhai made Te Koutu their home. The pa was on an important trading route with portages linking the lakes Tarawera, Okataina, Rotoiti and Rotorua.

Te Koutu was renowned for the skill of its waka builders and was famous for carving. Carvers there were early and enthusiastic adopters of European carving tools, and one of the pa's most famous carvings is the magnificent gateway now in the Rotorua Museum. Once this huge gateway stood on the narrow isthmus that links the pa to the mainland, but anxiety over the deterioration of the carving saw it removed, first to the Auckland Museum and, in more recent times, back to Rotorua.

During Hongi Hika's invasion of Rotorua in 1823, he sent a party of his men to bring back the head of Te Koutu's great tohunga Tamakoha, so he could eat his brains and thereby acquire Tamakoha's mana. However, Tamakoha was more than a match for Hongi and conjured up a great storm on the lake that so terrified Hongi's men that they abandoned the attack and fled.

The level of Lake Okataina varies considerably, and in the past was 12 metres lower than it is today. During the Hawkes Bay earthquake in 1931, the lake abruptly dropped nearly 4 metres.

During the Tarawera eruption in 1886, Te Koutu was thickly cloaked in a heavy layer of ash, though by that time the pa was virtually abandoned. Today the pa is covered by regenerating bush, but all the earthworks are clearly visible and, in particular, the pa is noted for its stone kumara storage pits and burial caves carved into the hillside.

The walk takes thirty minutes and begins through the archway by the carpark at the end of the Okataina Road and follows the shoreline of the lake through the bush to the small peninsula where the pa is located.

○ End of Lake Okataina Road, off SH 30, 25 km from Rotorua.

8. Tarawera Falls

Not far from Lake Tarawera, the river of the same name completely disappears underground into old lava tubes and emerges from cliffs formed over 10,000 years ago by lava flowing from Mt Tarawera. The highest drop of 65 metres is dependent on water flow so it is best to visit the falls when the lake level is high. Gushing over broken rocks, the river reforms to flow through native bush consisting of tawa, rata and pohutukawa. The clear waters are a fabulous teal green and are deep enough to swim in summer. A side road leads up to the lake and a simple camping ground.

It is quite a long haul by car to the Tarawera Falls from Rotorua and last stretch from Kawerau is gravel forestry road but the road is in good condition and well within the capabilities of any family car. From the carpark an easy walk follows the Tarawera River to the base of a volcanic cliff and the falls.

- From Rotorua drive to Kawerau where you need to buy a permit ($5) from the i-SITE to use the forestry road to the falls. Twenty-five kilometres (20 km is gravel) from Kawerau, the road to the falls is very clearly sign posted from the I-SITE and will take about 30 minutes to drive to the carpak.
- The i-SITE is open from 9 am to 5 pm and the road is only useable during daylight hours. Please note that some rental car insurances do not cover travel on gravel roads or private forestry roads such as this.

9. Waikiti Valley Thermal Pools

Tucked away in a quiet side valley, this mineral pool doesn't attract the tour buses and is considerably more relaxed than pools in the city. Consisting of a large family pool, small soaking pools and private spas, the complex is fed by the impressive hot spring Te Manaroa. Accessed by a short walkway this large spring, fringed by mosses and ferns, pulsates scalding hot water down a steaming narrow river past the pools. The swimming pool cools the soft calcite-laden water by a series of somewhat home-built cascades, more a testament to Kiwi ingenuity than to refined engineering. The complex has facilities for camper vans and is a very pleasant place to spend an evening, especially on a cold winter's night when the steaming hot river is particularly impressive.

- Take SH 5 27 km south to the Wai-o-Tapu turnoff.

The valley is 6 km from SH 5 down the road directly opposite the turnoff.

🕐 Open daily 10 am to 10 pm.
🌐 www.hotpools.co.nz
$ Entrance fee.

10. Rainbow Mountain/Maungakaramea

Maungakaramea or Rainbow Mountain lies about 25 kilometres south of Rotorua and is scarred and torn by a series of volcanic eruptions going back thousands of years. The lakes are old craters and the last eruption was believed to be around 1000 years ago. Today the mountain still steams and boils, and the geothermally active lake near the beginning of the track up the mountain presents a rare sight of ducks swimming unperturbed at one end of the lake, while at the other the water furiously boils. Above the lake tower raw cliffs of red, orange and brown multi-hued volcanic rock that that have been discoloured by continual exposure to steam, and now give this mountain its European name. Many of the plants found on the mountain are peculiar in that they specifically adapted to these harsh geothermal conditions. It takes about twenty minutes return to the lookout over the lake, but around two and hours to the top and back. Not a particularly hard climb, from the top the rewards are views over lakes Tarawera, Rotomahana and in the distance Taupo, and the mountains Tarawera, Tauhara, Ruapehu and Tongariro. The very top of the mountain is known as 'the owl's perch' or Tiho O Rua. After a hike to the top, reward yourself in the hot waters of Kerosine Creek, a naturally heated stream a few hundred metres down the road.

📍 Take SH 5 26 km south towards Taupo and Rainbow Mountain is clearly marked on the left, 500 metres past the Murapara/Waikaremoana turnoff.

11. Kerosine Creek

A popular swimming hole with locals, Kerosine Creek is a hot water stream heated by the water of the creek passing over hot rocks. The temperature of the water varies considerably, and you need to move up and down the creek to find a spot to suit. Particularly popular is the hot waterfall, great for a neck and back massage. Set amongst trees, the atmosphere on cold winter days or early evening can be magical.

There are no facilities here and it is best to change into swimming gear either before you arrive or by your car. Also the track can be pretty muddy so come prepared. At nighttime you will need a torch. This is a public reserve and as there is no knowing what might go in the water upstream, it is best not to put your head underwater. Relatively isolated, in recent years there have been considerable problems with cars being broken into.

> Kerosine Creek Road is on the right just past Rainbow Mountain Reserve. The hot stream is 2 km down this unsealed forestry road.

12. Wai-o-tapu Boardwalk Mud Pools

On the road to Taupo this huge pool of boiling mud is the best mud pool in Rotorua, it is free and well worth the short detour off SH 5. Here a very large pool of steaming shallow water constantly boils, bubbles and plops as gas escapes through the thick mud. Mini mud volcanoes are built up during the drier seasons while during wet times the mud is thrown several metres into the air.

> 27 km south of Rotorua off State Highway 5, turn left on Loop Road and drive a few 100 metres until you reach mud pools.

13. The Bridge Hot Pool, Wai-o-tapu

A bit further on from the mud pool and just past the main entrance to Wai-o-tapu, the road crosses a small bridge where a creek enters the main Kapakapa Stream. Here the local authorities have thoughtfully built several wooden steps down to the junction of the stream where water is heated by the hot rocks below. Naturally the temperature varies according to water flow and you need to find the right temperature for you. The bottom of the creek is sandy, and entry is free.

> One kilometre past the Wai-O-Tapu Geothermal Park just off State Highway 5.

14. Kaingaroa Forest

A native of California, Pinus radiata was first planted as far back as 1859 near Mt Peel in Canterbury, but it was not until the 1920s that serious planting began.

Taking advantage of unemployed workers, the government of the day oversaw the planting of radiata pine on a massive scale and by 1935 over 164,000 hectares were growing pines trees. Of this area, over 104,000 hectares were planted in the Kaingaroa plain north of Taupo, making it the largest planted forest in the world at the time. This was gradually expanded until in 1970 this one forest covered 122,000 hectares and today it is 290,000 hectares but there are now larger planted forests in other parts of the world.

Of the 1,750,000 ha of exotic forest in New Zealand, Pinus radiata accounts for 1,535,000 ha and the next most widely planted, Douglas Fir, is a mere 103,000 ha. Most of the planting is in the North Island with 1,204,000 hectares, with the Central North Island accounting for 567,000 ha.

The drive from SH 5 near Wai-o-tapu to Murapara along SH 38 passes right through the heart of this gigantic forest. While not perfectly straight the road continues through forest for around 30 kilometres with trees in various stages from small seedlings to felled giants, while some sections of the road are lined with Douglas fir and deciduous larch.

📍 SH 38 from Murapara to SH 5 near Waiotapu passes right through the heart of the forest.

TAUPO AND THE CENTRAL PLATEAU

1. Hatupatu's Rock/Te Kohatu O Hatupatu
2. Pohaturoa
3. Ohaaki Power Station
4. Wairakei Steamfields
5. Craters of the Moon
6. Huka Falls Walkway
7. AC Baths
8. Te Kooti at Taupo. Opepe Reserve and Te Porere Redoubt
9. Mine Bay Māori Rock Carvings
10. Tongariro River — Turangi
11. Tongariro National Trout Centre
12. Pihanga and Lake Rotopounamu
13. Raurimu Spiral
14. The Old Coach Road
15. Team Carrot Park
16. The Tangiwai Memorial

1. Hatupatu's Rock/Te Kohatu O Hatupatu

The story of Hatupatu and the Birdwoman is a dramatic and scary Maori legend and far too long to retell here. However, for those in the know, right here beside a busy road is the very rock that opened and saved Hatupatu from the terrifying Birdwoman when he uttered the magic words 'Matiti Matata' (Rock open for me open).

📍 SH 1, 23 km south of Tokoroa.

2. Pohaturoa

Pohaturoa is easy to distinguish as you whizz past in your car on SH 1. Just a single glance at Pohaturoa is all that is needed to know that this is the perfect place to build a pa, with the steep rocky cliffs encircling the summit that rises high above the swirling Waikato River.

In Maori legend Pohaturoa was the wife of Putauaki (Mt Edgecumbe), though this was only after he had been rejected by picky Pihanga.

Occupation goes back to Tia, who arrived on the Te Arawa waka and who settled in the area; though it is likely that the area only ever supported a very small population. Ngati Hotu ousted an earlier people, the Kahupungapunga, and established a formidable pa on the summit of Pohaturoa. Despite the superb defences, the pa fell to a coalition of Ngati Raukawa seeking revenge for the death of a Raukawa woman married to the chief living at Pohaturoa.

When the missionary Henry Williams visited the pa in January 1840, he found a small group of people living on the summit, though the pa seems to have been abandoned not long after. Palisades were still visible when the land was cleared to plant pines in 1927. In recent years the pines have been removed from the summit, though currently there is no public track to the top.

📍 Directly opposite the intersection of SH 30 and SH 1, 25 km south of Tokoroa.

3. Ohaaki Power Station

Rising over green paddocks this enormous cooling tower is the last thing you would expect in the open farmland on the road from Rotorua to Taupo. Just over 105 metres high, the natural draught cooling tower is the only one of its kind in New Zealand and, although the shell is thin, it is designed to resist both earthquakes and wind. Opened in 1989, Ohaaki is one of fourteen thermal power plants in the Taupo area and is unusual in that it also recycles most of the water it uses back into the steam field. There is a small viewing platform near the plant.

📍 Ohaaki Road, off SH 5, 35 km from Taupo.

4. Wairakei Steamfields

The Wairakei Geothermal Power Development was built in 1958, and later extended in 1996 and 2005. This was the first geothermal plant in the world to use hot water as a steam source to drive turbines. Spread over an area of 25 square kilometres, over fifty wells go down an average of 600 metres to tap into the vents of superheated steam which is then fed by a system of pipes into the geothermal power station down by the river.

Looking a bit like a demented hydro slide, the drive to the lookout leads through and under the fascinating maze of pipes, and at various points steam billows across the road and drifts through the tangle of pipes creating a surreal atmosphere that makes for great photos, especially in winter. The lookout provides an overview of the whole field and there is an excellent information board explaining just how the whole thing works.

📍 SH 1, 8 km north of Taupo.

5. Craters of the Moon

The Craters of the Moon is one the most recent and most active thermal fields in the area and is constantly changing. The most common thermal activity is steam vents, though there is one major crater of furiously boiling mud or water (depending on the water levels). The area is open, with intriguing low-growing plants that have adapted to the inhospitable environment.

To avoid disappointment, it is best to approach the Craters of the Moon as an interesting walk rather than a major geothermal experience.

📍 From Taupo take SH 1 north for 6 km, then turn left into Karapiti Road. The carpark is 1.7 km down this road.
$ Entrance fee.

6. Huka Falls Walkway

Huka Falls attracts huge numbers of visitors and who wouldn't be impressed by 200,000 litres of bright clear water rushing over a narrow 3 metre drop every second. However, if you have the time, the best way to approach the falls is not via a carpark jammed with camper vans and tour buses, but by walking from Spa Park in Taupo down the Waikato River. The river as it leaves Lake Taupo is magical; crystal clear with a sparkling teal tinge and great swathes of aquatic plants swaying in the current. It takes about an hour to walk to the falls and you will hear them long before you see them. For the more energetic, Aratiatia Rapids is another two hours' walk downstream.

If you fancy a swim even in cold weather, an added bonus is in the Spa Park at the Taupo end of the walkway – a hot spring that discharges into the river, creating a swirling mix of hot and cold water.

📍 From SH 1 turn into Spa Road, after 1.5 km turn left into Country Avenue and the track starts at the carpark at the end of this road.

7. AC Baths

This large modern pool complex uses thermal water for the main swimming pools and mineral water for the private pools. There are indoor and outdoor lap pools and family pools, smaller pools for quiet relaxation as well as private mineral pools. Part of the large family pool is set aside for 'bombing', and is particularly popular with younger males. In short this pool has something for everyone and unlike many other hot pools it is not expensive. 'AC' stands for the Armed Constabulary, who originally built a pool in 1886 on the site of a hot spring.

📍 Spa Road, Taupo.

8. Te Kooti at Taupo. Opepe Reserve and Te Porere Redoubt

After the defeat by militia and their Maori allies at Ngatapa in January 1869, Te Kooti escaped into the rugged Urewera country. However, the price his Tuhoe allies paid for sheltering Te Kooti became too much, with the government destroying Tuhoe villages and forcing their chiefs to surrender. When staying in the Urewera country was no longer tenable, Te

Kooti sought the protection of Tawhiao in the King Country and started to make his way west in the direction of Lake Taupo.

On 7 June 1869 at Opepe an advance party of Te Kooti's men came across the camp of the Bay of Plenty Cavalry. This unit was scouting the area for signs of Te Kooti, but despite this had failed to post sentries and was caught completely off guard by the attack. Nine men died at the camp and five others escaped, taking several days in bitterly cold weather to reach Fort Galatea.

The Opepe Reserve is cut in two by SH 5 from Taupo to Napier. On the northern side of the road it is an easy ten minute return walk through bush to the lonely graves of the soldiers, which later also became the burial place of local settlers. Across the road another ten minute return walk will take you to the old redoubt, of which very little remains apart from an old well. Deep gullies on three sides made this an easily defended spot, though it saw no further action as Te Kooti had already moved further west.

The government troops were desperate to capture Te Kooti Arikirangi Te Turuki as he was travelling west to seek the protection of the Maori King Tawhiao. However, Tawhiao was aware of the price that the Tuhoe people had paid for sheltering Te Kooti and was reluctant to bring further bloodshed to his people, who had suffered badly at the hands of the British just a few years before.

With protection in the King Country denied him, Te Kooti had no choice but to make a stand, and he chose Te Porere, southwest of Turangi. He ordered two redoubts to be built. What makes these forts so interesting is that the old-style defensive pa was by this time redundant. These two fortifications externally resemble a British-style redoubt but the layout inside the fort is cleverly enhanced by lacing the interior with very deep trenches to protect the defenders from rifle and cannon fire.

Led by Lieutenant Colonel Thomas McDonnell, 500 government soldiers and their Maori allies, armed with rifles and cannons, attacked Te Kooti and his Tuwharetoa allies at Te Porere on 4 October 1869. The lower redoubt fell quickly and the defenders retreated to the upper redoubt, which was in turn easily overrun, and Te Kooti just barely escaped with his life. Of the forty-one casualties that day, thirty-seven of Te Kooti's men died and just four government soldiers. Te Kooti's highly symbolic flag was also captured; it can now be seen on display at Te Papa.

Both redoubts are in a very good state of preservation and the experience enhanced by excellent information boards and a lookout point over the upper redoubt.

📍 Opepe Reserve: SH 5, 14 km from the junction with SH 1 in Taupo.
Te Porere Redoubt: 26 km from Turangi on SH 47.

9. Mine Bay Māori Rock Carvings

Without doubt one of the most dramatic modern Maori works of art, rising on a cliff face 14 metres above the waters of Lake Taupo, is the ta moko-like face of the great tohunga Ngātoroirangi. The brain child of Matahi Brightwell, who led a team of four artists, the carving began in 1980 and took four years to complete.

Brightwell himself is descended from Ngātoroirangi, who arrived on the waka Te Arawa, which originally landed at Maketu on the Bay of Plenty coast. Legends about Ngatoroirangi vary considerably, but in one version he is responsible for creating the lake, though all agree that the lake's name is Taupo nui a Tia, 'the cloak of Tia'. At that time Taupo had no fish, and one day when he became hungry, Ngātoroirangi unravelled the threads of his cloak and threw them into the water, where they came alive as inanga and kokopu fish.

The carvings can only be seen from the water and several boat operators in Taupo run cruises out to the cliff. Another option is by kayak and these too can be hired in Taupo.

10. Tongariro River – Turangi

Regarded as one of the best stretches of trout water in the world, the Tongariro River has hosted the rich and famous, including royalty (this was one of the late Queen Mother's favourite fishing spots), but at the same time is accessible to the everyday fisherperson. While rainbow trout predominate, brown trout are also caught in this very attractive fast-flowing river. There is a lengthy track along the eastern side of the river giving access to many excellent fishing spots, and the Turangi Information Centre has a free and comprehensive map of the river. Several local fishing shops hire fishing gear and local guided trips are also available. A specific licence is required to fish in the Taupo Fishing District. These are available from fishing shops and the Information Centres.

- The river runs along the northern side of Turangi township.

11. Tongariro National Trout Centre

Trout in the Taupo area are sustained by wild trout spawning in the rivers and lakes, and while trout usually spend some time during their life at sea, in this area Lake Taupo acts as a substitute ocean. The hatchery is a safeguard should a natural disaster seriously affect the trout numbers in the area. The complex raises trout from eggs and at all times of the year there are usually trout in some growth stage on show. The Visitors Centre has excellent displays on all aspects of the trout fishery including a fascinating collection of rods and flies and a native fish freshwater aquarium. A series of paths link the various pools and lead down to the Tongariro River, and an underground glass viewing chamber allows visitors to see the trout below water.

- SH 1, 4 km south of Turangi.
- Open daily 10 am to 3 pm.
- www.troutcentre.com
- Entrance fee.

12. Pihanga and Lake Rotopounamu

While the legend of the battle of the mountains is well known, Pihanga, the cause of all the trouble, is often overlooked. Originally there were seven mountains in the area to the south of Lake Taupo, and all were passionately in love with gorgeous Pihanga. Eventually the rivalry erupted into an all-out fight and the seven mountains fought each other with fire, boiling water, eruptions of smoke and lava, and by throwing searing hot rocks. For days earthquakes shook the land and the air was full of smoke and ash until a victor emerged. Tongariro had triumphed, but it had cost him the top half of the mountain, which he had pulled apart to throw at his rivals, and today Tongariro is not the tallest peak.

With defeat came banishment, and that very night after the battle the defeated mountains were forced to leave. Ngauruhoe and Ruapehu moved off just to the south, while Putauaki fled far to the east and now towers over the Kaingaroa plain. Hapless Tauhara, unable to bear the thought of being without Pihanga, moved slowly and when dawn came, he remained forever looking across the lake to his lost love. The last mountain, Taranaki, was also the angriest and had fought the hardest and in his rage he stormed south, gouging out the Whanganui River, before turning west and settling by the sea.

Pihanga lies just southwest of Turangi, rising to a modest 1326 metres, with SH47 crossing just to the north. Within the folds of her bush-clad slopes lies a small lake, Rotopounamu, and this is the perfect place to experience first-hand the beauty that caused all the fighting in the first place.

While the name means greenstone lake, the reference is to the colour of the water as no greenstone is found here (the water, however, is not always green). From the road it is a short but steady climb up to the lake, which has no visible outlet; the water drains away through the porous volcanic rock. Untouched, the forest around the lake is mature red beech, kahikatea, rimu and matai. On the eastern side of the lake is Long Beach, an ideal picnic spot and a good place for a swim on a hot summer's day. The track follows the lake edge and is easy walking.

> Travelling on SH 47 from Turangi, the track is located on the left on the downhill side of the Te Ponanga Saddle.

13. Raurimu Spiral

This famous spiral solved a problem in the construction of the main trunk railway from Auckland to Wellington and is still considered an 'engineering masterpiece'. Completed in 1908 the spiral, using horseshoe curves, loops and tunnels, climbs over 139 metres within the short distance of 2 km, but it is hard to see the spiral except from the air. The lookout has a distant view of parts of the track, but even that is not easy to see unless there is a train on the track. However, the homemade model, in the 'No. 8 wire, do it yourself' tradition, in front of the lookout is a gem of Kiwiana.

> Spiral Lookout, SH 4, Raurimu, south of Taumarunui.

14. The Old Coach Road

Not so long ago Ohakune was considered a winter town providing accommodation and services for winter sports enthusiasts, mostly skiers. Now summer is just as busy as the town has becoming a popular centre for mountain bikers. For the truly hardy there is the 'The Mountains to the Sea' cycle trail which begins high on the slopes of Mt Ruapehu, and traversing mountain bush and river finally ends on the beach at Whanganui.

Much more manageable is the Old Coach Road, a 15 km one-way trail from Ohakune to Horopito. The cobblestone road was constructed in 1906 to prepare for the completion of the railway line through the area, but it was only used for two years and once the railway line was finished, the road became redundant and overgrown. Largely forgotten, in 2005, work began on restoring the road for cycling and walking, including using the old iron Hapuawhenua rail viaduct which was replaced in 1987 by an new concrete bridge.

> Walking the trail will take about four and half hours one way

and cycling two hours and most cyclist prefer to take the shuttle from Ohakune to Horopito and then cycle back into town. Bikes and cycling gear can be rented from TCB who can also organise shuttles but you need to book ahead.

📞 06 3858433

🌐 www.tcb.nz

15. Team Carrot Park

Rich volcanic soil and cold winters are the ideal climate to grow the very best and juiciest carrots. The first carrots were grown in the 1920s by Chinese gardeners and now two thirds of the North Island's carrots come from this area. To celebrate this humble vegetable, in 1984 a giant carrot was erected on the outskirts of town and continue to draw so many visitors that in 2016 a park, playground and toilets were built in the new Carrot Park.

You'd think that one giant vegetable would be enough. Clearly not for the good folk of Ohakune who have added swede, parsnip, potato and brussel sprout characters to keep the big carrot company. Unlike the carrot these humanoid vegetables have happy faces with arms and legs and together they make up 'Team Carrot'. With the playground and nice clean toilets, not to mention a short bush walk and an historic railway bridge across the road, this is an excellent spot to take a break from your travels, particular if you have energetic children in tow.

📍 On SH 49 just east of the centre of town.

16. The Tangiwai Memorial

On Christmas 1953, New Zealanders waking up to open Christmas presents were shocked by the news of a dreadful railway disaster that occurred at 10.21 pm the night before. That evening, high on the slopes of Mt Ruapehu, a tephra dam gave way and the lahar, the ash laden waters of the mountain's crater lake, surged down the Whangaehu River, destroying one of the piers of the railway bridge over the river at Tangiwai just minutes before the Wellington to Auckland passenger express train was due to arrive. Despite the valiant efforts of a passer-by to stop the train, the locomotive and the first six carriages plunged into the raging dirty water, killing 151 people, New Zealand's worst rail accident. Tangiwai in English means 'weeping water'.

The first reaction when arriving at the site is how small the river is, little wider than a large creek, but a photograph on the display board of a similar lahar in 2007, shakes you back to reality. In that event the entire memorial area is covered in deep water and volcanic debris and then you realise that it would be impossible to survive in such a torrent. Along with a commorative plinth, the memorial area has the number plate of K949 and a bogie of the original train. A track along the river leads to a lookout over the bridge. It is a very sobering place to visit.

📍 18 km east of Ohakune on SH 49.

EAST CAPE, GISBORNE AND TE UREWERA

1. East Cape Highway
2. Gisborne Beaches
3. Kaiti Hill
4. Te Poho O Rawiri Wharenui
5. The Star of Canada – Te Moana Maritime Gallery, Tairawhiti Museum, Gisborne
6. Gray's Bush Scenic Reserve
7. Millton Vineyard, Manutuke
8. Manutuke
9. Eastwoodhill Arboretum
10. Rere Falls and Rere Rockslide
11. Morere Hot Springs and Nature Reserve
12. Te Urewera

1. East Cape Highway

Once well and truly off the beaten track, this road from Opotiki to Gisborne is attracting more and more visitors, but it still doesn't have the coach loads of package holiday tourists and manages to retain a rugged identity all its own. Usually treated as one entity, the East Cape is two distinct regions. From Opotiki to Cape Runaway the road hugs the rugged coast, weaving in and out of sandy bays and small rocky coves. The climate is wetter, the landscape more forested and the iwi here is Whanau-a-Apanui. In contrast, the eastern side of the cape is drier, more barren and the road is mainly inland, only touching the coast occasionally. The beaches are wider, more sheltered, and sandy and this is also home to the Ngati Porou iwi. A notable feature of the East Cape is the numerous marae, often with historic carved meeting houses/wharenui. Meeting houses are not tourist attractions or public halls, but a living representation of the ancestors of local people. You should no more walk on to a marae than walk uninvited into someone's house. Please seek permission before entering a marae. Accommodation and facilities in general are limited so it pays to plan ahead, even in the off-season.

The following are the highlights from the Bay of Plenty to Gisborne.

Motu River

The wild rugged river is one of the last untouched rivers in the country as it winds its way through bush-covered hills from the foothills of the Urewera country to the sea. Jet-boat trips up the river are available.

Christ Church, Raukokore

This small photogenic Anglican church sits on a flat promontory jutting out to sea and is decorated in Maori carvings and beautiful woven tukituki panels. In the graveyard behind are the graves of Eruera and Amira Stirling, two notable twentieth-century Maori leaders. It even manages to accommodate nesting penguins under the floor.

Natural Solutions, Te Araroa

Manuka was once regarded as little more than a weed or at best a source of good firewood. Today the humble tree plays a vital role in rehabilitating vast areas of marginal land cleared of forest and Manuka honey and oil are now recognised for their outstanding natural anti-bacterial and anti-fungal properties. At Te Araroa Natural Solutions is a manuka factory which has a Visitor Centre that includes information about manuka, a retail outlet for the range of manuka products as well as a café. Tours of the factory are available, though it is necessary for visitors to book tours ahead.

 Natural Solutions, 3 km north of Te Araroa on SH 35.
 www.manukaproducts.co.nz

Te Waha O Rerehou

Located on the beach front at Te Araroa, is the largest pohutukawa in the world, known as Te Waha O Rerehou. Over 20 metres high and 40 metres at its widest point, the tree is believed to be over 600 years old. It is also tapu so please do not climb on the tree.

East Cape Lighthouse

Now located on the easternmost point of mainland New Zealand, the original lighthouse was first built in 1900 on nearby East Island. Ignoring local Maori advice that the island was tapu, the lighthouse was plagued with problems. Four men were drowned building the lighthouse, access was difficult and finally, after continuing landslides and earthquakes, the lighthouse was dismantled and moved to its present position in 1922.

 The lighthouse is 20 km from Te Araroa on a pretty rough gravel road.

St Mary's Church

Situated below the fortified pa site, Pukemarie, this small church is without a doubt one of the finest carved churches in the country. Constructed in 1924 under the encouragement of Sir Apirana Ngata, the church is a memorial to Ngati Porou soldiers who died in the First World War. Ngata was keen to revive dying arts and craft, so local weavers and carvers were employed in creating the fine interior, while the carved pulpit was a gift from the Arawa people to Ngati Porou.

Waipiro Bay

In 1900 this was the largest settlement on the East Coast, shipping out sheep, cattle and timber, and it was here that Robert Kerridge opened his first picture theatre in 1923. Now almost a ghost town, the centre of the settlement is the Iritekura marae with its fine meetinghouse carved in the traditional Ngati Porou style by master carver Pine Taiapa.

Tokomaru Bay

A magnificent sweep of sandy beach with plenty of room for everyone, it is the ruins of the old Tokomaru bay Freezing Works along with the Tokamaru Bay wharf and the New Zealand Shipping Company Offices and Wool Store at the northern end of the bay that have special appeal (all three are registered heritage buildings). Although now crumbling the surprisingly large and extensive freezing works is testament to the size and importance of sheep and cattle farming to this part of the country and the vital role that coastal shipping played before road transport became the norm. Despite the wonderful beach, time has not been kind to Tokomaru Bay and today most of this small township is abandoned businesses and shuttered shops.

Anaura Bay

Considered to be one of the finest beaches on the East Coast, this is a beautiful spot for swimming, fishing, walk, diving or just not doing much at all. This bay was Cook's second landing place in New Zealand, though bad weather prevented him from provisioning his ship and after two days, on the advice of local Maori, sailed south to Tolaga Bay. Today the bay supports only a small population, swelled over the summer by holidaymakers.

📍 15 km north of Tolaga Bay, turn off SH 35 into Anaura Bay.

Tolaga Bay

Built in 1929 at considerable expense and over 600 metres long, the Tolaga Bay wharf is an indication of the vital role that sea shipping played in the development of New Zealand. For much of New Zealand's early history, it was the sea and not roads that provided the link between the country's settlements. Wharves such as the one at Tolaga Bay were key to the success of the fledging agriculture industry and without sea access it was virtually impossible to get goods to market. With the advent of better roading, sea transport went rapidly into decline and all along the East Cape flourishing seaside communities such as Tokomaru Bay, Waipiro Bay, Hicks Bay, and Te Araroa saw both their importance and populations dwindle.

On the southern side of Tolaga Bay is Cook's Cove Walkway. Captain James Cook's first landing at the Turanganui River at modern day Gisborne was, through a series of misunderstandings, uncharactistically a disaster, and in desperate need of water and firewood he sailed north to this cove in October 1769. This walk – mainly through farmland – takes two and a half hours return, and from the track there are fantastic views north over the bay.

Whangara Beach

Made famous by Witi Ihimaera's novel *The Whale Rider* and the film of the same name, the centre of this small community is the meeting house crowned by the famous ancestor Paikea riding a whale.

Dive Tatapouri

Just 100 metres of Tatapouri beach is a reef that becomes almost exposed at low tide and is home to stingrays that live in the deep channels of the reef to avoid predators. Dive Taupouri take reef tours and snorkeling trips where the rays come right up to people and will even 'cuddle' them. Other sea creatures include the shy cougar eel, kahawai, kingfish and very occasionally orcas.

📍 Tatapouri Beach, 10 km north of Gisborne.
🌐 www.divetatapouri.com

2. Gisborne Beaches

With a hot summer climate, Gisborne is the ideal base for a beach holiday and within 20 km of the city are several excellent beaches, notable for both good surf and excellent swimming. These beaches are listed are in order of distance from Gisborne.

Waikanae and Midway Beach

Stretching for miles from the Turanganui River to the Waipaoa River mouth, this great uncrowded beach is within walking distance of downtown. Both Waikanae and Midway have patrolled swimming in summer, unlike some of the beaches further north. However, after easterly storms this beach can turn ugly with piles of driftwood washed down the Waipaoa River.

Wainui Beach

Famous for its surf, this long sandy beach has waves to suit everyone from the apprentice surfer to the very experienced.

📍 5 km east of Gisborne.

Makorori Beach

The pick of the beaches north of Gisborne and almost undeveloped, there are numerous points to access this golden sandy beach from the road.

📍 10 km north of Gisborne.

Tatapouri

A short stretch of sandy beach, with an excellent boat ramp for those going fishing or diving.

📍 13 km north of Gisborne.

Pouawa

The last sandy and easily accessible beach north of Gisborne, Pouawa has good surf in an easterly swell.

📍 19 km north of Gisborne.

3. Kaiti Hill

The base of Kaiti Hill holds a special place in the story of Polynesian migration to Aotearoa, as it is here at the mouth of the Turanganui River that two voyaging waka arrived: Horouta and Te Ikaroa a Raura. As with Cook, many centuries later in 1769, the Horouta's first sight of land was the cliffs of the great headland across the bay, which the captain Paoa named after his dog, Te Kuri a Paoa, later to be renamed by Cook as Young Nick's Head.

However, Kaiti is also associated with a great love story. A young man living at Kaiti fell in love with a girl living at Opape, near Opotiki, but he had been unable to declare his love for her before she returned to her home. Confused about what he should do, an idea came to him while walking along the beach that by chance he might be able to send a message to his love by way of a shellfish. Picking up a live shellfish he whispered a message of passion and love and put the shell back in the water. Entrusted with such an important mission, the shellfish made the long and difficult journey around the coast to Opape.

After the long journey the valiant shellfish washed up on the beach at Opape. One day, while out gathering shellfish, the girl came upon the messenger of love, picked it up, but quickly threw it back in favour of a bigger specimen. Undaunted the plucky shell constantly contrived to place itself in the path of the girl until, one day, she realised that she had seen this one shellfish time and time again. This time she picked it up and with a length of flax hung the shellfish around her neck, where it came to rest on above her heart. Finally the shellfish was able to convey the message entrusted to it on the faraway beach below Kaiti Hill. Now aware of her distant lover's true feelings, the girl set off alone to travel the difficult path through the Waioeka Gorge to be finally reunited with her true love on Kaiti Hill.

The walk uphill is in two stages. The first is a steady to steep uphill climb to the lookout Te Kuri a Paoa, which has views over Gisborne city, inland and across Turanganui. From this point it will take another 10 minutes to the carpark lookout further uphill. There are two options to reach the carpark lookout: a steep 'fitness trail' that is shorter but all steps to the top; and the 'Shady Oaks' track which is much more gradual.

Road access: Titirangi Drive off Queens Drive, Kaiti.
Walking Track: Kaiti Beach Road, opposite the Cook Memorial.

4. Te Poho O Rawiri Wharenui

Elaborately carved both inside and out, Te Poho O Rawiri at the foot of Kaiti Hill in Gisborne is New Zealand's largest carved meetinghouse. Opened in 1930, the building at the time was exceptionally modern, being the first meetinghouse to have a steel ridgepole, electrical wiring and a galvanised iron roof. The carvings are a mixture of styles with many of the pieces carved by Arawa craftsmen in Rotorua and some carvings coming from an older house, Poho O Mahaki built in 1830. The tekoteko figure is the revered ancestor Rawiri Te Eke Tu A Terangi, while inside another ancestor Kahungungu faces the visitors as they come through the door. Notable Maori leaders Sir Apirana Ngata and Dr Peter Buck attended the opening and both Queen Elizabeth II and Princess Diana have been welcomed at Poho O Te Rawiri.

📍 Queens Drive, Kaiti, Gisborne.

5. The Star of Canada – Te Moana Maritime Gallery, Tairawhiti Museum, Gisborne

This museum within a museum is the wheelhouse and captain's cabin of the ship The Star of Canada. Built in Belfast in 1909, the ship ran aground on rocks on the Gisborne foreshore in June 1912 and could not be refloated. The next best thing was to salvage what was possible to save, and local jeweller William Good purchased the wheelhouse, which included part of the deck and a very large cabin crowned by the wheelhouse. Towing the wheelhouse through town he placed it on an empty section next to his house in Childers Road where it became a local attraction its own right to many generations of Gisborne people. In 1983 The Star was left to the city of Gisborne and moved to its present location right on the river (the best view of the wheelhouse is on the river bank opposite the museum). This is not a small building and it is the surprising that the fine leadlight windows survive both the grounding and two subsequent moves.

This section of the Tairawhiti museum naturally houses the maritime history exhibits and includes an amazing collection of old surfboards.

- 10 Stout Street, Gisborne.
- Open 10 am to 4 pm Monday - Saturday, 1.30 pm to 4 pm Sunday.
- 06 867 3832
- www.tairawhitimuseum.org.nz

6. Gray's Bush Scenic Reserve

Set aside as a reserve in 1926 and the only remaining lowland bush on the Poverty Bay plain, tiny Gray's Bush has long been recognised as botanically unique. The highlights of this impressive subtropical forest are the massive kahikatea and puriri and what makes it highly unusual is the combination of these two trees growing together. Puriri tend to favour well-drained soils while kahikatea thrive in wet conditions. Furthermore, the height of the kahikatea has resulted in the puriri growing much taller and straighter than their usual spreading habit. The larger kahikatea are up to 40 m tall and 400-500 years old and the understorey is nikau palms and kawakawa. The tracks are not clearly marked, but the reserve is so small that it is impossible to get lost.

- 10 km from Gisborne on the Back Ormond Road.

7. Millton Vineyard, Manutuke

The Millton Vineyard, near Gisborne is possibly the best-known organic vineyard in New Zealand. Covering 30 hectares in four separate vineyards in the Manutuke region, The Millton Vineyard was established as a biodynamic organic vineyard in 1984, though grapes had been grown on the property since the 1960s. This means that no insecticide, herbicide, systemic fungicide or soluble fertilizers are used in the vineyard.

As with most Poverty Bay vineyards, The Millton Vineyard is strong on white wine, though they also produce merlot, pinot noir, malbec and syrah. All the wines are from single vineyards and these are identified on the label (e.g. Te Arai Chenin Blanc, Opou Vineyard Chardonnay). The Millton's Vineyards premium wines are produced under the Clos De Ste. Anne label that come from Naboth's Vineyard, a north-eastern facing hill slope in the foot-hills of Poverty Bay. They also produce two dessert wines from viognier and chardonnay grapes.

In addition to its reputation as leading organic wine producer, the tasting room at Millton is set in a beautiful garden with clipped hedges, old olive trees and large shade trees, ideal for a leisurely picnic.

- 119 Papatu Road, Manutuke, Gisborne.
- 06 862 8680
- www.millton.co.nz

8. Manutuke

Maori were very quick to adapt European building techniques and craft and the introduction of iron tools fueled a flowering of Maori carving and art in the mid nineteenth century. At Manutuke near Gisborne, the iwi Rongowhakaata built three extraordinary wharenui, Te Hau ki Turanga (1842), Te Mana ki Turanga (1883) and Te Poho Rukupo (1887).

The oldest of these three, Te Hau ki Turanga, was constructed by Raharuhi Rukupo, rangitira and master carver in rememberance of his brother Tamaki Waka Mangere, a signatory of the Treaty of Waitangi. Built of totara, the government of the day pressured Rukupo to sell the building, but he steadfastly refused and in 1867, JC Richmond, the then native minister and quasi director of the Colonial Museum had the building confiscated during the land wars. Now in Te Papa Museum of New Zealand, there are plans to return this house back to Rongowhakaata.

Te Mana-ki-Turanga and Te Poho Rukupo were both carved in the distinctive local Turanga style under the influence of local chief Raharuhi Rukupo. Te Mana-ki-Turanga is the older house, built in 1883, and features carvings of the separation of Rangi and Papa, and Maui hauling his fish from the sea. Te Poho Rukupo was built not long after in 1887 at nearby Pakirikiri to honour Rukupo and originally stood near his grave, but was moved to the present site in 1913. The Maori Battalion building in the centre was constructed in 1945 and the handsome church dating back to 1888 has recently been restored with a highly ornate interior.

While visitors are welcome at Manutuke, please show respect and do not enter when there is a hui in progress.

📍 14 km south of Gisborne on SH 2.

9. Eastwoodhill Arboretum

Billed as 'the largest collection of northern hemisphere trees in the southern hemisphere', Eastwoodhill has over 4000 exotic trees and shrubs covering 131 ha. The arboretum is the life work of William Douglas Cook, who at best could be described as eccentric.

Born in New Plymouth in 1884 to an affluent family, Cook developed an interest in plants from an early age. At just eighteen he established an orchard at Hastings with money borrowed from his family, but his venture failed and after taking labouring jobs, sold the orchard and in 1910 bought 250 hectares of rough land at Ngatapa west of Gisborne. No sooner had Cook established himself on the farm, that he was called to join the army at the outbreak of World War One. Wounded at Gallipoli in 1915, he then served in France and at one stage lost the sight in his right eye. While recuperating with relatives in Scotland, Cook became inspired by the great gardens of Britain and once he returned to New Zealand began a lifetime of collecting and planting trees and plants from the northern hemisphere.

On regular trips to Europe he bought thousands of plants including tulips, peonies and hyacinths from the Netherlands. In addition he collected an impressive library of books on horticulture.

In 1927 he employed Bill Crooks, who remained at Eastwoodhill for forty-seven years tending the farm, leaving Douglas to tend his trees. He married in 1930, but the marriage was not a success and ended just a few years later. During this time he enlarged his farm, but sold parts of it again in the 1950s to fund his tree buying expeditions. At that time the threat of nuclear war made him even more determined to preserve this oasis of northern flora in the south Pacific. In 1951 Cook established the Pukeiti Rhododendron Trust in Taranaki as rhododendrons did not flourish at Eastwoodhill. If Cook's tree collecting was unusual then his habit of working naked wearing just a sunhat and a boot on his right foot certainly confirmed him as distinctly odd with his neighbours. Over the half century until his death in 1967, it is estimated that Cook's tree collecting cost him in excess of 55,000 pounds. After his death from a heart attack the arboretum was left to a trust, but the vast area gradually became neglected. In 1984 a group of local women formed a garden group to help restore Eastwoodhill to its former glory.

Today the one-hectare Homestead Garden is recognised as a Garden of National Significance and at every time of the year there is some thing special to see, though autumn is a particularly popular time to visit. Numerous tracks throughout Eastwoodhill allow the visitor to spend any time from a thirty minute walk to half a day. There is also a café and accommodation available.

- 2392 Wharekopae Road, Ngatapa – 35 km from Gisborne.
- Open 9 am to 5 pm.
- 06 863 9003
- wwww.eastwoodhill.org.nz
- Entrance fee.

10. Rere Falls and Rere Rockslide

Travelling on this backroad, the traveller first comes to the Rere Falls and these are not to be confused with the Rere Rockslide which is another 2 km further on. At the falls the Wharekopae River tumbles down an escarpment to form the very attractive Rere Falls. While not particular high they are very broad and pour into a wide pool, which is a very popular swimming hole in summer. There is off road parking, toilets and a grassed picnic area.

Neither long nor steep, the Rere rockslide is more like a gentle hydro slide, though the speed is determined by the volume of water in the river. Very popular in summer, once school has returned the weekdays are a good deal quieter. The river is partially shaded by old willow trees and there is a large picnic area with tables and off-road parking.

It's a long drive, but the road is good and sealed all the way. Water quality at both the rockslide and falls is questionable.

◉ Wharekopae Road, Rere, 13 km past the Eastwoodhill Arboretum.

11. Morere Hot Springs and Nature Reserve

New Zealand has more than its fair share of hot springs, but these hot springs are unique for several reasons. They are located in a 364-hectare nature reserve and surrounded by fine native bush that is particularly famous for the luxurious growth of the nikau palms. The reserve has several tracks that take thirty minutes to three hours to walk, so this is your chance to feel very virtuous and go on a brisk bush walk, rewarded by a soak in hot pools. It you are there at night, then take a walk in the bush to see the glow-worms. The springs produce an astounding 250,000 litres of water per day, bubbling up through a crack in the fault-line that cuts across the Mangakawa Valley. Even more incredible is that the water is actually ancient seawater that has been trapped for thousands of years underground, even though Morere is situated inland and at quite a distance from the ocean. There are a number of pools indoor and out, for both families and those wanting a more relaxed soak. The mineral pools are reputed to have therapeutic value, though the water temperature is more warm than hot. The small spa-like pools known as the Nikau Pools are located in a wonderful bush setting thick with nikau and well away from the larger family pool.

On SH 2, Morere, just north of Nuhaka.
Open daily 10 am to 6 pm.
06 837 8856
www.morerehotsprings.co.nz

12. Te Urewera

Te Urewera has always been isolated country. Rugged and bush covered this is a land of steep hills, deep valleys and a tough climate. Te Urewera is also the land of the Tuhoe people, known as the 'Children of the Mist', fiercely independent and the last Maori iwi to be influenced by Europeans and even today well known for their individuality. The Urewera National Park encompasses much of this inland country and at the heart of the park is Lake Waikaremoana. This large lake, second only to Taupo and formed only 2000 years ago by a massive landslide across the Waitakeheke River, is over 240 m deep and has deep bays that reach far into rugged bush-covered terrain. Over 600 native plants have been recorded in the area, and the bush is mostly untouched.

At the eastern end of the lake, below the distinctive Panakiri Bluff, is the site of the Armed Constabulary Redoubt. Today the bush has reclaimed the land and all that remains is the old parade ground, an historic cemetery and a limestone rock poignantly carved with the names and dates of soldiers stationed here the 1860s and 1870s.

The Lake Waikaremoana Great Walk follows the shore for most of its 46 km. It is by no means flat, but is within the reach of a moderately fit tramper who is prepared for a three to four day trip. The weather in the area is very changeable and can be cold and wet even in summer, and it is not unusual to have snow in winter. This tramp is becoming increasingly popular, so it is necessary to book huts and campsites well ahead in the busy season. A water taxi service is available for those who wish to shorten their trip or even do sections of the walk as a day trip.

If you are not up for something so demanding, there are numerous shorter walks ranging from ten minutes to half a day, most within a short distance of the Visitor's Centre.

The pick of these walks are as follows and the distances are from the Visitors Centre.

> The easiest way to the park by car is the sealed road from Wairoa 72 km away. The road via Murapara from the north is something else. Narrow, relentlessly winding and gravel for 100 kilometres, this road needs real patience and careful driving, but passes through some of the most wild and untouched bush country in New Zealand.

Hinerau Track/Aniwaniwa Falls

This short walk through beech forest (thirty minutes return) leads to three cascades known as the Aniwaniwa Falls, together over 40 m high. There is also a viewpoint over the lake and Panekiri Bluff.

> Track begins from the carpark of the Visitor Centre.

Lake Waikareiti Track

About one hour each way this moderate-grade walk leads through red and silver beech to Lake Waikareiti, which is free from introduced aquatic plants and is known for its remarkable water clarity.

📍 The track begins 200 m from the Visitor Centre.

Papakorito Falls

Only a few minutes' walk from the carpark along a grassed track, this attractive waterfall tumbles 20 metres over rocky outcrops into the pool below.

📍 1.2 km from the Visitor Centre down Aniwaniwa Road.

Giant Rata/Tawa Walk

This loop takes around thirty minutes return, and features mature tawa that can grow up to 25 m. They also have an attractive open canopy, giving a light green feel to the usually dense New Zealand bush. A short detour leads to a massive rata with a convoluted and twisted trunk, believed to be over 1000 years old.

📍 The loop track is just off the Ngamoko Track 2 km from the Visitor Centre on the road to Wairoa.

Whatapo Bay

One of the best sandy beaches with excellent views over the lake, Whatapo Bay is an easy ten minute walk from the road.

📍 The track to the bay is 5.5 km from the Visitor Centre on the road to Wairoa.

Lou's Lookout

A steady uphill climb through a jumble of limestone boulders to an impressive lookout point over the lake.

📍 8.5 km south of the Visitor Centre.

Onepoto Caves

A complex of caves, rocky overhangs, arches and tunnels created by the giant landslide that created the lake and once used by Maori as a refuge in times of trouble. The convoluted track is frequently slippery and you will need a torch to explore the caves.

📍 12 km south of the Visitor Centre.

Lake Kiriopukae

A tiny lake in wetland that continually expands and shrinks with the season and surrounded by limestone outcrops and boulders that give the lake the appearance of a Japanese garden.

📍 12 km south of the Visitor Centre at the beginnig of the Great Walk at Onepoto.

HAWKES BAY

1. Kahungunu Wharenui
2. Mahia Peninsula
3. Giant Puka, Waiatai Reserve
4. Gaiety Theatre, East End Café and Saloon Bar
5. Mohaka Viaduct
6. Waikare Beach
7. Shine Falls
8. Lake Tutira and the Gutherie Smith Arboretum
9. Rorookuri Hill, Whakamaharatanga Walkway
10. Pania of the Reef
11. Napier Botanical Gardens
12. Napier Prison
13. Otatara Pa Historic Reserve
14. Tutaekuri River
15. Ocean Beach
16. The Faraday Centre
17. Arataki Honey
18. Birdwoods Gallery
19. Rush Munro Ice Cream Garden
20. Spanish Mission, Hastings
21. Hawke's Bay Wineries
22. Pekapeka Wetlands
23. The Public Toilets, Onga Onga
24. Norsewood
25. The Wop Wops Wetland Park
26. Danish Hair Embroidery - Dannevirke Gallery of History
27. Fantasy Cave, Dannevike
28. Wimbledon Tavern
29. Taumata whakatangi hangakoauau o tamatea turi pukakapiki maunga horo nuku pokai whenua kitanatahu
30. Waihi Falls

1. Kahungunu Wharenui

This magnificent meeting house in Nuhaka was built as a war memorial after the Second World War to honour the large contingent of Maori soldiers from this area who fought overseas during the war. Traditionally styled and elaborately carved, in pride of place at the apex of the front of the house is the Kahungungu himself, the central ancestor after which the iwi of the Hawke's Bay and Wairarapa take their name. The traditional style of this house contrasts with the modern and more colourful meetinghouse Tane Nui A Rangi two miles north of Nuhaka.

📍 300 m from the roundabout on SH 2, Nuhaka.

2. Mahia Peninsula

Jutting out into the Pacific, the wild and barren Mahia Peninsula separates Poverty Bay from Hawke Bay and is a popular fishing, diving and surfing area. The north side of the peninsula is characterised by small rocky bays and has a good boat-launching ramp, while on the southern side the wide sweep of Opoutama Beach is a favourite swimming and surfing spot, though Blacks Beach further south has the best surf. The Mangawhio Lagoon is an important wetland reserve and, for the more energetic, there is a two hour walk through the Mahia Peninsula Scenic Reserve, a rare remnant of coastland forest in this bare landscape.

In the Maori legend of Maui hauling up his great fish (the North Island), Mahia is known as Te matau a Maui, the fishhook of Maui. In the fourteenth century the great waka Takitimu landed here, and Ruawharo, the tohunga on the waka, decided to end his voyaging and he settled on the peninsula. Tradition also has it that Ruawharo brought whales to the bay, and the wharenui at Opoutama is named in his honour.

Coronation Reserve or Piko o Te Rangi on the eastern side of the peninsula is a natural rock basin that was once used by Bishop William

Williams to baptise local Maori. A small cleft in the rocks was said to have been used to store bibles.

No longer is Mahia all about the past and beaches; this is the home of Rocket Lab. Not mucking about, Rocket Lab decided on the peninsula for the location of the launch facility for its Electron rocket in November 2015. By mid-2016 most of the infrastructure was in place and on 26 September 2016, Rocket Lab Launch Complex 1 was officially opened. The first test flight was carried out on 25 May 2017 and the rest is history; Mahia, once a quiet backwater, is now at the cutting edge of space technology. From Maui's fishhook to the stars.

⚲ Mahia is 20 km from Nuhaka on SH 2.

3. Giant Puka, Waiatai Reserve

If you want to see the largest puka tree in New Zealand, you need to come prepared for a bit of bush bashing. The size of this puka will come as a surprise to those who consider this tree suitable for the small city garden. Standing 10 metres tall, this broad multi-branched tree has much smaller leaves in the mature form than the more familiar wide leaves of the younger tree. The reserve is overgrown, the track almost impossible to find, the tree is not marked, and you won't be able to do this in your jandals. After crossing the stile, follow the fence line up the hill to some steps which lead to an indistinct track. The puka is not marked but it is right next to the dilapidated picnic table. The reserve is very small, and it is impossible to get lost.

⚲ Waiata Road, just off SH 2, 4 km north of Wairoa.

4. Gaiety Theatre, East End Café and Saloon Bar

These three places are all in the same and adjoining buildings and together they make a stopover in Wairoa more than worthwhile. The historic Gaiety theatre is the heart of this trio and has regular film screenings, the occasional live show and can host any event that will attract a decent crowd. Built in 1925, six years later it was flattened in the Hawkes Bay Earthquake, but by the 1930s no town could be without a movie theatre and it was rebuilt immediately. Television took its toll and, along with hundreds of other small theatres around the country, it closed its doors in the late 1960s. However, unlike the other theatres Wairoa rallied around and restored the theatre to its modest former glory, and it reopened again in the mid-1990s.

The East End Café with its fresh tasty food is in the same building and has double doors leading into the theatre. Even if you are only passing through Wairoa, this café is the pick of the town's small number of eateries. Next door to that is The Saloon, which originally was the town's billiard saloon and is now a bar, live music venue and restaurant. The style, if it has one, is best called eclectic, but if you are staying in Wairoa on a Friday night there is a very good chance you will end up here.

📍 Marine Parade, Wairoa.
🌐 www.gaietytheatre.co.nz

5. Mohaka Viaduct

As with tunnels it's the railways that steal the show when it comes to big bridges. The railway line from Napier to Gisborne crosses the Mohaka River over a viaduct 97 metres above the water, the highest bridge in New Zealand. Built in 1937, the bridge is so exposed that windbreaks are necessary to protect the trains from being blown off the tracks into the river far below. By comparison, road bridges are pretty lowly affairs with the deck of the Auckland Harbour Bridge a mere 43.7 metres above the water. There is an excellent view of the viaduct from the main highway.

📍 SH 2, 38 km south of Wairoa.

6. Waikare Beach

Wild and empty, Waikare beach was once the main highway down the coast both in pre-European times for Maori, and for Pakeha prior to the road further inland being built. Today the long sweep of beach with mounds of driftwood and backed by high cliffs mainly attracts just a few fisher folk, but it has an untamed beauty all of its own and is an ideal place to just slow down and do not much at all. The flat farmland on the other side of the river from the camping ground was the location of an early whaling station, though nothing now remains. Behind the beach are huge crumbling cliffs, and clearly visible to the south is the massive Moeangiangi Slip, created when a 3-kilometre section of the cliffs collapsed during the 1931 earthquake.

📍 To get to Waikare Beach at Putorino 60 km north of Napier on SH 2, turn into Waikare Road and follow this narrow and unsealed road for 13 km to a camping ground by the river at the very end of the road.

7. Shine Falls

Picture a hot Hawke's Bay summer's day, with a deep blue sky and a temperature nudging thirty. Now imagine the picture-perfect waterfall, with water tumbling down a rocky face into a large cool swimming hole, surrounded by native bush alive with birds. Now you have Shine Falls. At 58 metres this is the highest waterfall in Hawkes Bay, and certainly one of the most attractive in the North Island with two streams breaking into myriad rivulets spreading down over a broad rock face into a wide and deep pool. The falls are in an 800 hectare 'Mainland Island', an area where predators are intensely managed, resulting in an obvious recovery of both bird and plant life in the reserve, and where recently both kokako and kiwi have been reintroduced. It is a bit of a walk to get there, but it is not hard and the track meanders through a handsome limestone gorge with rocky bluffs towering above the stream and deep green cool native bush. You don't get to see the falls until you are there which increases the appeal of the walk. The falls are about a forty-five minute walk from the road.

It's a bit of journey to get to Shine Falls, and much of the road from Tutira is winding and gravel, but it is worth the effort and you can stop off for a short walk around the very pretty Opouahi Lake just down the road.

At the Tutira Store on SH 2 45 km north of Napier, turn into Matahorua Road. At the junction with Pohokura veer to the right (this is still Matahorua Road), and after 5 km veer to the left into Heays Access Road and the beginning of the track is on the left 7 km down this road.

8. Lake Tutira and the Gutherie Smith Arboretum

This popular swimming and picnic spot was originally part of the Tutira Station owned by farmer and author Herbert Guthrie-Smith. Guthrie-Smith early on recognised the need for conservation of native plants and birds, and in 1921 published his massive book, Tutira: the story of a New Zealand sheep station, based on years of painstaking observation and note-taking. The picnic area at the southern end of the lake was the site of the station's woolshed and is now the beginning of several tracks in the Tutira Country Park. The walks include the Lake Waikopiro Loop Track, a thirty minute circular walk around this small lake adjoining Tutira, and the three hour tramp to Table Mountain Trig with spectacular views both inland and over Hawke Bay.

The narrow strip of land that runs between lakes Tutira and Waikopiro was the site of a very unusual pa called Te Rewa. Taking advantage of the location, the pa was built up with tree trunks and then protected by a moat. Even in 1882 few signs of the pa remained, and today a raised mound is the only trace. Several other pa sites can be found on the eastern side of the lake.

Water quality in both lakes has been compromised by developments along the shore but is currently undergoing restoration.

Across the other side of SH 2 is the Gutherie-Smith Arboretum covering 90 hectares on what remains on original Gutherie-Smith sheep station. Since 2002 over 20,000 trees have planted in series of grouping from different countries and geographical regions, all linked by walkways. There are also collections of single genra and blocks of timber trees and tree crops for potential commercial development. Providing a backdrop to the arboretum is an area known as The Hanger. In 1896, Gutherie-Smith set aside a 10 hectare block of rough land so he could observe the natural regeneration back to forest and the area has been largely untouched since.

📍 SH 2, 44 km north of Napier.

🕐 The arboretum is opened to the public 9 am to 5 pm Sundays only and entry is free.

9. Rorookuri Hill, Whakamaharatanga Walkway

The Hawkes Bay earthquake needs little introduction, but nearly 90 years later it is hard to grasp both the scale of destruction and the dramatic changes to the landscape. One place, that in itself is rather ordinary, but is actually the best spot to take in what happened that day on February 3 1931 when a 7.8 magnitude earthquake struck Hawkes Bay.

The Whakamaharatanga Walkway leads up the modest 71 metre Rorookuri Hill. Prior to that fateful February day, you would have been standing on an island and the flat land around you and all the way to Bluff Hill six kilometres distant, a vast lagoon and tidal flats. The violent earthquake lifted the ground by over 2.7 metres, instantly draining most of the area in front of you. Subsequent reclamation for farming and the airport reduced the wetland further still, and now only a small tidal lagoon remains just south of the airport.

The summit was once occupied by a pa with another on a headland and these were key to controlling the important food resource of the lagoon. Strategically placed, the wide terraces and defensive ditches are still very clear today.

The walkway is across farmland and is easy walking, though the tracks are closed for lambing during July, August and September.

Take SH 2 north from Napier. Just before Bay View turn left into Onehunga Road.
The walkway begins on the left 1km down this road.

10. Pania of the Reef

Without a doubt Pania is one of the most famous and tragic Maori legends. It is very close in sentiment to the Hans Christian Andersen tale The Little Mermaid and while it is remotely possible that Andersen could have heard of Pania (he wrote the story in 1836), it is highly unlikely.

Pania lived in the sea, but she was fascinated by life on land. Every evening she swam to the shore to explore the world of humans, faithfully returning to the sea at dawn. One evening a local chief, Karitoke, came down to a spring at the foot of the cliff and there he caught sight of Pania hiding in the flax. Immediately he fell in love with Pania and they secretly married that very night, though when dawn came Pania returned as usual to the sea.

So their married life began with Pania joining Karitoki in his whare every night and in the morning returning to the sea. Eventually Pania gave birth to a strange child, a son completely without hair who was named Moremore, the hairless one. Karitoki was now even more anxious that he might lose both his wife and son to the sea. He consulted a tohunga for help. The tohunga told him that if Pania and his son were to touch cooked food they would never be able to return to the sea. That night Karitoki went ahead with the plan. However, as he was about to place the food on them, Ruru the morepork cried out a warning which woke Pania. Horrified, she fled back to the sea where her own people greeted her and took her down to the depths, never to return.

Pania was turned into a reef, where she lies with her arms outstretched, though no one is sure if she is pleading with Karitoki to explain his actions or if she is still expressing her love. Her son Moremore was transformed into a taniwha in the shape of shark and acts as a kaitiaki of the bay.

The statue of Pania was unveiled in 1954 and is a firm favourite with both locals and visitors. When the statue was stolen in October 2005, the uproar was such that the thieves abandoned the statue and it was restored the following month. The motivation for the theft was never made clear.

The reef itself lies about 500 metres north of the port, is 1600 metres long running in a northeast direction, and is marked by two large buoys at either end. Walking from the statue on Marine Parade to the point overlooking the reef is an easy stroll of about 30 minutes.

📍 The statue is located in the gardens on the Marine Parade next to the Tom Parker fountain.

11. Napier Botanical Gardens

One of New Zealand's oldest botanical gardens are tucked away in a gully on Bluff Hill, and often bypassed by visitors who flock to the famed Art Deco wonders of Napier. Established as early as 1855, the gardens contain a number of very large specimen trees that must count among the oldest exotic trees in the country. The gardens had a tough start, as the site was steep and difficult to work. As always public money was short, and the development had to rely on prison labour. Today the gardens are an attractive mix of wonderful old trees, specialised plantings such as the sub-tropical garden with palms and cycad, formal gardens, a duck pond and an aviary that unfortunately is a bit tired. Right next door is the oldest cemetery in the area, established just a year before the gardens in 1854 and includes the graves of early missionaries William Colenso and Bishop William Williams. In keeping with custom of the time, most gravestones are large and elaborate, but there are also a number of very rare wooden memorials dating from the 1860s. As was typical for the period, the cemetery is carefully laid by religious denomination. The gardens are a good place to start a walk on Bluff Hill.

📍 Spencer Street, off Chaucer Road South.

12. Napier Prison

In 1858 125 pounds was allocated for the construction of a prison in Napier and in 1862 the prison opened with inmates that totalled twenty-five men and twenty-four women, but included lunatics, alcoholics, children and dispossessed Maori. The prison was harsh and the regime included hard labour in the quarry opposite under the watchful eye of Officer Jack 'the Bastard' Adams. The quarry is now the Centennial Gardens. New Zealand's oldest existing prison, the current building constructed of sandstone blocks is still largely in original condition and includes the solitary confinement cells, the hanging yard with a public gallery, a small graveyard, and cells complete with original bunks. It was in this prison that those found guilty of killing the Reverend Volkner in Opotiki were hanged. Finally closed in 1993, the prison offers a range of tours and three Escape Rooms, and there are regular ghost sightings. You need to book for a guided tour and the monthly night tour, both of which are dependent on numbers. Self-guided tours can be taken any time.

📍 55 Coote Road.
🕐 Open daily 9 am to 5 pm.
📞 06 835 9933
🌐 www.napierprison.com
$ Entrance fee.

13. Otatara Pa Historic Reserve

One of New Zealand's oldest and largest pa (only Mangakiekie in Auckland is bigger), the location alone of Otatara indicates its importance. Situated high above the Tutaekuri River, the views from Hikurangi Pa at the top of the hill are superb and encompass all of the Heretaunga Plain and far inland.

The pa were established around 1400, and over time various iwi have occupied this site, including Te Tini o Awa, Ngati Koaupari, Ngati Mamoe and Ngati Ira, until the pa came under attack in the seventeenth century by Ngati Kahungunu under the leadership of Taraia. While Hikurangi fell, Taraia was unable to take Otatara and built a new pa at Pakowhai. A short time later he again began a siege of Otatara and finally captured the pa by tricking the defenders, after which the pa was abandoned.

The pa are perfectly situated to take advantage of the vast resources on the shallow lagoons between the pa and the ocean, while the river gave access to the forest resources further inland. The site is huge, covering 40 hectares, and everywhere there are terraces, house sites, kumara pits and defensive earthworks. Hikurangi occupies the summit while Otatara is more in the style of headland pa and has been partially destroyed by quarrying.

A large tidal lagoon, Te Whanganui a Orotu, an extension of the enormous Ahuriri Lagoon, originally came right up to the foot of the pa, but the 1931 earthquake effectively drained the land.

The recent addition of a carved gateway, palisades and tall pou give this reserve an ancient air, and the open grassy site allows a clear view of terraces, defensive ditches, house sites and kumara pits.

📍 Springfield Road where Gloucester Street crosses the Tutaekuri River.

14. Tutaekuri River

What's in a name? A lot if the English translation of Tutaekuri is 'Dogshit River'. Apparently, the name refers to the muddy brown colour of the river after heavy rainfall which is highly likely as the 100 km river does begin in the steep Kaweka ranges which are subject to periodic heavy rain events.

📍 The Tutaekuri River runs just south of Taradale and joins the Ngaruroro River as it enters the ocean between Napier and Clive.

15. Ocean Beach

For the first time visitor to Hawkes Bay, the central coastline is a disappointment. Instead of a typical long sandy New Zealand beach, the beaches here are deep shingle, like something seen on miserable cold British coastline. However, all is not lost, as not so far away on the other side of Cape Kidnappers is Ocean Beach, a huge sweep of golden sand that stretches for miles. Although very popular in the summer months, it is largely undeveloped and never crowded.

📍 25 kms east of Havelock North.

16. The Faraday Centre/Hawkes Bay Museum of Technology

The building now housing the Hawkes Bay Museum of Technology began life in 1912 as the Napier Power Station. It expanded significantly in 1927 with the installation of the massive Fullgar engine which was installed specifically to supply electricity to the city's trams based next door. Solidly built of reinforced concrete, the building survived the 1931 earthquake, and with functioning machinery, the power station supplied electricity to those people sheltering in nearby Nelson Park. While the station made a major contribution to the revival of Napier, the tram system never recovered. Functioning until 1975, just four years after its closure, an organisation was set up to preserve the unique engines.

Today the small, but perfectly formed Faraday Centre focuses on hands-on displays, whether it is operating a machine, handling old appliances, or stepping into the Tardis.

The heart of the displays is the massive Fullgar Engine, the only working example in the world, but equally appealing is the Teslar Coil and then there is the opportunity to time travel in the Tardis. Regardless of your interest in technology, this place is enormously appealing and knowledgeable and friendly volunteers make it even better.

- 2b Faraday Street, Napier
- Entrance fee.
- www.faradaycentre.org.nz

17. Arataki Honey

Arataki Honey is New Zealand's best-known honey producer, which is not surprising since it is also the largest honey enterprise in the Southern Hemisphere. Established in 1944 and now with 20,000 hives across New Zealand, the business is in two distinct parts. The Hawke's Bay operation produces honey for the local and export market and provides local pollination services, while the Rotorua Division specialises in live bee exports, queen bees, packing honey and providing pollination services.

As expected, the Visitor Centre at Havelock North is packed with information about bees and honey and along with a live beehive, also provides a range of honeys and honey related gifts. What comes as real surprise is the honey tasting. We all know that there are a variety of honeys depending on the plants the bees collect honey from and that these honeys taste different. However, few of us really take that much notice and even fewer have tried tasting a range of honeys. What is unexpected is just how different these flavours are and here at Arataki you can taste ten honeys from very different flowering plants. The flavours are so distinct, and in much the same way as wine picks up the flavour of individual grapes, honey does much the same. So on your wine tasting tour of Hawkes Bay, add in a stop at Arataki for a honey tasting, you will not be disappointed.

- 66 Arataki Road, Havelock North.
- Open 7 Days from 9 am to 5 pm.
- 06 877 7300
- www.aratakihoneyhb.co.nz

18. Birdwoods Gallery

It is very rare for one place to please everyone, but Birdwoods manages to do just that. Whether you are eight or eighty, a smart city doctor or a small town chippie, Birdwoods just seems to appeal to everyone. Even their own website can't quite put a finger on why.

In 2005, Bruce and Louise Stobart moved the old 1894 church hall from St Peter's in Waipawa to a site on the outskirts of Havelock North, added a large outdoor terrace and developed a large sunny garden featuring works of art. The following year they added a tiny colonial style cottage built from recycled materials. The church hall became a gallery and café, while the cottage became a sweet shop. Nothing so remarkable there.

The gallery is stocked with a truly individual and unique range of artwork and gifts sourced from both New Zealand and Africa and you will be guaranteed to find something here, for even the most discerning and difficult person. The café terrace is the perfect place to enjoy both good coffee and food and from there to stroll through the sculpture garden with creations that range from the stylish and to the amusing.

Next door in the cottage is a shop which Birdwoods claim to be 'an old-fashioned sweet shop just like you remember'. Honestly, no one remembers a sweet shop like this, as no shop was ever this good. The walls are stacked floor to ceiling with jars of sweets, some familiar and some never seen before, and more incredible is that most of these are made in New Zealand. Where have these incredible lollies been hiding all the time?

- 298 Middle Road, 3 km from the centre of Havelock North.
- Open daily 10 am to 5 pm December to March, 10 am to 4 pm April to October.
- 06 877 1395
- www.birdwoods.co.nz

19. Rush Munro Ice Cream Garden

Having worked with his father in the confectionary business Frederick Rush Munro arrived in Hawkes Bay, from Britain in 1926. With just 10 pounds to his name he started selling handmade ice cream, taking advantage of the abundance of local fresh fruit. From this small beginning he established his Ice Cream Garden in Heretaunga Street, only to have the building destroyed in the 1931 earthquake. Drawing large crowds, visitors travelling long distances to experience the delights of the Ice Cream Garden, though in this more sophisticated age the gardens might seem a bit ordinary, though the ice cream is certainly not. Rush Munro ice cream is superb. Still made to the original recipes with no artificial flavouring or additives, the Rush Munro uses only natural ingredients and the fruit ice cream contains a minimum of 25 per cent real fruit. The range today also includes organic ice creams.

- 704 Heretaunga Street West, Hastings.
- Open 11 am to 5.30 pm Wednesday to Sunday.
- 06 878 9634
- www.rushmunro.co.nz

20. Spanish Mission, Hastings

The people of Hastings have always seemed slightly put out that Napier received more attention than Hastings did in regard to the 1931 earthquake. Even the recent name change from Napier Earthquake to Hawke's Bay Earthquake was on the insistence that the quake damaged much more than just Napier. This was true, but Napier was doubly devastated by the fire that followed when the water system failed. Hastings, however, was able to contain any fires immediately.

With all that said Hastings, like other towns in the region, suffered major damage and, like Napier, was rebuilt in the style of the day. In the case of Hastings, though, the style was more Spanish mission than Art Deco. Hastings has, in the Westermans Department Store (1932), one of the finest period buildings in the province, unique in the fact that not only the facade has been preserved but also the glass shop front, the interior oak panelling and even some of the original signage. The building now houses the Hastings Information Centre, from which visitors can obtain a self-guide leaflet for a walking tour of Spanish mission Hastings.

- Cnr Russell & Heretaunga St, Hastings.

21. Hawke's Bay Wineries

The Hawke's Bay climate with its hot dry summers combined with excellent grape-growing soils produces some of the best wines in the world. Of all the grape-growing areas in New Zealand, Hawke's Bay grows the widest range of varieties, including pinot noir, merlot, syrah, chardonnay, sauvignon blanc, riesling and pinot gris. The Gimmlett Gravels area is famous for its superb red wines. In all there are seventy wineries and a further seventy-one grape growers in the area, all with their own style ranging from large sophisticated affairs with top-of-the-range restaurants to more homely or historic vineyards where a picnic among the vines is more the order of the day. The wineries are well spread out and you will need a sober driver if travelling by car.

Craggy Range Giants Winery

As monumental as the landscape it occupies, Craggy Range is a striking winery set on a wide river terrace above the Tukituki River and below Te Mata peak. Designed by architect John Blair, the winery hints at the grand European chateau, but retains a distinctly New Zealand feel. Although large in scale, Craggy Range maintains a degree of intimacy with a small, formal courtyard garden, and a spare but elegant tasting room. The restaurant is recognised as one of New Zealand's finest vineyard restaurants.

253 Waimarama Road, Havelock North
www.craggyrange.com

Mission Estate Winery

New Zealand's oldest winery, Mission Estate was originally established in nearby Meeanee in 1851 primarily to produce altar wine. Superbly situated with broad views over Napier, the winery is housed in the beautifully restored seminary building originally constructed in the early twentieth century. In addition to the stylish restaurant overlooking the gardens, the Mission provides free wine tasting and conducts tours of the historic building.

📍 198 Church Road, Taradale.
🌐 www.missionestate.co.nz

Askerne

A small intimate winery, Askerne grows all its grapes on a single vineyard just outside Havelock North and has a good reputation for producing fine wines but also has been bottling some head-turning dessert wines. The wine tasting room is simple and friendly, set among the huge gum trees which feature on their label.

📍 267 Te Mata-Mangateretere Road, Havelock North.
🌐 www.askernewines.co.nz

Te Mata

Established in 1892, Te Mata is one of New Zealand's oldest and best-known wineries, made famous in the 1970s by the striking Ian Athfield designed house set among the vines just across the road from the current winery. Ian Athfield was also the architect who designed Te Mata's main building. From vineyards scattered across Hawkes Bay, the winery produces a wide variety of wine types from syrah and cabernet/merlot to chardonnay and sauvignon blanc.

📍 349 Te Mata Road, Hastings
🌐 www.temata.co.nz

Sileni Estates

Internationally recognised for its stylish modern architecture, Sileni offers a first-class restaurant, wine-tasting, a vineyard tour, and one of the country's best gourmet stores, which stocks an amazing selection of cheeses as well as locally made olive oils.

📍 2016 Maraekakaho Road, Bridge Pa.
🌐 www.sileni.co.nz

Alpha Domus

Producing single-estate wines from two vineyard within three kilometres of each other Alpha Domus has established an excellent reputation for Bordeaux-style reds, but also has won awards for its whites and dessert wines. Wine tasting is a simple affair with the tasting area located in the winery itself, surrounded by tanks of fermenting grape juice, while outside a pleasant shaded area is just the spot for a relaxing picnic or glass of wine.

📍 1829 Maraekakaho Road, Bridge Pa, Hasting.
🌐 www.alphadomus.co.nz

Trinity Hill Winery

Located in the famous Gimblett Gravels vine-growing area, this vineyard produces wine from sixteen different varieties, more than any other vineyard in New Zealand. The handsome modern winery built in 1997 was designed by Auckland architect Richard Priest and was honoured in 2002 as a 'stand-out' building by the New Zealand Institute of Architects. In addition to cellar sales and tastings, the cellar is a venue for exhibitions of contemporary New Zealand art, and behind the winery is an extensive picnic area (platters are also available).

📍 2396 State Highway 50, Hastings.
🌐 www.trinityhill.com

Lime Rock Wines

Situated on limestone much further inland than the majority of wineries and at a higher altitude, the Lime Rock vineyard is ideal for growing sauvignon blanc but also produces pinot noir, merlot and pinot gris. The crumbling limestone is full of fossilised sea life and some of these fossils are on display in the tasting room. From the top of the hill within the winery is a spectacular view over central Hawkes Bay.

- 601 Tikokino Road, Waipawa.
- www.limerock.co.nz

22. Pekapeka Wetlands

The Pekapeka wetlands is a very odd shape. Covering almost 100 ha, the swamp follows a long valley extending 4.5 km long but very narrow, at best a few hundred metres wide. Making it even more odd, there is a railway line running right down the middle of the wetland. All that aside, it is one of few remaining inland wetlands in the Hawkes Bay and has been extensively restored; the removal of willow trees was a herculean effort that helped regulate flood waters and improved its natural biodiversity.

Access is only to a small part of the wetland where raised boardwalks weave through the dense raupo, over deep ponds and along winding waterways, giving visitors a close up view of the many water birds. A small rise allows an excellent view of the whole area, but will gradually be obscured by thick planting.

Take care to secure your car in the carpark and take your valuables with you.

- Well signed posted on SH 50, 12 km south of Hastings.

23. The Public Toilets, Ongaonga

Once a thriving farming community, progress bypassed Ongaonga and what a good thing too. This small township has eleven registered historic buildings and some of the buildings such as the old butcher's shop and school are tiny. Several buildings have been shifted to an historic park next to the Department of Conservation office, including a backcountry hut. However, you need to remember to save your toilet stop for Ongaonga. Not to let a good historic building go to waste, the public toilets are housed in the old police cells. Built to last the sturdy wooden cells still have barred windows over the heavy doors but thank goodness the peephole covers in the doors have been firmly closed.

- Ongaonga is off SH 50, 18 km west of Waipawa, Central Hawke's Bay.
- The toilets are part of a larger museum complex that is open on Sunday afternoons from 1 pm to 3 pm.

24. Norsewood

Not that long ago, travellers would have been justified in giving Norsewood a miss, but this is one small town that has really lifted its game and is well worth the short detour off SH 2.

On 15 September 1872 two ships carrying Scandinavian immigrants landed at Napier. They were the Hovding from Christiania (now Oslo) and the Ballarat from London, and their passengers were Norwegian and Danish families sponsored by the New Zealand government and destined to develop the rugged southern Hawke's Bay. Initially nineteen families settled in Norsewood and Dannevirke, but over the years 3000 more Norwegians, Danes and Swedes joined them.

As time passed the immigrants gradually assimilated into the general New Zealand population with the Scandinavian heritage largely confined to surnames and street names, but not entirely forgotten. Norsewood leads a new wave of Nordic pride and it has given this town a much-needed lift. Now the town has a lively celebration to mark Norway Day, (the closest Sunday to May 17), Norwegian flags flutter in the main street and at the southern end of town is replica wooden Norse church.

The museum is a good place for visitors to start, and like the best museums it is small and not overwhelming. Spread over several buildings the museum contains a wide range of items reflecting a colonial heritage with a strong Scandinavian flavour. The main building is an old cottage and among the items is a nineteenth-century Royal Copenhagen porcelain communion jug used in the local Lutheran Church, as well as the pulpit from the old Dannevirke Lutheran Church. Behind the cottage, but still part of the main building is an old smithy and in the garage display is the fascinating Scandi wagon, an early horse-drawn cart used locally and of distinctive Scandinavian design.

Just down the road is replicate of a bindalsfaering, a type of Norwegian fishing boat, looking for all the world like a mini Viking ship and clearly not much used in landlocked Norsewood. This vessel was presented to Norsewood by the Norwegian government in 1972 on the occasion of the centenary of the settlement of the district.

The nearby Norsewood cemetery is believed to be the largest Scandinavian cemetery in Australasia, and mainly contains the graves of Norwegian settlers. Across the highway in 'Lower Norsewood' is the Natural Clothing Company, where Norsewear socks and gloves are still made in the factory behind the shop. Clearly it's now time for a sit down and in the main street, Café Norsewood has excellent coffee and homemade food.

Norsewood is just off SH 2, 20 km north of Dannevirke.

25. The Wop Wops Wetland Park

Located behind the Natural Clothing Company, this tiny restored wetland can't fail to appeal to the passing visitor. The entrance is through a highly unusual and certainly unique gateway. Created by Jeff Byran, the carved and tattooed totara wood panels merge Nordic, Maori and Celtic traditions. The lefthand panel weaves native flora and fauna into a design representing the migration of tuna (eels). On the right the panel depicts Scandinavian migration, interwoven with Celtic knots. In the centre of the arch is the mask of Papatuanuku, the Earth Mother.

Once this area was part of a busy town, but now a languid stream winds through regenerating native plants. The highlight are the enormous native longfin eels that congregate in a small pool waiting to be fed. Do not feed the eels bread, they are not vegetarians and much prefer fine slivers of meat.

📍 75-79 Hovdig Street, Lower Norsewood.

26. Danish Hair Embroidery - Dannevirke Gallery of History

Dannevirke, meaning Danes work, is named after a fortification in Schleswig (now part of Germany) and, like Norsewood, was settled by Scandinavians, the Norwegians in Norsewood and the Danes in Dannevirke.

In the local museum, known as the Dannevirke Gallery of History, is the 'Danish Hair Embroidery'. While ornaments made of human hair were not uncommon in Victorian times, the pieces were usually confined to rings, lockets and small personal items. What makes this piece so special is that not only is it large, but it is also totally created using human hair. Technically it is not an embroidery but uses very fine, short pieces of hair that with tweezers have been precisely and delicately glued to glass.

The embroidery celebrates the marriage of Brendt and Lisbet Johannsen and their offspring and was completed in 1886. What is not known is just whose hair was used and whether each name was embroidered using the hair of the person mentioned.

In a glass case is the sad sight of a fine pair of huia, shot in 1889 in the Pohangina Valley and believed to be the last pair in the area. If that is not enough, in May 2012, a thief carefully prised open the glass case and stole the two tail feathers from the huia in front; each feather valued at $8000 on the open market.

14 Gordon Street, Dannevirke.
Open 9.30 am to 4 pm Monday to Friday.
06 374 6300

27. Fantasy Cave, Dannevike

First opened in 1989, the The Dannevirke Fantasy Cave began modestly as a Christmas promotion and consisted of small Christmas caves where local children could come and visit Santa. Gradually the idea grew, and the Santa Cave became the Fantasy Cave and from one small grotto, the complex now covers three and half floors in the heart of Dannevirke and is open throughout the year. Entirely constructed and operated by volunteer 'Cave Dwellers', the idea has moved beyond Christmas and now covers popular fairytale, storybook and nursery rhyme characters. The displays constantly change and are frequently replaced and more recently model trains have been added, known as 'Little Southern Hawke's Bay Railway'.

Santa is certainly not forgotten, and every December he returns to the cave where this all started.

The cave is open throughout the year on Saturdays only as well as during the school holidays and most of December. The opening days and hours vary so it is best to check the website first.

Currently in recess pending relocation to a new building.
Check www.fantasycave.org for the latest details Entrance fee.

28. Wimbledon Tavern

Typical of late nineteenth century rural hotels the Wimbledon is quite possibly the most original pub in New Zealand. The exterior is no different from when it was built in 1889, apart from a couple of chimneys that toppled after earthquakes and were never replaced. The narrow front bar is typical of the older hotels with just standing room for drinkers and with a separate small dining room for meals. The walls are still lined in scrim and piles are still the original wooden blocks, so if you find you are a bit unsteady on your feet after a beer or two it may not be the drink alone.

Like most small pubs not only did the pub provide drink, food and lodgings, but also provided a wide range of services for both the local community and for travellers, and the publican often doubled as postmaster, storekeeper, and even local magistrate. This is not the first hotel on the site; an earlier hotel built around 1880 went up in flames and the current pub was rebuilt in 1889. The narrow bar occupies the entire front of the building, with a pleasant outdoor area off the eastern end of the building. With wooden fixtures, historic photos and local farming memorabilia, including a small collection of old shearing combs, the Wimbledon Tavern is worth the long 65 km drive from Dannevirke (the road is sealed but winding).

The township of Wimbledon takes its name from Wimbledon England, which was originally better known for rifle shooting championships rather than tennis. Local legend has it that the name stuck after a farmer shot a cattle beast at such a distance that a local remarked that the shot 'was good enough for Wimbledon'.

📍 6333, Route 52, Wimbledon.
📞 06 374 3504

29. Taumatawhakatangihangakoauauotamatea- turipukakapikimaungahoronukupokaiwhenu- akitanatahu

This place name is officially accepted as the longest in the world and belongs to a hill in southern Hawke's Bay. The hill itself is unremarkable and would hardly warrant a second glance if it wasn't for the length of the name. The notable chief Tamatea lost his brother in a battle nearby and retreated to the summit of the hill to play his flute and lament his dead sibling. Usually shortened to Taumata Hill, the accepted English translation is 'the place where Tamatea, the man with the big knees, who slid, climbed and swallowed mountains, known as land eater, played his flute to his loved one'.

Usually written as one word, a breakdown of individual words will help with pronunciation - Taumata-whaka-tangihanga-koauau-o-Tamatea-turi-pukaka-pikimaunga-horonuku-pokai-whenua-kitana-tahu

◉ Wimbledon Road, 5 km south of Porangahau, Southern Hawkes Bay.

30. Waihi Falls

It's a a bit of a drive out to these falls but it's a pleasant excursion especially when you can work in a swim on a warm summers day. In 1899 this was the first scenic reserve established in Hawke's Bay as locals recognised early on the need to protect a local attraction where the Waihi River cascades 25 m over a wide bluff into a large pool (ideal for swimming). Although not particular high, the falls are wide and are especially spectacular after heavy rain. From the car park and picnic area the track is a short downhill walk through thin native bush that nonetheless contains some handsome old kowhai trees, leading to a grassy picnic area by the falls.

◉ From Dannevirke take the Weber road for 30 km, then turn right into Oporae Road for a further 12 km to the short Waihi Falls Road on the left. A substantial section of Oporae Road is unsealed.

TARANAKI

1. Forgotten World Highway
2. Pukerangiora Pa
3. Awatetake Pa
4. Manutahi Taxidermy Museum
5. Hillsborough Car Museum
6. The Rewa Rewa Bridge and the Coastal Walkway
7. Abraham Salaman Tomb, Te Henui Cemetery
8. Govett-Brewster Art Gallery and the Len Lye Centre, New Plymouth
9. The Swanndri Collection - Puke Ariki Museum
10. New Plymouth Power Station Chimney
11. Paritutu Rock and the Sugar Loaf Island
12. Ratapihipihi Reserve
13. The Vineyard Bistro at Okurukuru
14. Te Koru Pa, Oakura
15. Parihaka Village
16. Cape Egmont Lighthouse
17. Opunake Beach
18. Peter Snell Statue
19. Hollard Gardens, Kaponga
20. Manaia Blockhouse and Redoubt
21. Tawhiti Museum
22. Elvis Presley Museum
23. Butterfly Tree, King Edward Park, Hawera
24. Hawera Water Tower
25. Aotea Monument Patea
26. The Garden of Tutunui, Patea
27. EC Dallison and Sons, Waverley

1. Forgotten World Highway

For a backcountry driving experience it is hard to beat SH 43 that runs between Stratford and Taumarunui and is now known as the Forgotten World Highway. Rich in both natural and human history, this is not a fast road, continuously twisting and turning through broken hill country and over numerous saddles. From the higher points along the road there are marvellous views of Taranaki and the mountains of the central North Island. Even though it is now sealed all the way, it will take at least three hours to travel the 155 km.

Highlights along the road include:

The Moki Tunnel

Known as the Hobbit's Hole long before the Lord of the Rings film was even made, this narrow 180 metre one way road tunnel was built in 1936 and has wooden beams supporting the portals and peaked roof.

Mt Damper Falls

A 16 km detour off the highway near Whangamomona, these falls at 74 metres are the highest single drop falls in the North Island. A local story tells of the discovery of the falls by a local sheep farmer who lost his prize sheep dog after it was dragged over the cliff by a wild boar. From the road it is a forty-five minute return walk mainly across farmland to the falls. Though not hard the track is pretty rough and muddy.

Whangamomona

Established in 1895, this historic village is now famous for its January Republic Day Festival that attracts thousands of people to the township that normally has a popular of sixteen. The festival was first held in 1989 and declared the Whangamomona area a republic (complete with its own passport) as a protest against regional government boundary changes that took the district out of Taranaki and into Manawatu. The centre of the rebellion was the Whangamomona Hotel, one of New Zealand's most famous iconic pubs.

2. Pukerangiora Pa

A major pa on a high bluff overlooking the Waitara River, Pukerangiora saw bitter fighting during the Musket Wars period of the 1820s and 1830s. At one stage the pa fell to invaders, forcing many of the defenders, including women and children, to try and escape by leaping from the cliffs above the river.

During the New Zealand Wars of the 1860s, the pa was the centre of a campaign led by the elderly Major General Pratt, who adopted slow siege tactics including a series of redoubts and a long sap, which are still clearly visible. Pratt's technique, described as 'a mile a month', drew criticism from the colonists; one report said, 'The war in Taranaki maintains its peaceful course.' However, the British were not slow to adapt to Maori fighting techniques developed in response to the use of gun and cannon. Pa were built to withstand cannon fire and engineered to ensure that a full-frontal assault was near suicidal. Moreover, Maori defenders would use a pa to slow down the attack and then quickly abandon the position to avoid heavy casualties in the face of an attacking force that had greater numbers and was better armed. In reality Major General Pratt knew that a drawn-out fight with careful advances was one tactic that would wear down his enemy, and when the sap eventually reached the palisading, a truce was agreed, and the defenders abandoned the pa to Pratt.

The site is not well maintained, and the signage is minimal and confusing, but don't be put off by that. The main carpark is about 200 metres past the first sign and is easy to miss. The military sap to the pa is behind the trees to the left of the first sign. The road from the turnoff is also signposted with the location of the redoubts built as part of the attack on the pa. From the point where the pa overlooks the river there are wide views back to the coast.

Q From SH 3 east of Waitara, turn into Waitara Road and then continue for 7 km and the pa is on the left.

3. Awatetake Pa

Located on a cliff high above the Waitara River, this pa is ringed on three sides by a single defensive ditch that is one of the most impressive of any pa in the country. The description 'ditch' does these earthworks a great injustice, as even now they are still very deep and broad, much more moat-like and still very difficult to scale. Once they would have been topped by a bank and palisading, making a very impressive and, to enemies, formidable sight. Rua or food pits are still visible throughout the pa, though today the site is covered in trees that include many old karaka and a very old totara that would date back to when the pa was occupied.

The track begins over a stile at the back of the gravel yard (and not down the farm track). From there it crosses farmland, marked by orange triangles, and is easy walking, but expect electric fences gates and boisterous stock.

📍 From SH 3 at Waitara take Princess Street, which eventually becomes Ngatimaru Road.
The track begins on the corner where Ngatimaru Road meets Tikorangi Road West.

4. Manutahi Taxidermy Museum

What began as a curious boyhood interest, John Ward's fascination with stuffed animals really started when his grandmother gave him a book on taxidermy. Now, with 2000 items in his vast collection, John's enthusiasm has grown, not diminished.

First impressions are not the best as you swing off the road and face what appears to be a large and rather ordinary farm implement shed with a small door at one end. Stepping through that door takes you to another world and you are immediately overwhelmed by hundreds of animal heads peering down from the walls. Every wall, cabinet, and large areas of the floor are covered by animals of every description. You need to stand for a moment and wait as it sets in just how much stuff is here. Flying birds, domestic and wild animals, spiders, seashells, fish and snakes and even a rock collection. A few exhibits such as the rhino head and the standing polar bear make you shudder, but John is very particular that each and every one of his animals complies with the strict CITES (Convention on International Trade in Endangered Species). The building is climate controlled to protect the animals and the birds are mostly in glass cases to keep them dust free and preserve their colour.

John is a bird taxidermist and on display is his very first specimen, an Eastern Rosella. Curiosities abound from the double headed lamb to the last cattle beast through the Waitara freezing works. Not everything is labelled but that hardly matters, John knows what everything is and where it is. Come with an open mind and prepare to be fascinated.

- 360 Manutahi Road, Lepperton.
- Open Saturday and Sunday 10 am to 4 pm.
- 06 752 0569
- Entrance Fee.

5. Hillsborough Car Museum

New Zealand's only Holden car museum and the largest private collection in New Zealand dedicated to that Aussie motoring icon, this is the life work of local builder, Steve Fabish. Definitely not an ageing farm shed filled with a few old cars, this is a superb purpose-built, state of the art museum with not a speck of dust or an item out of place. In pristine condition the paint work gleams and with the bonnets up, the engines look like new.

Generations of Holden memorabilia, clothing, posters and historic video clips complement the forty-five vehicles on display. Covering the entire history of Holden, among the rare cars is the oldest registered Holden in New Zealand, dating back to 1949. It might come as a surprise that the Holden history in Australia dates back much further to 1852 when James Holden first stepped ashore in Adelaide.

Adding to the appeal is the mini golf course based on the famous Mt Panorama track at Bathurst and, like the museum, this is a superb facility that will appeal to everyone regardless of age.

- 📍 683 Egmont Road, Lepperton.
- 🕒 Museum open weekends and public holidays 10 am to 4 pm. Mini-Putt open daily 10 am to late.
- 📞 0274 470 708
- 🌐 www.hillsboroughholdenmuseum.co.nz
- $ Entrance fee.

6. The Rewa Rewa Bridge and the Coastal Walkway

In a country where nowhere is far from the sea, it is odd that so few New Zealand towns and cities manage easily to connect their urban centre with the sea. New Plymouth is the exception. Running almost 13 km from the port to the north outskirts of the city at Bell Block, the Coastal Walkway is a gem and the locals know it. Young, old, people pushing prams, skateboarders, joggers, scooter folk, cyclists, walkers, runners and those who just want to sit by the sea all use this magnificent walkway. Winning too many awards to list here, the walkway deserves every one of them.

The most recent section, opened in 2010, extended the walkway three kilometres from the city to Bell Block and includes the striking Rewa Rewa bridge. Crossing the Waiwhakaiho River, the 68 metre long bridge, constructed of steel and concrete, was designed by Peter Mulqueen. Reflecting the prevailing westly wind, the structure is open and touches lightly on the northern side which is an historic pa and burial ground. The design cleverly frames Mount Taranaki in the curving arch when viewed from the far side.

If a 13 km one-way walk sounds like a bit much, make sure you visit this section.

📍 The walkway is accessible at numerous points along the coast, but parking can be a bit tricky at the city centre.
The bridge is at the northern end of Clemow Road, Fitzroy.

7. Abraham Salaman Tomb, Te Henui Cemetery

The grand tomb of Abraham Salaman takes you by surprise. Mausoleums of any type are uncommon in New Zealand cemeteries, most kiwis preferring their final resting place to be marked with a plain, undecorated tombstone. Not so Mr Salaman, who lies in at peace in a grand edifice in the shape of a mosque. Even more surprising is that this grave dates from the 1940s, when it would have been even more striking than it is now.

Born in Amritsar around 1880, Salaman arrived in New Zealand about 1903 and by 1914 was a well-established silk merchant, but later set up a pharmacy despite having little formal education of any sort. His herbal medicines attracted a wide and loyal clientele. However, most of his remedies were opium based and he fell foul of the law on two occasions and twice ended up in prison.

In 1930 he moved to New Plymouth where he again attracted numerous customers who swore by his herbal medicines. Married three times he died in New Plymouth in February 1941, but even in death he was a larger than life character. Prior to his death he designed and had built an elaborate tomb in the Islamic style with the blue dome topped by a brass star and crescent. In the complete opposite to the traditional Islamic burial, Salaman lay in state for a week dressed in equally elaborate clothing. Over 2000 people gathered in the cemetery to watch the Muslim funeral ceremony as Salaman's coffin was placed in the tomb. Although the tomb has been occasionally vandalised over the years, it is still an impressive edifice and impossible to miss.

📍 Te Urenui Cemetery, end of Watson Road, off SH 3, Strandon.

8. Govett-Brewster Art Gallery and the Len Lye Centre, New Plymouth

In 1963 Monica Brewster bequeathed to the New Plymouth City Council 50,000 pounds to create a trust to set up a gallery named the Govett-Brewster Art Gallery (combining both her maiden name, Govett, and her married name). Now one of the finest contemporary art institutions in the country, the gallery is dedicated to showing exhibitions that are both intellectually challenging, exciting and cutting edge. This is no collection of modern paintings, but a mixture of contemporary art expression in the broadest possible terms. There is no permanent collection and the gallery excels in presenting a continual series of exhibitions (at least three a year) that showcase the best in contemporary art in the widest possible definition.

But how did such a cutting-edge gallery come to be established in New Plymouth? Although a private person, Monica Brewster was a shrewd woman. From a long-established local family, she travelled widely and developed a love of modern art, which she much preferred to the more traditional art styles more common in the grand European art galleries. An art collector herself and with no children, the 50,000 pound gift came with a deed that included some carefully chosen provisions to ensure the gallery would focus on contemporary work, especially that the director of the gallery should be an art professional with a national reputation.

The opening of the initial exhibition in February 1970 shocked locals, but fifty years later New Plymouth folk take new installations at the gallery in their stride and today the gallery is one of the most visited attractions in Taranaki. Monica Brewster died in 1973 and was buried without a headstone, considering the art gallery to be her memorial. You may love or hate the Govett-Brewster, but one thing you won't be is indifferent.

Adjoining the gallery, but with the same entrance, is the Len Lye Centre easily recognised by the series of tall reflective columns that distort and illuminate the surrounding streetscape and sky. This is the only gallery in New Zealand totally dedicated to a single artist. Best known as a kinetic sculptor, artist and film maker, Lye left his estate to the New Plymouth-based Len Lye Foundation weeks before his death in May 1980, although he had no personal connection with the city. Described as 'the coolest building in New Zealand', the gallery was designed by Patterson Architects and consists of two large galleries, archives and a film theatre. Like the Govett-Brewster gallery, the Len Lye exhibitions are constantly revolving.

In direct contrast to the modernist gallery, the wooden White Hart hotel directly across the road is one of New Zealand's finest old pubs, though today it houses a mix of business and eateries.

📍 40 Queen Street, New Plymouth.
🕐 Open daily 10.00 am to 5 pm.
📞 06 759 6060
🌐 www.govettbrewster.com
💲 Entrance fee.

9. The Swanndri Collection - Puke Ariki Museum

In 1913 local Taranaki tailor William Broome developed a garment for farmers and bushmen, a strong woollen over shirt that he waterproofed with secret formula and registered the name Swanndri. The origins of the formula are unclear, but a recipe for waterproofing clothing was available in a book that William owned called Fortunes in Formulas and Facts and it is belived that a formula from this book was adapted and developed to produce the Swanndri shirt. Made in limited quantities in Taranaki until 1952, when new techniques allowed much greater production, the Swanndri became hugely popular during the 1950s and 60s, and anyone who worked or played outdoors owned a 'swannie'. Mostly they were long, almost reaching the knee and always an olive-green colour, though later check Swanndris become more common. Eventually production moved to the South Island and more recently overseas. No one now knows the reason for the double 'n' in Swanndri and whether the spelling was deliberate or, as some might say, just a spelling mistake.

Puke Ariki have been proactive in collecting Swanndri, the oldest of which dates back to the 1950s and of which around five are on display at any one time. Swannies were not the sort of clothing that was left hanging in the cupboard but were worn until they fell apart and then just biffed out, making older versions very rare.

- Puke Ariki. 1 Ariki Street, New Plymouth.
- Open Monday to Friday 9 am to 6 pm, weekends 9 am to 5 pm.
- 06 759 6060
- www.pukeariki.com
- Koha/donation.

10. New Plymouth Power Station Chimney

The chimney of the New Plymouth Power Station is by far the tallest in New Zealand. Built in 1972, the chimney is a massive 198 metres in height — 48 metres taller than the two chimneys of the Huntly Power Station. The construction of the 30-metre-wide chimney used 16,400 tonnes of concrete and 1200 tonnes of reinforcing steel, while the five individual flues within the single stack are lined with almost one million bricks. In high winds the chimney can sway almost 10 centimetres. The station was decommissioned in 2008.

Still, this tall smokestack is dwarfed by the tallest chimney in the world on the GRES-2 Power Station in Kazakhstan which is over double that of New Plymouth at 419.7 metres high. The tallest in Europe is the Trbovlje Chimney in Slovenia at 360 metres, and in Australia the MIM Smelter Stack at 270 metres.

- Port Taranaki, hard to miss really.

11. Paritutu Rock and the Sugar Loaf Island

Looming over the modern-day port of Taranaki is the sharp rocky pinnacle of Paritutu. The flat area at the top is not very large, but anyone who has climbed the rock will know how difficult it would have been for any invading force to capture this pa.

Used by Te Atiawa right up until the 1830s, the pa held out against attack from Waikato in 1832 while other pa in the area fell to the invaders. Try as they might, nothing that the Waikato warriors offered could induce the defenders to come down from their eyrie. Paritutu was well stocked with food, but water was the greatest problem as the only source was halfway down on the western face. This difficulty was solved by lowering a person down the cliff at night with calabashes, which were then hauled back to the summit. Any attempt to disrupt this process by the enemy drew musket fire from the offshore island pa of Mataora and Motu o Tamatea. The pa survived the siege.

While the climb is steep and not for those afraid of heights, the rocky scramble to the summit is made easier by numerous steps and wire railings near the top. The views are spectacular, south along the coast, southeast to the mountain and north over the port and city.

To the south of Paritutu is Back Beach, a local favourite, though often overlooked by visitors. Noted for its surf and the occasional seal lolling on the black sand, swimming is tricky and suited to the more confident swimmer as the beach has no surf patrol.

Paritutu (154 m), along with five small offshore islands and rocky outcrops, is a volcanic plug – cooled magma that has hardened in a volcanic tube following an eruption over 1.7 million years ago. Beneath the water, the seascape is as rugged as the land above and is a maze of caves, deep canyons and rocky peaks, the perfect environment for 400 types of fish as well as seaweeds, sponges and shellfish. The rich waters attract New Zealand fur seals, dolphins, orca and occasionally whales.

> Now protected by the Sugar Loaf Islands Marine Protected Area and the adjoining 1400 ha Tapuae marine reserve just to

the south, Chaddy's Charters offers a scenic cruise as well as the hire of kayaks and paddleboards, Centennial Drive, New Plymouth.

🌐 www.chaddyscharters.co.nz

12. Ratapihipihi Reserve

This small reserve is one of the fewer remaining patches of lowland bush in Taranaki and takes its name from a traditional method of hunting birds. By blowing through a leaf, a hunter perched high in a tree would attract birds such as kaka to come very close, where the birds were easily killed by a blow from a short club.

Ratapihipihi was also the name of a nearby kainga that was destroyed during the New Zealand Wars in the 1860s by the Taranaki Rifle Volunteers. Today the kaka, kainga and the lowland forest of Taranaki are all long gone, but this beautiful reserve is a rare view of what the bush around Taranaki was like before the coming of people. There are two loop tracks on excellent paths and the walking is easy, with just some steps to climb.

📍 At the end of Ratapihi Road off Cowling Road on the south side of New Plymouth.

13. The Vineyard Bistro at Okurukuru

Located high above the sea on the Taranaki coast, Okurukuru has one of the most spectacular sites of any New Zealand vineyard, but what a tough place to grow grapes. In contrast to the warm, dry climate usually associated with grape growing Okurukuru is exposed to the cool prevailing westerly winds, and receives high rainfall, a test to any grape grower. Planted in pinotage and pinot gris, the vineyard produced their first vintage in 2006 with a Taranaki rosé.

Okurukuru has taken full advantage of a stunning site by building a modern and very stylish restaurant accentuating views of both the coastline and of the mountain. Blending into the hillside and imitating an ocean wave, extensive use of huge glass windows ensures a view in every direction. Whether it is for weekend brunch, lunch, dinner, coffee and cake or just a relaxing glass of wine, Okurukuru is not to be missed in any visit to the Taranaki. If you are very lucky, you might spot a passing whale just offshore.

📍 738 Surf Highway, Oakura.
🕒 Open Wednesday to Sunday 11.30 to late.
📞 06 751 0787
🌐 www.bistro.net.nz

14. Te Koru Pa, Oakura

Occupied from around 1000AD to 1826, this is one of New Zealand's most ancient pa sites. Overlooking the Oakura River, Te Koru pa is also unusual in that stone has been used extensively. This is very rare for pa in Aotearoa, where wood was much more readily available. Occupied by Nga Mahanga a Tairi for many centuries, the pa fell to an overwhelming force of Te Atiawa in the early nineteenth century, and was finally abandoned in the face of the Waikato invasion in the 1820s. One of the finest examples of Taranaki carving, a carved paepae was found at Te Koru in 1898 and is now held at Puke Ariki Museum in New Plymouth.

The pa is well preserved with terraces, food pits and defensive ditches all clearly outlined. The stones from the river below were used extensively on the outer facings of the defensive ditches and for kumara pits. The pa is bush covered, which makes exploration of the pa more intriguing, though there is a good view of the river from a lookout point. The use of stone is an indication to some theorists that Aotearoa was inhabited by an ancient stone-using culture long before 1000AD.

The walk to the pa is through a grassy open paddock and then through bush on the pa itself. Do not climb on the steep banks as the stonework is fragile and easily damaged.

📍 At Oakura turn left into Wairau Road and follow the signposts 4 km down this road.

15. Parihaka Village

Parihaka, south of New Plymouth has today become the symbol to many of the power of peaceful protest. The village grew up after the confiscations of the 1860s and was at the time the largest Maori village in New Zealand. In 1880, in a series of remarkable actions, the people of Parihaka began protesting continued land sales. Time and time again, under the leadership of Te Whiti o Rongomai and Tohu Kakahi they met armed force with peaceful action and courteous resistance, using tactics such as pulling up survey pegs and ploughing confiscated land, but never resorting to violence. By September 1880, hundreds of men were exiled or imprisoned in the South Island, and finally on November 5 1881, in front of a silent crowd of 2000 Maori, the army moved in, arresting the leaders Te Whiti and Tohu and then spent two months destroying the houses and crops. Many of the men never returned from the south, and of those who did, the last arrived back in Parihaka in July 1898.

Parihaka never recovered and today is a small cluster of houses around a central monument, the tomb of Te Whiti O Rongomai. While the protest eventually failed, the actions at Parihaka and the leaders Tohu and Te Whiti have come to symbolise the fight for indigenous rights through nonviolent resistance. The actions at Parihaka have inspired books, music and art, and the tiny village is the location of the Parihaka International Peace Fesitival held in January each year (www.parihaka.com), fulfilling Te Whiti's prophetic words 'Those who are bent by the wind shall rise again when the wind softens.' A plough used by the Parihaka men to remove survey pegs is held in the Puke Ariki Museum.

Visitors are welcome at Parihaka, but these are people's homes not a tourist attraction so please show respect.

📍 Mid- Parihaka Road off SH 45, Pungarehu south of New Plymouth.

16. Cape Egmont Lighthouse

Built solidly to withstand the furious westerly, this cast-iron lighthouse was made in sections in London in 1864 and shipped out to New Zealand in pieces. Originally erected on Mana Island north of Wellington, in 1887 it was dismantled and rebuilt at Cape Egmont where it stands today. It was converted to electricity in the late 1950s and automated in 1986. The lighthouse is now part of the Cape Egmont Boat Club.

Despite what it looks like on the map, the cape is not the most westerly point in mainland New Zealand, nor in the North Island; those distinctions belong to Cape Maria van Diemen in Northland and West Cape in the South Island.

📍 From New Plymouth drive 45 km south on SH 45. Just south of Pungarehu turn right into Cape Road. The lighthouse is 5 km at the end of this road.

🕓 Open Friday, Saturday, Sunday and Monday 11am to 3pm.

17. Opunake Beach

Opunake Beach lies in a broad cove below the town and is open to strong westerly swells that make the beach one of New Zealand's top surf destinations. An artificial reef has ensured even better waves. Situated on SH 45 (now known as the Surf Highway), Opunake is just one of Taranaki's famed surf beaches and in virtually every weather a good swell will be running somewhere in the province.

📍 Beach Road, Opunake.

18. Peter Snell Statue

Striding out in the main street of Opunake is the lean athletic figure of Peter Snell cast in bronze in mid-stride. Born in the town in 1938, Snell moved to the Waikato nine years later and the peak of his career was his double gold medal win in the 800 and 1500 metres at the Tokyo Olympics in 1964. Slightly larger than life, the statue depicts Snell breaking the world record for the mile in early 1962 at Whanganui. Designed by New Plymouth sculptor Fridtjof Hanson, Snell unveiled the statue in May 2007.

📍 Outside the Opunake Library, Tasman Street/SH 45, Opunake.

19. Hollard Gardens, Kaponga

Bernie Hollard's interest in gardening started young when at the age of four his grandfather dug a small garden for him and his grandmother gave him a plain yellow abutilon cutting to plant. However, it wasn't until he and his wife Rose became dairy farmers in 1927 that Bernie had a real chance of creating an exceptional garden. Although the land was rough, overgrown and without much shelter, Bernie was not afraid of hard work, coming in from the farm or garden well after dark and then sitting down, not to listen to the radio but to read plant manuals and nursery catalogues. Even today the 'collector plantsman' is evident in at the Hollard gardens. While design and effect are not overlooked, the variety of plants is exceptional and what is especially appealing is that the garden is an interwoven mixture of native and exotic plants, a style currently in rapid decline, especially in public parks and gardens.

Covering 4.5 hectares, the garden is divided into three chronological parts: 1927 the Old Garden, 1982 The New Garden, 1992 The New Zealand Garden. Free to the public it is one of three gardens owned by the Taranaki Regional Council – the other two are Pukeiti and Tupare.

Clearly gardening and clean Taranaki air had its benefits as Bernie died in 1996 aged ninety-four and would have seen his garden develop from weedy paddocks to an internationally acclaimed garden attracting thousands of visitors a year.

Hollard Gardens are also part of the spring Taranaki Rhododendron and Garden Festival. The heart of the festival is the rhododendron collection at Pukeiti, but over forty gardens are open to the public, ranging in type from coastal and subtropical to alpine. Although some of the gardens are open all year round, most are only open during the festival or by appointment.

📍 1686 Upper Manaia Road, Kaponga.

🕒 Open daily 9 am to 5 pm.

20. Manaia Blockhouse and Redoubt

A fort or blockhouse immediately suggests a structure, simply built, but substantial and strong. These two blockhouses are simple and strong but look more like small garden sheds. Looks are deceiving and blockhouses were cleverly designed to be built quickly with double skinned walls filled with gravel through which bullets were unable to penetrate. The gun holes are cleverly tapered to present the smallest aperture to the attacking forces. Sitting diagonally opposite each other, the Manaia redoubt was built in 1880 when tensions between Maori and settlers in the province increased. The central concrete tower is essentially a folly and was built in 1915 to replace an older wooden tower which blew down in storm (clearly not as well built as the blockhouses).

Oddly, the redoubt, blockhouses and tower sit in the middle of the Manaia Golf Course and are diagonally opposite the club house – take care not to be clonked in the head by a golf ball.

Q Manaia Golf Club, end of Bennett Drive, Manaia.

21. Tawhiti Museum

In 1975 Nigel and Teresa Ogle bought the old Tawhiti cheese factory and eventually turned the factory into one of New Zealand's best private museums. What makes this museum special are the wonderful models, both miniature and life-sized models, that are dazzling in their attention to detail. The diorama of a Maori raiding party, comprising of hundreds of tiny figures threading their way through a variety of landscapes, is just superb. The life size models will make you jump with surprise.

While the museum focuses on South Taranaki history, this museum has an appeal way beyond the region. The latest addition is Traders and Whalers, where life size models and meticulously crafted artefacts recreate the world of the Taranaki coast during 1820 and 1940. Without giving too much away, visitors actually float through the exhibition.

Don't miss the special display on Chinese settler and entrepreneur Chow Chong (Chau Tseung), who developed a fungi export business that gave local farmers a much-needed source of cash during difficult times.

Worth a trip to Taranaki all on its own.

Q 401 Ohangai Road, well signposted from both Normanby

(north) and Hawera (south).

🕐 Open Friday, Saturday, Sunday, Monday 10 am to 4 pm, January every day 10 am to 4 pm, Winter (June, July, August), open Sundays only.

📞 0800 921 921

🌐 www.tawhitimuseum.co.nz

$ Entrance fee.

22. Elvis Presley Museum

Born and bred in Hawera and a rocker from way back when, Kevin Wasley is a long-time Elvis fan and has created in his garage a monumental collection dedicated to 'The King'. Previously known as the Elvis Presley Memorial Record Room, the garage is absolutely packed floor to ceiling with both Elvis and rock-n-rock memorabilia and souvenirs including over 5000 recordings and a juke box that only has Elvis records. Kevin has been to Elvis's home, Gracelands, no less than nineteen times and the highlights of his collection are a 1968 autographed Christmas album, original concert tickets and a scarf from a 1974 Memphis concert. While this is a private collection and viewing is strictly by appointment only, Kevin is a friendly and accommodating guy.

📍 51 Argyle Street, Hawera.

🕐 Appointment only.

📞 027 498 2942

🌐 www.elvismuseum.co.nz

$ Koha/Donation.

23. Butterfly Tree, King Edward Park, Hawera

Edward in name and Edwardian in style, this fine park opened in August 1904 with the formal inauguration of the elaborate gateway, and today is a combination of formal gardens, playgrounds and a sports field, and is home to the famous butterfly tree.

For some reason this rather ordinary totara tree has become the wintering place of local monarch butterflies. With wings folded, the butterflies cluster together overnight, dispersing during the sunny afternoons and returning in the late afternoon to gather together in preparation for the chilly frosty nights of southern Taranaki.

No one is really sure when or how monarch butterflies came to New Zealand, but the first reported sightings appear in the 1870s and now they can be found in every part of the country. Numbers though have drastically diminished since the arrival of the Asian paper wasp, which feeds on the eggs, caterpillars and adults.

In their native North America, the monarchs undertake an impressive migration from their wintering boltholes in Mexico to their feeding and breeding ground in Canada. In the mild New Zealand climate, the butterflies have opted more sensibly to stay closer to home. Studies show that in New Zealand they rarely travel more than 20 kilometres, though in areas of the country where temperatures fall below -10c they will cluster at night on a particular tree, often numbering in their thousands, for warmth and protection. It is believed that tiny vibrations of their wings keep the temperature from dropping too low and the dense foliage of the totara shields them from the worst weather. They are unable to fly in temperatures below 13°C.

While in the park, take time to admire the impressive and still healthy totara hedge, planted in 1904 at a time when using native plants for hedging was highly unusual. The totara tree is between the children's playground and the rose garden.

> King Edward Park, corner of High Street and Camberwell Road.

24. Hawera Water Tower

The cry of 'Fire!' sent early New Zealand settlers into a panic. Not only were there very few fire brigades, but also there was rarely an adequate water supply to quell the flames. Once alight, most buildings burnt to the ground and frequently took with them neighbouring buildings and, at times, whole town blocks. In 1884, 1888 and 1912, fires in Hawera burnt down significant parts of the business area, and exasperated insurance companies refused to cover new buildings until the town provided a proper water supply and improved its ability to fight fires.

The striking 54.2 m water tower was completed in January 1914, at the cost of PDS 4,510 including PDS520 for the curious cost of 'deleaning' the tower (the tower still leans 8cm). Still supplying water to the town from the 680,000 litre holding tank at the top, the tower has fine views over the surrounding countryside if you are happy to climb the 215 steep stairs to a gallery under the tank. Accessed is gained from the i-SITE directly in front of the tower.

There is something about Hawera and fire as the name Hawera is the shortened version of Te Hawera, meaning 'burnt place' and refers to a conflict between two iwi which resulted in a village being destroyed by fire.

- 📍 55 High Street, Hawera.
- 💲 Entrance fee.

25. Aotea Monument, Patea

New Zealand doesn't really have a tradition of folk art but the memorial to the Aotea waka is one of New Zealand's best known such works and was constructed (and possibly designed) by Jones Brothers, monumental masons based in nearby Hawera. Built of concrete with paua shell inlays, the monument is nearly 17 metres long and was originally the gateway to the Town Hall (since demolished). Unveiled on April 2 1933, the monument was the brainchild of Mr Panenui, Mr Tupito and Mr Wakarua, and commemorates the settlement of the district in the fourteenth century by Turi and his wife Rongorongo. The figures, all resolutely facing forward – no doubt excited at the prospect of settling in Patea – were originally carved from punga wood.

Turi was one of the great early navigators who journeyed from Hawaiki to Aotearoa to settle. He was later acknowledged as 'Turi he patea paipo moana' or 'Turi who drinks the ocean'. He was specifically told about the land around the Patea River by the explorer Kupe, although the waka landed at Kawhia far to the north. After taking some time to establish the kumara plants they had brought on the waka, Turi and his hapu travelled through dense bush and rugged hill country to settle at Patea, a walk that even today would be a challenge. Today the marae at Patea still bears his name, Wai o Turi.

The park behind the monument holds an annual Waitangi Day celebration called Paepae in the Park that attracts top musical acts and large crowds.

The Aotea Monument is just one view of the arrival of Turi at Patea. Stroll across the road to the smart Patea Museum and see two strikingly different depictions of this epic event. Decorating the entrance foyer of the museum is a long series of Maori carvings and tukutuku panels of Turi, his family, his fellow travellers and the story of Patea Maori. These stunning carvings and panels were specifically commissioned for the museum and have been executed in the Taranaki style. Turi is easily recognised as holding a black adze. In contrast is an oil painting also dating from 1933, showing Turi and his band making their way up the Patea River. Unusually the painting was executed by two people: Oriwa Haddon and Charles Hay-Campbell.

SH 3, Patea. Impossible to miss.

26. The Garden of Tutunui, Patea

In the centre of Patea is a highly stylised garden featuring upright replica whale bones. The garden commemorates the story of Tutunui, a whale that was the pet of the famous chief Tinirau. When Tinirau's son was born, the birth rites were performed by the tohunga Kae, and as part of the ceremony the priest was fed a tiny piece of the flesh of the whale, Tutunui.

Sometime later, after much persuasion Tinirau allowed Kae to take Tutunui to his home on another island; but this was a mere trick, as Kae had never forgotten the delicious taste of whale meat. Engineering the death of Tutunui by stranding, Kae then cooked his flesh, wrapped in koromiko leaves to hold the fat and flavour. However, Tinirau discovered the true fate of the death of his pet and, in revenge, had the deceitful Kae put to death. That, unfortunately, is not the end of the story, as Kae's family avenged his death by killing Tinirau's young son. This legend gave rise to a saying, 'Tena te karaka a Tutunui', 'there rises the savoury smell of Tutunui', which is used when someone's guilty actions are exposed.

◉ Cnr of Egmont Street and SH 3.

27. EC Dallison and Sons, Waverley

Many generations of local families have trod the three worn wooden steps to this general store selling clothing, furniture and flooring in the heart of the small South Taranaki town of Waverley.

In 1919 EC Dallison took over the local store and the shop has been in the family ever since. The store itself is much older, built in 1890, and it is extraordinary that the building has kept its essential Victorian character ever since, apart from the 'new' extension in 1938 to accommodate the expansion into the furniture business. Large skylights let in natural light to the interior of the store, which retains it old tongue and grove wood lining. The long counters from where staff once handed merchandise to their customers from wooden shelves and deep drawers still remain, though the style of retailing is thoroughly modern. In the heart of the store is a wood burner, guarantee to fight off the coldest winter frost.

However, there is nothing dated about the stock, with the current owners Brett and Barbara Dallison keeping on top of fashions and current styles including a very sharp looking website. One thing that does match the original style of the store is the commitment to good old-fashioned service.

- 52 Weraroa Road, Waverly/SH 3.
- Open Monday to Friday 8.30 am to 5 pm.
- 06 346 5005
- www.dallisonandsons.co.nz

WHANGANUI

1. Whanganui River Road
2. Waimaire Paddle Steamer and Centre
3. Durie Hill Elevator and Tower
4. Lindauer Gallery - Whanganui Regional Museum
5. Whanganui War Memorial Hall
6. Ladies Rest
7. Cooks Garden
8. Cameron Blockhouse
9. Ratana Temple, Ratana

Whats in a name?

In legend the Whanganui River was created by Taranaki as he was driven from his home in the centre of the island after his epic battle with Tongariro over the love of Pihanga. As he left he first headed south and carved out the course of the river and, on reaching the coast, turned west and travelled to where he is today. Behind him the deep valley filled with his tears.

Kupe was said to have discovered the mouth of the river, but it was the people of the Takitimu, captained by Tamatea, who first explored the river itself, closely followed by the waka Aotea, whose people later settled in the area.

There has been much, and often bitter, discussion over the spelling of the name of both the river and the city. In the local Maori dialect the 'h' is silent, replaced by a short glottal stop as is common in other Polynesian languages. Ideally the word should be written 'W'anganui' to indicate the silent letter, but it came to be written as Wanganui, reflecting the local pronunciation. However, in written form the word makes no sense as the name means 'large harbour' and therefore should be written Whanganui.

Following the wishes of the local iwi, the New Zealand Geographic Board changed the name of the river to Whanganui, but in a referendum the vote strongly favoured the retention of the spelling Wanganui; the mayor, Michael Laws, stated that the city over the years had developed 'its own identity, its own history, its own pride, its own mana'. Gradually names are changing to 'Whanganui'. Ironically with the change to Whanganui, it is now pronounced by many people incorrectly with the 'wh' fully sounded as 'f'.

1. Whanganui River Road

The legendary Whanganui River Road begins at Upokongaro, just north of Whanganui on SH 4 and ends 91 km later at Raetihi, and covers some of New Zealand's most fascinating backcountry. Settlements along the river were originally only accessible by river boat, but once the road was built in 1935, the river traffic slumped. Following the course of the river for much of its length, this is not a road that can be hurried as it is narrow and winding, and a long stretch is still unsealed with few facilities. What's more the locals drive fast and are disinclined to give way. Many of the names of the settlements along the river are of biblical origin – Hiruharama (Jerusalem), Atene (Athens), Koriniti (Corinth) – a legacy of their origins as mission settlements. Though quite how Ranana (London) crept in is anyone's guess. In recent years, the population has drifted away and now these once thriving villages are today little more than a tiny collection of old houses.

Highlights along the river include:

Jerusalem/Hiruharama

Once a thriving settlement, Jerusalem is set in a bend of the river above which sits the pretty church of Hato Hohepa (St Joseph), one of New Zealand's most photographed churches. The convent next to the church was the home of Mother Aubert (1835–1926), who came from France and established the order of The Sisters of Compassion in 1892. Mother Aubert was well known in the district for her charitable work and use of native plants for medicinal purpose. James K Baxter, the acclaimed poet, established a short-lived commune settlement in 1969, and Jerusalem Sonnets and Jerusalem Daybook were written there. Just downriver from Jerusalem is Moutoa Island, site of the historic battle of 1864 when upriver supporters of the anti-British Hauhau were defeated by their lower-river opponents.

Kawana Flour Mill

In 1854 Governor (Kawana) Grey presented the Poutama people with the machinery to build a flour mill. The mill operated until 1913, then fell into disrepair until recent years when it was faithfully restored. The mill contains the original millstones and upstairs the walls are lined with historic photographs and an excellent diagram as to how the mill operated. The cottage next to the mill was moved to the site from its original position across the road.

📍 9 km south of Jerusalem

Koriniti

This beautiful historic marae features three carved meeting houses, Poutama (1888), Te Waherehere (1845) and Hikurangi Wharerata (1975). The marae is open to visitors except when a function is being held. A koha is appreciated.

Pipiriki

The stretch of the river above Pipiriki, which is not accessible by road, is considered to be the most attractive part of the Whanganui as it meanders through the Whanganui National Park. Once a busy river port, Pipiriki is now the base for tramping, jet boating, kayaking and other adventure trips along the river, and is the access point to the Bridge To Nowhere.

2. Waimarie Paddle Steamer and Centre

This restored river boat the *Waimarie*, now based in Whanganui City, was built in 1899 as a kitset in London, and was one of a fleet of twelve riverboats owned by Alexander Hatrick working the river between the coast and Taumarunui. Once the road opened in 1934, patronage on the river boats declined and the *Waimarie* was finally taken out of service in 1949. Abandoned on the riverbank, the *Waimaire* was rescued from the mud in 1993 and she was back on the river in 2001. Now New Zealand's only authentic coal-fired paddle steamer, Waimarie runs cruises up the river to Upokongaro.

One very appealing aspect of the trip is that on the 11 am cruise the boat carries homing pigeons. Visitors write messages and at the furthest point of the trip the pigeons are released and the messages collected back at Whanganui. This may be the only place in New Zealand which still uses homing pigeons.

At the departure dock is a small museum, the Waimaire Centre, which tells the story of the river boats through photographs and memorabilia. Built in 1881 and an historic building in its own right, the centre was formerly the Wanganui Rowing Club. Like so many buildings at the time, it had a formal wooden façade facing the street, but the rest of the building is clad in corrugated iron which at the time was cheap and fireproof.

Trip times vary considerably throughout the year, though are more frequent in summer, so it pays to phone ahead or check the website.

- 1a Taupo Quay, Whanganui.
- Open day 10 am to 3 pm October to April.
- 06 3471863
- www.waimarie.co.nz

3. Durie Hill Elevator and Tower

Across the river from the city and giving access to the suburb of Durie Hill is the only public underground elevator in New Zealand. Durie Hill became part of Wanganui Borough in 1910, but there was no easy access to the area high above the river. Dismissing a cable car as too costly the council opted for a unique solution, an underground tunnel to an elevator. Work began in 1916 and the elevator finally opened in August 1919. The 205 metre long tunnel and the 66 metre elevator are now a Category One Historic Place. Not fast, the elevator rattles and shakes but it is much more convenient than the path with 191 steps from the river to the top.

The 33 metre tower was not part of the elevator development but rather a World War I memorial opened in 1925. From the top, views include not only the city and environs, but also on a fine day Taranaki and Mt Ruapehu.

The suburb of Durie Hill is also unique as it was New Zealand's first planned modern suburb and is properly known as the Durie Hill Garden Suburb.

- The tunnel to the elevator is opposite the City Bridge at the end of Victoria Street.

🕐 Open Monday to Friday 7.30 am to 6 pm,
Saturday 9 am to 5 pm, Sundays and public holidays 10 am to 5 pm.

$ Small charge.

4. Lindauer Gallery - Whanganui Regional Museum

While this excellent regional museum focuses on the Whanganui distinct, it contains some of the country's most important artefacts, and is not too big to be overwhelming.

Not to be missed is Lindauer Gallery, one of the largest collections of Lindauer paintings in the country with around twenty paintings on display at any one time. Most Lindauer paintings are in private collections and only the Auckland Art Gallery has a larger collection.

Sir Walter Buller commissioned Gottfried Lindauer to paint a series of portraits of rangatira for a London exhibition and after the exhibition the paintings were returned to New Zealand and have been displayed at the museum since 1928. While today Lindauer is best known as a painter of Maori subjects, only a third of his 1000 painting are about Maori, the majority being family portraits of important and wealthy Europeans. He repeated many of his most popular painting several times so what might appear to be copies are in fact originals.

Gottfried Lindauer was born in Bohemia (modern day Czech Republic) and began painting at a young age, and in 1860 painted a series of large murals for a church in Morovia where they remain today. In 1874 to escape the army he jumped aboard the first ship leaving Hamburg, thinking he was going to America, but instead landed in Wellington in August of that year. Lindauer wandered around New Zealand picking up painting commissions from leading colonialists and eventually settled in Woodville, built a studio and continue to paint until his death in 1926.

In addition to the Lindauer Collection the museum holds one of the most important collections of moa bones with several complete skeletons of several species. Located in the central hall is the magnificent waka taua (war canoe) Te Mata. Over 22 metres in length, this waka was built before 1810 from a single totara log and took part in several battles, with the musket holes to show for it.

- Watt Street, adjacent to Queen's Park.
- Open daily 10 am to 4.30 pm.
- www.wrm.org.nz
- Donation/Koha.

5. Whanganui War Memorial Hall

Well-known for its Victorian and Edwardian architecture, Whanganui is home to a startling example of New Zealand modernist architect. Construction on a new city hall started in 1956 after a public competition surprisingly chose the ultra-modern design of Gordon Smith, a partner in the Auckland firm of Greenhough, Smith and Newman. Described as 'a white clean-lined floating block, a visual mass supported by setback concrete pilotis', the hall opened in 1960 and in the following year won New Zealand Institute of Architects Gold Medal.

- Watt Street, Whanganui.

6. Ladies Rest

Euphemistically called 'Ladies Rest', this is the first women's public toilet in New Zealand and naturally the immediate question is 'how did women cope before?' Opened in 1930 and still operating today, the toilet is Art Deco in design, a style all the rage at the time. Stylish it may have been, but it was not cheap, costing threepence to use when the going rate for men was just a penny. While still 1930s on the outside, today the interior is now thoroughly modern and free.

📍 Below Cooks Garden, Saint Hill Street, Whanganui.

7. Cook's Garden

The origins of the name are a bit clouded, but it is believed the area was once a vegetable garden and today Cook's Gardens is now known as an athletic stadium made famous when Peter Snell ran New Zealand's first sub-four-minute mile in 1962. The gardens began their life as a sports arena in 1896, when the local athletics, cycling, rugby and cricket clubs got together to jointly develop the area for their club activities. The Gardens rocketed to fame in January 1962 when Peter Snell ran the first sub four-minute mile in the world in front of a packed crowd of over 13,000 people. Generally, the gardens are open to the public and anyone can test their pace over the very track that Snell ran (though don't get in the way of the real athletes training!). If the stadium is closed there is an excellent view over the grounds by the old wooden fire-tower with bells dated back to 1874.

📍 Saint Hill Street, Whanganui.

8. Cameron Blockhouse

Unlike most blockhouses from the nineteenth century, the Cameron Blockhouse is a rare example of a privately built fort from that time. In the 1860s New Zealand was convulsed by the war over land and all around the country blockhouses were constructed. John Cameron built this blockhouse in 1868 for his family and neighbours. With two storeys, consisting of two rooms and a loft, the construction was typical with double wooden walls infilled with 15 cm of clay which prevented fire and protected the interior from bullets, along with a fireproof corrugated iron roof. Built on high ground, the Cameron blockhouse was sited so it could signal to two nearby families, the Morgans and the Campbells. Never used under attack, the building was open to the public in 1990.

SH 3, 6.5 km from Whanganui.

9. Ratana Temple, Ratana

Every year in February Ratana Pa springs into the news headlines, as politicians vie for attention and support of the influential Ratana church. For the rest of the year, this is a quiet place dominated by the distinctive Ratana temple that is well worth a short detour off State Highway Three just south of Whanganui. During the 1918 Influenza epidemic, the very worldly Tahupotiki Wiremu Ratana was told, during a vision, that he was to unite Maori and return them to God, for now Maori were to replace the Jews as God's Chosen people. After studying the bible, Ratana, now known as the Mangai (Mouthpiece of God), began preaching and quickly began attracting ever growing congregations. In order to improve the conditions of Maori, Ratana gradually turned to politics, and through the 1920s and 1930s become increasingly more influential to the point of taking two seats at the 1935 election. In 1936 Ratana and the Labour Prime Minister Michael Savage brokered a deal that saw the political arm of the Ratana movement come under the Labour banner. TW Ratana died on September 18th 1939, and while the influence of the Ratana movement has waned during the second half of the twentieth century, it still claims to have around 65,000 adherents.

Te Tempara Tapu O Ihoa (Holy Temple of Jehovah) was dedicated in 1928 and, while it has many features common to Christian churches, it is at the same time distinctly different. The interior of the church is very simple, but very strong in symbolism and in particular the five pointed star and the crescent moon representing divine enlightenment are repeated throughout the church. The carefully chosen colours all have meaning:

blue – The Father, white – The Son, red – The Holy Spirit, purple – angels, and pink Ratana himself. The symbol of the sun unusually represents both the second coming of Christ, but also a unique spiritual relationship established in 1924 between Ratana and Bishop Juji Nakada of Japan. On the two domed towers are written Arepa (Alpha) and Omeka (Omega). Set in beautifully kept gardens, the grave of the Mangai is in front of the church and while visitors are welcome they are requested not to take photos inside the gates.

📍 23 km south of Whanganui on SH 3, turn into Ratana Road and drive for 2 km.

MANAWATU/ RANGITIKEI/ HOROWHENUA

1. Taihape Gumboot Sculpture
2. Stormy Point Lookout, Rangitikei
3. Te Apiti and Tararua Wind Farms
4. Railway Houses
5. Hoffman Kiln
6. The Log Cabin
7. The Bald Kiwi - New Zealand Rugby Museum
8. Regent on Broadway
9. Savage Crescent
10. Mini Railway Victoria Esplanade
11. Caccia Birch House
12. Mt Cleese, Awapuni Landfill
13. Feilding Sales Yards
14. The Coach House Museum
15. De Molen and Nieuwe Stroom
16. Foxton Flax Stripper
17. Foxton Beach — Manawatu Estuary
18. Waitarere Beach Shipwreck
19. Mangahao Power Station
20. RJ's Licorice
21. Lake Papaitonga
22. Ohau Wines
23. Our Lady of Lourdes, Paraparaumu
24. Kapiti Island

1. Taihape Gumboot Sculpture

Odd is the only word to describe a giant corrugated-iron sculpture of gumboot to symbolise a town, but to New Zealanders it makes perfect sense.

Taihape was hit hard by economic changes in the 1970s and 80s, especially with the decline of railways and later the radical change to agricultural subsidies. From a population of 3500 in 1960, the population was less than 2000 in 1985.

Given the rural nature of the district with the gumboot as the preferred footware, and inspired by John Clarke's 'Gumboot' song (along with his reference to the 'Taihape University Seat of Joinery'), locals decided to extend the theme and Gumboot Day was born.

The first Gumboot Day was held on April 9, 1985 at the renamed Gumboot Park and is now an annual event including gumboot races, gumboot decorating and of course the annual attempt on the world gumboot-throwing record. In 2019 Taihape hosted the World Gumboot Throwing Championship and to date the New Zealand record is 34.45 m for women and 52.22 m for men, though sadly the world records for both men (63.98 m) and women (40.87 m) are held by people from Finland. Known as Welly Wanging in Britain, there are serious rules for both national records and the world cup **(www.bootthrowing.net)**

In 2000 Jeff Thomson completed his huge thrown gumboot sculpture which was eventually relocated to the SH 1 where the sign Taihape was added in 2015 just to make sure everyone knew where they were. Now a compulsory photo stop on any trip through Taihape, children love to clamber over the corrugated iron monument and to add to the attraction there are picnic tables and toilets.

The word gumboot is peculiar to New Zealand, having arisen from the rubber boots worn by Dalmatian gum diggers in Northland.

On SH 1 on the north side of Taihape.

2. Stormy Point Lookout, Rangitikei

Driving along SH 54 from the south, the steady rise in the road is hardly noticeable so when you round the bend at Stormy Point, the stunning vista comes as a surprise. While there are any number of good viewpoints overlooking Rangitikei, by far the most spectacular view is from Stormy Point. Of particular interest are the broad river terraces considered to be one of the best-preserved sequences of river terraces in the world and each formed during a period of climatic cooling, the oldest of which is 350,000 years. They have trouble keeping the signage that indicates the points of interest and considering the location, the signs are most likely blown away by the ferocious winds that give the lookout its name.

📍 On SH 54, 15 km from the turnoff on SH 1, 6 km north of Hunterville.

3. Te Apiti and Tararua Wind Farms

These three wind farms, located north and south of the Manawatu Gorge, are the largest such farms in the southern hemisphere. With the hills rising to 1500 metres and exposed to the prevailing westerly winds, the farms take advantage of one of the windiest places in the country. The windmills are of Danish design, which is most appropriate in a district settled by large numbers of Scandinavian immigrants.

First commissioned in 1999, today Te Apiti has 55 turbines, while Tararua has 134 and Te Rere Hau 97. The tallest are over 65 metres high and with blades 45 metres long.

📍 Information site, Saddle Road, 25 km from Palmerston North.

4. Railway Houses

Just over the railway line at the northern end of Fairs Road in Palmerston North is a mini museum of railway houses. While not all are original many are and, once considered an inferior sort of house, today an original railway house is an early example of domestic New Zealand architecture.

Manufactured in kitset form at a factory in Frankton Hamilton, railway houses were transported all over the country to provide accommodation for railway workers often in isolated areas. The railways had provided housing as early as 1880, though the cottages regarded today as a typical railway house were built in the 1920s and were based on the American bungalow, fashionable at the time. In all, the factory produced nearly 1600 houses until its closure in 1929. Most of these simple wooden houses are long gone or altered beyond recognition, but this group in Palmerston North is particularly extensive.

9   Fairs Road, Palmerston North.

5. Hoffman Kiln

Despite being listed by the Historic Places Trust as one of the country's ten most important industrial sites, the forlorn Hoffman Kiln has little protection from vandalism and no information or signage. And it has been neglected like this for years. This type of kiln was developed in Germany in the 1850s, though the Palmerston North kiln is an updated version of the original design. The kiln was unique in that it was fired continuously with each chamber being loaded, heated and unloaded one after the other. While most firings were around six weeks, the longest continuous firing for this kiln was three months and when running at full capacity produced an incredible 9000 bricks per day (the distinctive Log Cabin was built with bricks from the kiln). To keep the kilns running, coal was fed into the chambers through small holes in the top of the kiln by men working under the corrugated iron roof structure. Talk about hot work!

📍 615 Featherston Street, Palmerston North.

6. The Log Cabin

Log shaped concrete fences are not uncommon in Palmerston North and while it is not known who built these distinctive fences, they are all very similar in style and most likely built by the same person. However, this house is the 'mother ship' of concrete log construction in the city and to experts is known as dendromorphic (wood form) architecture. Constructed by local building contractor and owner of the house Les Arnott in 1923, the house is a simple California bungalow with a Canadian log cabin façade of concrete and plaster over double brick walls. The fence is a different construction with rough concrete over a wire netting frame coated in a smoother plaster finish. The only such building in New Zealand, it is clearly a style that never caught on. Private property, the house is clearly seen from the street.

📍 Corner of Grey and Russell Street.

7. The Bald Kiwi - New Zealand Rugby Museum

Regardless of your interest in rugby, this small museum is crammed full of every conceivable type of rugby memorabilia and is well worth a visit, though rugby fans should plan to spend a few hours here. But what is a stuffed kiwi with a bald patch doing in a rugby museum? On the 1925/26 tour of Britain the New Zealand team took along a stuffed kiwi in a glass case to give to the first team that beat them. But the All Blacks won game after game and the kiwi in its glass case kept touring on and on. Unfortunately, the kiwi was just a bit too tall for the case and every time it moved its head rubbed against the top of the glass case. Undefeated the All

Blacks returned home, still clutching the glass case holding the kiwi. By this time the kiwi had lost all the feathers on the top of its head and today is bald but proud to be part of the extraordinary team.

Now that the Rugby Museum has moved into the main Te Manawa Museum building, it finally has space to properly display most of its vast collection, much of it unique and irreplaceable including the extraordinary size 20 rugby boot and New Zealand rugby caps dating back to 1883, not long after the game was established in this country.

📍 The Rugby Museum is in the same building but it not part of Te Manawa Museum and there is an Entrance fee to the rugby exhibits. 326 Main Street.
🕒 Open daily 10 am to 5 pm, but closed main public holidays.
📞 06 358 6947
🌐 www.rugbymuseum.co.nz
$ Entrance fee.

8. Regent on Broadway

Grey concrete and not much to look at from the outside, stepping inside the Regent Theatre is like entering a world of opulent Italian grandeur. Architect Charles Hollingshed drew on diverse styles from Europe, Byzantium and the Mediterranean and when the theatre opened in July 1930, the newspaper reports were ecstatic, 'Creating an entirely new standard of Entertainment, the Luxurious Regent will become the Mecca of all Devotees of the Magic Talking Screen because of its Compelling Worth and Regal Magnificence.'

However, time passed the Regent by and in 1991 the once 'Wonder Theatre' was dilapidated, run down and finally closed. Public reaction to save the theatre was unprecedented and in 1993 city council purchased the building and fundraising for the restoration began. Returned to it early glory, the theatre is one of the top four performing arts spaces in the country.

📍 59-71 Broadway.
🌐 www.regent.co.nz

9. Savage Crescent

Few communities in New Zealand are without a little or large neighbourhood of state houses. Actively promoted by the first Labour Government under Michael Joseph Savage state houses appeared everywhere and today in the age of the leaking house syndrome, are considered to very well built if a little lacking in style. What makes Savage Crescent unique in that the whole development is largely still original. Containing 245 houses and developed from 1939 to 1944, the crescent is a mixture of housing designs from this period, with some of the houses being quite different in style from those typically associated with state housing. A walk round the entire crescent will take less than an hour.

📍 Savage Crescent can be accessed off either Park Street or College Street, both of which run off Fitzherbert Avenue.

10. Mini Railway Victoria Esplanade

A grand park indeed, Victoria Esplanade covering 26 hectares on the western bank of the Manawatu Esplanade has it all: bush walks, playgrounds, bird aviaries, a flying fox, arboretum, sports fields, café, fernery, aquatic centre, and of course a mini railway. Miniature railways are not unusual in New Zealand parks, but most are very small, taking just a few minutes to complete a circuit. What makes the Esplanade's railway so special is that the track is 2.2 kilometres long and takes twenty minutes to do the full trip. There is even a station halfway just in case your little one has had enough (or your big one has cramped up sitting in the small seats). Opened in 1969 and extended in 1998, the two engines are miniaturised versions of New Zealand railway diesel engines.

○ The 'main station' is most easily accessed off Fitzherbert Ave.

11. Caccia Birch House

In the late nineteenth century thousands of Scandinavians, mainly of Danish and Norwegian origin, settled in the Manawatu, southern Hawkes Bay and northern Wairarapa. Quick to assimilate, their legacy was largely forgotten and only now is the contribution made to this country by these industrious people being recognised. Despite its name, Caccia Birch House is unique in that it is built in a distinctly Scandinavian style. Designed by Danish architect Ludolp Georg West for Norwegian sawmiller Jacob Nannestad and his wife Anna in 1895, the house was part of an 8-hectare property overlooking the Hokowhitu Lagoon.

However, Nannestad's fortunes declined and he sold the house in 1903 to wealthy businessman John Strang who commissioned substantial additions to the house (also designed by West) including the conservatories and a billiard room along with a polo ground and stables for the polo ponies. Renamed 'Woodhey' from 1908 to 1910, the house became the official residence of the Governor-General William Plunket after fire destroyed the government buildings in Wellington.

The house changed hands in 1921 and was owned by William and Maud Caccia Birch until 1940, when the recently widowed Maud gifted the house to the government to support the war effort. In subsequent years the house was used as an army barracks, convalescent home, university buildings and finally as part of the Teachers' College. Eventually left derelict it was sold to the Palmerston North City Council for community use and restored. It is now listed as a Category One Historic Building and is used for weddings and conferences. In addition to the house, Caccia

Birch boasts a number of impressive trees including horse chestnuts and elms.

The grounds are open to the public, and check the website for regular open days to the interior of the house. The Coach House building has a permanent archive display of the history of the house.

- 112-130 Te Awe Awe Street, Palmerston North.
- www.caccia-birch-house.co.nz

12. Mt Cleese, Awapuni Landfill

Comedian John Cleese should have kept his mouth shut. Clearly in a bad frame of mind and perhaps a little tired, Mr Cleese commented after his show in Palmerston North in November 2005 that he had a 'thoroughly bloody miserable time' and that 'if you wish to kill yourself but lack the courage to, I think a visit to Palmerston North will do the trick.'

Locals were mostly amused, but also slightly miffed and it was another comedian John Clarke, aka Fred Dagg, born in Palmerston North, who came up with a very novel idea of renaming the local Awapuni Landfill as the John Cleese Memorial Tip, as it was a place where 'All manner of crap happily recycled'. Some time later a sign appeared proclaiming the tip as Mt Cleese. The landfill is now closed but the Mt Cleese sign still remains on the lofty summit of 45 metres.

- The sign is right by the entrance to the Awapuni Resource Recovery Park, Tip Road, Palmerston North.

13. Feilding Sales Yards

While many smaller sales yards have disappeared, they are still a vital ingredient of the rural economy, not only for trading sheep and cattle but also for a place where rural folk can meet. However, for those not directly involved in agriculture, the operation of a sales yard can be just noisy and plain confusing.

Feilding in the Manawatu still has one of New Zealand's largest sales yards and possibly one of the biggest in the world. Each week on a Friday morning around 12,000 sheep and 1100 cattle are sold with a smaller sale on Monday. Established in 1880, the yards were once part of the local Denbigh Hotel, which correctly figured it could boost hotel patronage by building a stockyards right next door. Oddly the hotel initially did not sell alcohol, though that quickly changed.

There is a raised walkway which overlooks the yards but even better at a small price for the uninitiated, a tour is available with local farmers acting as guides. This personable and friendly tour unlocks the mystery of how a sales yard works and how these sales are a key indicator as to the health of the rural economy. The tours are on Friday at 11 am, bookings are essential and don't forget sensible shoes and to bring a rainproof jacket. Small charge.

Right next door is the Saleyards Café, where they are very used to serving hearty breakfasts to farmers and truck drivers who have already been up and working for several hours. You won't walk away hungry.

---

10 Manchester Street.
06 323 3318
www.feilding.co.nz

14. The Coach House Museum

From the outside, first impressions are not great; another small-town museum in a large, plain shed that looks like a packing house, and full of well-meaning but only vaguely interesting donated material – and they want you to pay for it as well. Put all your preconceived ideas aside as you are in for a treat and you won't regret your time spent here.

Professional is one word to describe the Coach House Museum; not so much that it follows the modern museum philosophy of 'less is more' but in that everything in this museum is so carefully thought through. What makes this museum work, when many others don't? The answer is an army of over ninety committed volunteers who really know what they are doing. Most displays are 'curated' by a single group who decide what should be displayed, how it should look and provide excellent concise information. The result is a superb experience for the visitor and there is plenty of variety.

The John Deere tractor and implement display is outstanding and the largest in the Southern Hemisphere (all vehicles are operational). The nineteenth century horse drawn vehicles look almost brand new (the largest collection in the country) and the 1912 Burford Lorry is the only such vehicle left in the world and yes, like the John Deer tractors, it too still goes. It's not all about machinery as the volunteers understand that behind all this is a human touch. Historic photos reach out across the decades and remind us of the backbreaking work and isolation of generations past. Particularly touching is a hawker's van owned by Peter Kerouz. Built in 1900 Kerouz, of Syrian extraction, toured all over the Manawatu selling house goods from the horse drawn cart and sleeping overnight in the narrow space in the centre. Finally retiring in 1957 he left the district in 1960 and was never heard of again.

Well worth a trip to Feilding.

📍 121 South Street, Feilding.
🕐 Open daily 10 am to 4 pm.
📞 06 323 6401

🌐 www.coachhousemuseum.org
💲 Entrance fee.

15. De Molen and Nieuwe Stroom

Some men build sensible things like decks and a spare room but for Dutch immigrant Jan Langen nothing but a full-sized seventeenth-century Dutch windmill would do. After years of fund raising and planning the main street of Foxton carries the sight and sound of windmill arms whirring in the wind. This working windmill was built from actual Dutch plans from the seventeenth century with only small adaptations to the New Zealand building code and with the working machinery imported from the Netherlands. De Molen (The Windmill) operates during opening hours (except in very high winds) and processes New Zealand wheat into three types of flour (organic wholemeal, rye, millers mix), which can be purchased at the shop on the ground floor of the mill. There is a small charge for a tour of the working areas of the mill. Finding a full-sized seventeenth-century Dutch windmill with arms turning in the wind in the main street of a small New Zealand town is a sight not to be missed.

The windmill has spurred on several other Dutch related attractions with a café The Dutch Oven run by Dutch owners and specialising in Dutch food and delicacies and, as to be expected, great coffee. Alongside the windmill is a Dutch museum, Nieuwe Stroom, the New Stream. This is part of a larger complex, Te Awahou, which houses the Foxton Library and Museum, along with the Nieuwe Stroom (all are free to enter). Not large, this Dutch museum focuses on immigration to New Zealand particularly the period between 1951 and 1954 when 10,500 arrived. The café in Te Awahou Nieuwe Stroom also houses a café with Dutch food.

📍 96 Main Street, Foxton.
🕐 Open daily 10 am to 4 pm
📞 06 363 560
🌐 www.foxtonwindmill.co.nz

16. Foxton Flax Stripper

In the heyday of the flax industry the stretch of the Manawatu River between Foxton and Palmerston North supported seventy flax mills, and flax was an important industry not just in the Manawatu but throughout colonial New Zealand. Foxton alone had eight flax mills as late as 1912 sourcing huge amounts of flax from the vast swamps along the river. Different regions produced different types of flax fibre which was used for everything from rope to very attractive flax matting. Most mills were small, usually just one or two strippers but labour intensive and provided work for over twenty men.

Today flax has long been superseded by imported and synthetic yarns, and this museum now houses the only working stripping and scutching machines in the country. This noisy machine strips the flax down to soft fibre/muka, ready for weaving and is one of the most intriguing museum experiences in the country. There is a Flax Walkway along the Manawatu River Loop behind the museum.

- Main Street, Foxton (behind the windmill).
- Open daily 1 pm to 3 pm Closed June and July and main public holidays.
- 06 363 6846
- www.foxton.org.nz
- Entrance fee.

17. Foxton Beach – Manawatu Estuary

One of the top five most polluted rivers in the country may not sound like much of an attraction and while is best avoided for swimming, the estuary of this river is one of the most important aquatic and wading bird habitats in New Zealand.

Where the 180 km long Manawatu River empties into the Tasman Sea at Foxton Beach, the river forms a wide shallow estuary of saltmarsh, tidal flats and sand dunes and more bird species (over 110) have been recorded here than anywhere else in New Zealand including twenty-eight species of bird are listed as nationally critical or nationally threatened. Native plants and fish are found here in abundance as well. Of the twenty-four fish species recorded here, four are regarded as endangered.

Once neglected, in recent years this area improved considerably and the path along the estuary has a bird hide, a lookout point at Dawick Ave and excellent information. There are basically two choices of walk, both flat and easy. The first leads upriver along the estuary to the boat club and it is here that you will see the most birds. An advantage is that most of the path is above the tidal flats, so the birds are easy to spot. The second walk heads down to the sea and forms a loop through the partially protected dunes and along the river mouth.

Declared a Wetland of International Importance in 2005, if you are bird watcher, then Foxton Beach is a compulsory stop.

📍 Carpark at the end of Pinewood Road, off Holben Esplanade, Foxton Beach.

18. Waitarere Beach Shipwreck

There is nothing quite as appealing as a shipwreck and while New Zealand has nearly 3000 recorded wrecks, most have long gone or are difficult to access. In 1879 the sailing ship the *Hydrabad* was wrecked on Waitarere Beach. Unable to be salvaged, much of the ship was stripped of its more valuable items, leaving the hulk to slowly decay. The wreck is high on the beach, a short walk south of the carpark but even viewing the *Hydrabad* is a lucky chance as it alternates between being exposed and being entirely covered in sand.

📍 Waitarere Beach, 7 km from the turnoff on SH 1 north of Levin.

19. Mangahao Power Station

Little known outside of the Manawatu, this was not only New Zealand's first major power plant, but also one of the most complex and is now recognised for its architectural, technological and historic importance. Rather than just dam a river, the eastward flowing Mangahao River deep in the Tararua ranges was diverted through a tunnel to a reservoir on the westward flowing Tokomaru stream and from there two massive pipes directed the water downhill to the power station above Mangaore Stream. The tunnel and the pipes together cover 4.8 kilometres.

Looming above the stream the powerhouse, opened in 1924, is a striking example of contemporary industrial architecture. Advancing down the steep hills, the huge pen stocks are difficult to see and are best viewed from the small Mangahao village built to service workers at the station. The reservoirs are some distance from the power station and the road is narrow, winding gravel. Mostly one way and with little opportunity to turn around, is best suited to confident drivers.

Right below the power station is the Mangahao White Water Park, a 300 metre world class kayaking facility established in the 1970s on the Mangaore Stream, aided by the constant flow of water.

📍 From SH 57 at Shannon take the Mangahao Road five kilometres to the power station.

20. RJ's Licorice

The licorice plant, *Glycyrrhiza glabra* is a herbaceous perennial native to southern Europe, the Middle East and parts of Asia and can be easily grown in New Zealand. The root when dried is fifty times sweeter than sugar, has distinct flavour and aroma, and has a long history of being used as a sweetener and herbal medicine. In New Zealand licorice straps, a long piece of licorice around 10 cm wide and 30 cm long have been a favourite sweet treat.

Roger Halliwell bought the Grannies Licorice factory when in it went into receivership in 1983 and began producing a range of soft licorice under the RJ brand. The company changed hands several times and in 1994 Halliwell bought the company back and moved it to Levin. Rather than stick to the traditional licorice allsorts and sticky licorice sweets, RJ's have greatly expanded the market to include raspberry and chocolate flavours.

At the factory at Levin is a shop dedicated to licorice in all forms and here you will find the complete RJ's range as well as the harder black knight licorice, now made by RJ's. In October 2016 RJ's produced the world's largest licorice allsort. Made from 75 kg sugar, 624 kg of icing sugar/cornflour, 27 kg of desiccated coconut and 156 litres of glucose syrup, the sweet weighed 1.1 tonne and was 800m square. The company is now owned by an Australian family.

Licorice is the American spelling, whereas liquorice is the British spelling.

- 5 Tirotiro Road, Levin.
- Open 8 am to 4 pm Monday to Friday.
- 06 366 0270
- www.rjslicorice.co.nz

21. Lake Papaitonga

For those used to the open and often windswept landscape of the Horowhenua, this small lake surrounded by the finest lowland bush remnant between Wanganui and Wellington will come as a surprise. Now just covering 122 hectares, including the lake, the reserve forest is dominated by titoki, kahikatea, nikau, karaka and kiekie. It is just so hard to believe that this whole coast was once covered in such dense and luxurious bush and so little has survived. Maori and European settlers were nothing if not thorough when the cleared the land for crops and farming.

Early in the nineteenth century the area was settled by the Muaopoko people who constructed two islands in the middle of the lake for their

Pa Motukiwi and Motungarara. In the early 1820s Ngati Toa chief Te Rauparaha visited the area with his family. They were hosted by Muaupoko at Te Wi near Papaitonga. Suspecting that Te Rauparaha's real intentions were to settle in the area long term, Muaupoko decided to kill the visitors. Unfortunately for Muaupoko, Te Rauparaha only narrowly escaped, though his son and daughter and many of his relatives died. Biding his time, Te Rauparaha finally sought revenge on both Muaupoko and their allies Ngati Apa, based on Kapiti Island, whom Te Rauparaha suspected as being behind the earlier ambush.

In 1823 Te Rauparaha attacked the two pa in the lake, and one after the other the pa fell to the Ngati Toa warriors. Only a handful managed to escape the fearful slaughter that followed. In the same year Te Rauparaha conquered Kapiti Island and Ngati Apa met the same fate.

However, Te Rauparaha remained unforgiving of the massacre of his family at Te Wi and was not yet finished with Mauapoko. After the 1823 attack, the few survivors returned to their lake pa. In 1827–28 they were again attacked by Ngati Toa and this time almost entirely annihilated, with just a few survivors fleeing into the mountains or finding refuge with other tribes. The lake pa were never reoccupied.

In 1897 the land was acquired rather deviously by the noted naturalist, Sir Walter Buller, though it was Buller who recognised its value and preserved this small piece of bush for future generations. Today the lake is an important bush and wetland preserve.

📍 4km south of Levin turn off SH 1 into Hokio Beach Road. Lake Papaitonga is signposted to the left.

22. Ohau Wines

No slouch at making good wine, Ohau Wines are the only vineyard in a region not known for wine making yet their Woven Gold Pinot Gris won double gold at the prestigious San Francisco International Wine Competition in 2018. Double Gold is only awarded to wines that are awarded a gold medal by all the judges in the competition which is very difficult to pull off.

While the area is well known for vegetable and fruit growing it has never had a reputation for growing grapes yet viticulturalist Kate Gibbs identified the Ohau river soils as very similar to the Wairarapa wine growing area and ideal for producing excellent grapes. Established in 2009, the vineyard now covers in 40 ha, mostly in pinot gris, pinot noir, sauvignon blanc and gewürztraminer. Winemaker Jane Cooper, with an extensive background in winemaking in Italy, Chile, Australia and New Zealand creates wine that are drier, but still aromatic and more in tune with modern tastes which have moved away from sweeter style wines. In addition, Ohau produce a rosé and sparkling sauvignon blanc.

The small friendly tasting room is just a few metres off SH 1, but keep your eyes open, it is easy to miss.

- 6 Bishops Road, Ohau, off SH 1 six kilometres south of Levin.
- Open daily 11 am to 4.30 pm, closed weekends April to August.
- 06 367 5051
- www.ohauwines.co.nz

23. Our Lady of Lourdes, Paraparaumu

High on a hill overlooking the Kapiti Coast is an enormous 14 metre high statue of Our Lady of Lourdes. The idea for the statue came from local Waikanae Parish Priest Father Dunn, who wanted a monument to celebrate 100 years since the first appearance of the virgin Mary at Lourdes in 1848. Early in 1958 he commissioned Martin Roestenburg to build the statue, after a previous one built by enthusiastic but inexperienced Marist brothers blew down. Born in Eindhoven in the Netherlands in 1909, Roestenburg always had an interest in religious art, and intriguingly spent some time studying at the Munich Academy of Fine Arts in 1941 and 1942. In 1951 he immigrated to New Zealand and, while this statue is his most prominent work, he is best known for his stained glass windows.

Constructed over a period of six months, the statue is concrete plaster over a wooden frame and was dedicated in August 1958 to a crowd of over 6000 people. Roestenburg died at Palmerston North in 1966 aged just fifty-six years old. The statue is simplistic in form, with strong angular lines and rather roughly finished. Located on a small hill, the rather steep and bumpy track to the statue is lined by the fourteen Stations of the Cross in various states of repair. At night the statue is floodlit, though the halo is separately lit.

Tongariro Street, Paraparaumu.

24. Kapiti Island

One of New Zealand's most important bird sanctuaries, Kapiti Island, lies 5 km off the coast, is 1965 hectares in area, and its highest point, Tuteremoana, is 520 m.

For most people Kapiti Island is closely associated with the famous fighting chief Te Rauparaha, but the Maori history of the island goes back much further. According to tradition both Kapiti and Mana Island, just to the south, were created by Kupe with one strong blow from his patu. Several tribes occupied Kapiti, appreciating its natural qualities as a fortress and cultivating the sheltered and more accessible eastern side of the island. Kapiti became known as 'motu rongonui' or 'famous island' and whoever held Kapiti effectively controlled Te Moana a Raukawa/Cook Strait.

Kapiti is a contraction of Te Waewae Kapiti o Tara raua ko Rangitane, which acknowledges the island as marking a boundary between Ngati Tara and Rangitane, a boundary that was swept away with the arrival of Ngati Toa. After first settling in Otaki in 1823, Ngati Toa under Te Rauparaha decided to take the island. They were met with fierce resistance from Ngati Apa, who were well aware of the fate that had befallen their allies Mauapoko; but gradually pa after pa fell to the invaders and Te Rauparaha finally completed his conquest of the island with the capture of Waiorua, the last Ngati Apa stronghold. At the same time Te Rauparaha took Mana Island, which then became the home of Te Rangihaeata, a nephew of Te Rauparaha.

From his island base Te Rauparaha launched his conquest of Wellington and the South Island. While he was uncompromising in respect to his defeated enemies, he not only shared the island with Pakeha whalers, but actively encouraged them to set up a whaling station on the island. A small area of 13 hectares at Waiorua Bay is still held by Maori.

In 1987, the management of the island was handed over to the Department of Conservation who set about removing sheep and possums from the island. In a operation thought impossible rats were also eradicate in 1998 and now Kapiti is an important nature sanctuary and home to a wide range of native birds including many rare birds such as the little spotted kiwi (extinct on the mainland), weka, kaka, kakariki, tieke (saddleback) and hihi (stitchbird).

An excellent one-day trip is a tramp to Tuteremoana, the summit of the island (521 m). There is an option of two tracks to the top. The Wilkinson Track is better formed, has the easier grade, but takes longer (3.8 km) than the steeper and rougher Trig Track (2 km). Covering both tracks as a loop is a popular option with the fitter (up the Trig and down the Wilkinson) as both tracks meet a short distance from the top.

There are also several shorter walks on the flat for those who wish to visit the island but are less keen on the hike to the summit.

The island is reasonably accessible with two companies operating a ferry service to the island (weather dependent). Visitors numbers are regulated and you must obtain a visitor's permit from the Department of Conservation first (kapiti.island@doc.govt.nz for more information). It is also possible to stay overnight at the Nature Lodge in the north of the island.

WAIRARAPA

1. Tui Brewery, Mangatainoka, 'Yeah right'
2. Anzac Bridge, Kaiparoro
3. Eketahuna War Memorial Hall
4. Mt Bruce Pioneer Museum
5. The Alpaca Place
6. Castlepoint Lighthouse and Lagoon
7. Ten O'Clock Cookie Bakery and Café
8. The Cricket Oval and a Redwood stump, Queen Elizabeth Park, Masterton
9. The Wool Shed and the Golden Shears
10. Wairarapa Times Age Building
11. The Clareville Bakery
12. Stonehenge Aotearoa
13. Papawai Marae
14. Mountain Ash Gum Tree, Greytown
15. Tauherenikau Racecourse
16. Fell Locomotive Museum, Featherston
17. Wairarapa Wineries
18. Putangirua Pinnacles
19. Ngawi, South Wairarapa Coast

1. Tui Brewery, Mangatainoka, 'Yeah right'

The Tui Brewery comes as a surprise in the wide-open spaces of northern Wairarapa and southern Hawkes Bay. The brewery was originally established by Henry Wagstaff in 1889 to take advantage of the clean waters of the Mangatainoka Stream and beer was sold under the Wagstaff label. Wagstaff set up the brewery after he was fired from his job as cheesemaker as incompetent and he clearly he had more affinity with beer than cheese. Sold to Henry Cowan in 1903 who renamed the brewery the North Island Brewery, the business continued to expand with the introduction of Tui East India Pale Ale. This proved so popular the company changed its name to the Tui Brewery in 1923.

In 1931 a seven-storey brick building rose in the rural landscape of Northern Wairarapa where previously very few buildings were more than a single level. The height was needed to turn malt into beer beginning on the sixth floor where malt was mixed with water on the top floor. From there a series of gravity fed processes finally resulted in sparkling ale in the basement. Oddly the builders completely forgot to put in either stairs or a lift, something that wasn't rectified until 1938 when an external lift was added.

Sold to Dominion Breweries in 1969, Tui beer moved from being a regional brand to a major player in the market with its innovative 'Yeah right' billboard campaign. While 'Yeah right', indicating disbelief, has always been part of New Zealand English, this advertising campaign for Tui beer moved the saying into mainstream slang. In 2016 beer production ceased at Mangatinoka with only a small amount of boutique beer made on the site. The tour of the brewery includes beer tastings, and bookings are essential.

- SH 2, 6km north of Pahaitua.
- Open November to April Sunday to Thursday 11 am to 5 pm, Friday 11 am to 8 pm, Saturday 11 am to 6 pm.
  May to October: Sunday to Thursday 11 am to 4 pm, Friday 11 am to 8 pm, Saturday 11 am to 5 pm.

📞 06 376 0815
🌐 www.tuihq.co.nz

2. Anzac Bridge, Kaiparoro

It is easy to overlook this war memorial as you speed along SH 2 in the northern Wairarapa. The simple concrete Anzac Bridge was built in 1922 over the Makakahi River, and while a new bridge was a necessity, in joint community and government project the bridge was turned into a war memorial. The idea behind the bridge as a war memorial was to remind those who crossed the bridge of those who had died in war. The impetus for the bridge came from local mill owner Alfred Falkner, who had lost his youngest son Victor and his nephew Donald Pallant during World War I. Falkner, a draughtsman, drew up the plans while the local community provide half of the 800 pounds to build the bridge. The bridge was open in December 1922, and the plaques unveiled on Anzac Day the following year. After WWII further names were added to the bridge that was in regular use until 1956 when it was replaced with a new bridge. Anzac Day commemorations are still held each year at the bridge.

📍 Kaiparoro, on SH 2 just north of Pukaha Mt Bruce Wildlife Centre, Northern Wairarapa.

3. Eketahuna War Memorial Hall

Even in the most remote backblocks, the local hall is usually a decent size and it really makes you wonder what the folk of Eketahuna were thinking in the 1920s when they built their War Memorial Hall barely bigger than a good-sized lounge. It has all the attributes and design of a hall with a kitchen and toilets, but it is just so small that even with everyone standing up close together it would barely fit thirty or forty people. A very private wedding perhaps, the bridge club maybe, Irish dancing where they don't wave their arms about, but it certainly couldn't cope with boisterous girl guides or even indoor bowls. The tiny fireplace at one end, makes it look even more like a spacious living room. However, it is beautifully maintained, and the hall is still the town's official war memorial.

📍 Corners of SH 2 and Main Street, Eketahuna.

4. Mt Bruce Pioneer Museum

The sign directs you up a driveway to a farm house and you wonder if you have come to the wrong place so you keep driving up the track a little to a collection of sheds and a handmade sign declaring that you have indeed arrived at the Mt Bruce Pioneer Museum. Somewhere from one of the sheds emerges the cheerful and friendly Henry Christensen who then takes you on a magical mystery tour of more old stuff than you ever thought possible to cram into a series of interconnected sheds and even part of an old house. Henry began collecting in 1973 with most of his enormous collection coming from the local district and, from radios and dolls to ploughs and milking machines, Henry has it all. Most of the material is not labelled but Henry knows what and where everything is. Without Henry most of the district's history would have ended up in the farm's rubbish dump and in some sense the collection is a tribute to the innovation and resourcefulness of New Zealand farmers.

Situated on a working dairy farm, one of the most intriguing machines is a mechanical milking machine from 1891. Foot operated, it fundamentally works on the same principle as a modern milking machine, milking two cows at a time and twenty cows an hour, which compared with hand milking was incredibly speedy. On the same theme, the collection has a 1917 milking machine. This one however, was powered by diesel or petrol and later electricity.

If you are not in a hurry, enjoy good hospitality and love old things, this is the perfect place to stop.

- 📍 SH 2 18 km north of Masterton, 10 km south of Pukaha National Wildlife Centre.
- 🕐 As Henry says, *'When we are home, we are open'*, generally 9 am to 5 pm.
- 💲 Entrance fee.

5. The Alpaca Place

It started with just two alpacas in 2000 and now there are around fifty on this small farm northeast of Masterton. Used to a very tough environment in their native South America, alpacas are hardy animals who thrive in the more benign New Zealand conditions. New Zealand was the first country in the world to import alpacas for farming when, in 1985, the Chilean governments agreed to allow exports to New Zealand. Numbers have steadily risen, but industry remains small with around 26,000 animals being farmed for their prized wool.

Unarguably cute with cuddly fleece and a placid nature, this is the place to get up close and personal with the alpaca. Along with learning about alpaca history and farming, the tour allows visitors to take an alpaca for a walk, meet babies and feel that gorgeous wool. The Alpaca Place is a farm and not a petting zoo and the tour is not suitable for very young children. Tours are daily at 10 and 1 and last around an hour and half and bookings are essential.

- 📍 365 Bluff Rangitumau Road, Masterton.
- 🕐 Open daily except Thursday.
- 📞 06 372 5565
- 🌐 www.thealpacaplace.co.nz

6. Castlepoint Lighthouse and Lagoon

Known for safe swimming, surf and fishing, the setting of Castlepoint is dramatic. Facing the small settlement is a wide surf beach partially protected by the raw cliff face of Castle Point. High on the point is one of New Zealand's most stylish lighthouses with a slender taper from 5 m at its base to 3 m at the top. Built in 1912, the lighthouse can be seen 30 km out to sea and was automated in only 1988. Below the lighthouse huge waves, directly off the southern ocean, hammer the cliffs and thunder and crash over the rocky reef that protects the lagoon. In rough weather this place has a wild seascape that is nothing short of spectacular. The rocky reef, overlooking the reef and lagoon, is a very popular spot for fishing, but as a plaque commemorating the dead and injured testifies, this is a very dangerous spot; a powerful wave or a careless step and you are unlikely to come back in one piece.

It is appropriate that the dramatic landscape of Rangiwhakaoma/Castle Point was also the location of one of Kupe's most lively escapades. While sailing along this coast in the great waka Matahorua, Kupe disturbed a giant octopus that lived in a cave in the cliffs. Taking fright, the huge creature fled from the waka, heading first south and then north through Cook Strait with Kupe in hot pursuit. Finally the octopus had no choice but to turn and fight, attacking the waka with great fury, wrapping its enormous tentacles around Matahorua. Kupe had to act fast as the waka was in danger of being pulled apart. He flung a gourd far into the sea and the octopus, thinking a man had fallen overboard, released the waka and grabbed the gourd. Kupe seized his chance and killed the octopus with a blow to the head with his adze.

Castlepoint is also famous for its beach races, which have been held in March annually since 1872. The races apply the sweepstake form of betting where punters place their bets and are then allocated horse numbers after the tote has closed.

📍 65 km from Masterton on a sealed road.

7. Ten O'Clock Cookie Bakery and Café

How many awards can one bakery have? A lot if you are Ten O'Clock Cookie and those awards include the prestigious Bakery of the Year in 2016 and 2017. Yet when Dutchman John Kloeg arrived in New Zealand, his plan was to be a teacher. Unable to find a job he fell back on his baking background and took over an existing bakery in Masterton in 1987. More than thirty years later, the bakery is still in family hands and still packs in the locals who know a good thing when they have it.

Best to come here hungry, and while the cakes are to die for, all the food is top notch and the coffee is great too. If choosing is difficult, opt for the award-winning Opera Cake. Originally known as 'The Clichy' after the French creator Louis Clichy, Opera Cake is in many ways a refined version of the classic layered trifle and the Italian tiramisu. Thin slices of almond sponge are interspersed with layers of mocha cream and ganache (a rich chocolate cream). The result is a very rich but not overly sweet cake, worth a trip to Masterton itself.

- 180 Queen Street, Masterton.
- Open Monday to Friday 7 am to 4.30 pm, Saturday 8 am to 4 pm.
- 06 377 4551
- www.tenoclockcookie.co.nz

8. The Cricket Oval and a Redwood Stump, Queen Elizabeth Park, Masterton

For fans of the traditional cricket game, with men dressed in white and a polite audience lounging under leafy trees, the cricket oval in the Queen Elizabeth Park is the place to go. What must be the most attractive cricket ground in the country lies in the middle of this huge park, established in

1877 alongside the Waipoua River in the heart of Masterton. Traditionally English in style, this is a beautifully kept cricket green, surrounded by mature European trees (not a native tree in sight), a tiny Victorian grandstand built in 1895 and alongside, an Edwardian band rotunda built to celebrate the coronation of Edward VII in 1902.

Not far from the band rotunda is a curious shelter covering nothing but an old stump. This is no ordinary old stump, but the remains of a massive redwood tree struck by lightning in 1989 and so badly damaged that the tree was subsequently felled. The park staff were then able to date the tree back 114 years to when the park was first laid out. Masterton folk are a thrifty lot and not keen on seeing good timber go to waste, trimmed the huge stump to table height and with the timber built a pretty picnic shelter, including wooden roofing shingles, all from the fallen redwood.

The park was renamed to commemorate the visit of the young Queen Elizabeth in 1954 and, along with the cricket ground, also features attractive formal gardens, aviaries, a miniature railway, a children's playground, a swing bridge over the river, and across the road a modern swimming pool complex.

📍 Dixon Street, Masterton.

9. The Wool Shed and the Golden Shears

Shear Discovery is a fitting tribute to the sheep farming industry on which the prosperity of the Wairarapa region was founded. The first sheep arrived in region in 1844 after being driven around the coast by five Wellingtonians who had obtain leases from local Maori, and today the Wairarapa is home to three million sheep.

In 2005 Masterton folk were originally horrified at the sight of two dilapidated old woolsheds being dumped in the centre of town right across from their splendid Queen Elizabeth Park, but the museum now does the town real credit.

It is the only museum in the country dedicated entirely to the history of the wool industry, and the well-presented exhibitions covering of every aspect of this very Kiwi industry include the Trethewey statue 'Shearing a Ram' (commissioned in 1925 for the Great Empire Exhibition in London), a range of historic shearing gear and the Golden Shears Wall of Champions.

The Wool Shed is housed in a building that includes two complete historic shearing sheds, Glendonald (built 1903) and Roselea (built 1892). The older woolshed Roselea, built by Thomas Wilton, is possibly the only surviving building constructed from hand-adzed totara logs.

Off to the side of the sheds is the newer Stewart-Weston Gallery which houses a very rare split timber bushman's hut dating to around 1890 and a replica of a station cookhouse, which will send shudders down the spine of a modern cook.

Masterton is home to New Zealand's most famous shearing event, the Golden Shears. Attracting both national and international competitors to Masterton (and including a trans-Tasman test), the competition was first held in 1960 and quickly became a major event on the national calendar, especially when televised during the 1960s and 1970s. As well as shearing, other events include wool classing and wool handling, and there is also a 'wool triathlon', a combination of all three disciplines. The main events are held on the Saturday, which is always the first Saturday in March.

More than a museum, the Wool Shed is also a venue for craft groups such as the weavers and spinners and the dedicated felt makers. These groups welcome visitors; those interested can check the website for dates and details.

- 12 Dixon Street, Masterton.
- Open daily 10 am to 4 pm.
- 06 378 800
- www.thewoolshednz.com
- Entrance fee.

10. Wairarapa Times Age Building

Does the Wairarapa Times Age Building look line an ocean liner? Well in 1937 the architects Mitchell and Mitchell of Wellington certainly thought so. The Art Deco style, fashionable at the time, was fascinated by the great ocean-going passenger liners of the time and many buildings incorporated elements from ship design. The curved, double-storey main entrance accentuated by the flag pole represents a tall ship's prow, while the long single level facades on Chapel and Perry Streets fan back at an angle and with streamlined, horizontal banding give the impression of movement and speed.

Beautifully maintained and carefully painted it is one of New Zealand's most striking Art Deco buildings.

📍 Corner of Chapel and Perry Streets, Masterton.

11. The Clareville Bakery

From the day it opened in 2013, the Clareville Bakery started to scoop up the awards for its bread and pies including Best Regional Bakery in 2018. All the food here is fresh and the baking superb. Specialising in bread, the bakers pride themselves on using no preservatives or additives, allowing a long fermentation, and the bread is best eaten as fresh as possible.

Adding to the appeal of the food, the bakery is housed in an historic chapel built in 1872, a log burner keeps the interior toasty in winter and in summer a garden provides welcome shade.

📍 3340 SH 2 Clareville, three km north of Carterton.
🕐 Open Monday to Saturday 7.30 am to 4 pm.
📞 06 379 5333

12. Stonehenge Aotearoa

Looking completely lost in the foothills of the Wairarapa, anyone interested in astronomy will find immediate appeal in this full-scale model of Stonehenge. Opened in 2005, this southern Stonehenge is built on a hill overlooking the plains and has been adapted to function for the sky in this hemisphere. More than just a replica, Stonehenge Aotearoa also details ancient and modern methods of astronomy, time and navigation including early Polynesian celestial seafaring abilities, Maori astrology and Celtic, Egyptian and Babylonian astronomy.

- 51 Ahiaruhe Road, 11 km east of Carterton and well sign posted from SH 2.
- Opening times are seasonal and vary considerably so it is best to phone or check the website.
  Guided Tours are held at 11 am on Saturdays, Sundays and public holidays.
- 06 377 1600
- www.stonehenge-aotearoa.co.nz

13. Papawai Marae

Established only in the 1850s this marae under the leadership first of Te Manihera Te Rangi-taka-i-waho and then under Tamahau Mahupuka, became one of the most influential and important marae in the country. The marae played a major role in the Kotahitanga (Maori Parliament) movement in the late nineteenth century and early twentieth century and was the focus of many key meetings to address important Maori issues including an end to the sale of Maori land. The leadership also actively supported and encouraged close involvement with Europeans. The house Hikurangi was opened in 1888 and the lively Maori newspaper Te Puke ki Hikurangi was published here from 1897 to 1913.

Of particular note are the unique tekoteko. These carved figures representing ancestors on the palisading surrounding the marae usually face outwards to protect the pa. However, the eighteen tekoteko at Papawai erected in 1940 face inwards, representing peace between Maori and Pakeha and including a Pakeha Willam Mein Smith.

Through the remainder of the twentieth century Papawai declined in importance and fell into disrepair. However, in recent years the marae has revived, with the buildings restored and is now the centre of local Maori life.

📍 From Main Street Greytown, turn into Papawai Road and the marae is 2.5 km on the right.

14. Mountain Ash Gum Tree, Greytown

Stories regarding this old gum tree on the south side of Greytown vary somewhat but the heart of the story is agreed on. In January 1856 Samuel Oates arrived in Wellington and found employment with Charles Carter who had a farm near Masterton. Carter asked Oates to take a large wooden wheelbarrow of goods by foot to the farm includes ten gum tree seedlings. The trek took three days and not surprisingly Oates decided to call into the Rising Sun in Greytown for a cooling beer. Some say his stop was a quick one, while other versions have a much longer stay. However long, it was time enough for someone to pinch three of his gum trees from his barrow. Of the stolen trees, one was planted in what are now the grounds of St Luke's Anglican Church, though the church was not there at the time. Descendants of Samuel Oates still live in Greytown and have the wheel said to have come from the original barrow, though there are also rumours than another 'true' wheel also exists.

Now with a six-metre-diameter trunk and a wide canopy, the gum Eucalyptus regans is still flourishing, festooned with huge strips of bark up to 10 metres in length, a nightmare for those inclined to be tidy.

📍 St Luke's Church, 158 Main Street, (SH 2), Greytown.

15. Tauherenikau Racecourse

This popular country track is famous for the casual atmosphere of its summer race meets on January 2 and Waitangi Day (February 6) which attract tens of thousands of happy people and where picnics and barbecues under the massive totara and kahikatea trees are the order of the day.

Races have been held here since January 1874 on a track that, at the time, was noted as 'a very dangerous piece of ground to ride over owing to the number of holes thrown up during the earthquake of 1855'.

The elegant grandstand burnt down in 1955 during a race and, despite urgent calls of 'Fire!', patrons were reluctant to evacuate the grandstand until the race was finished. The historic ticket office and members stand still remain. Especially popular for Wellingtonians is to travel to the race meet by train – the atmosphere on the return journey becoming particularly festive after patrons have enjoyed some time at the legendary local pub known as 'The Tin Hut'.

📍 No 1 Line, Tauherenikau.
🌐 www.tauherenikau.co.nz

16. Fell Locomotive Museum, Featherston

The Rimutaka Ranges between Wellington and the Wairarapa presented a major obstacle to the easy movement of people and goods. The solution was the Fell railway system, which uses a third track to brake the train on the steep terrain. This small, smart museum tells the marvellous story of the famous Rimutaka Incline and John Fell's ingenious system designed to tackle the difficult 'Rimutakas'. Now housing the only remaining Fell engine in the world known as Mont Cenis H199 and built in Bristol in 1875, the museum also contains the only piece of the original track, the Fell brake van built in Petone in 1898, an audio-visual presentation of original archive film, and a great display of photographs. A small pit allows the visitor to look under the Fell engine and a model of the incline gives a graphic picture of the rugged terrain the railway line traversed.

For those feeling fit, the Rimutaka Rail Trail is a 17 km walk along the old railway line from Kaitoke to Cross Creek, 10 km south of Featherston.

- SH 2, Featherston (middle of the main street).
- Open daily 10 am to 4 pm mid-December to Easter. Rest of the year weekends and public holidays only.
- 06 308 9379
- www.fellmuseum.org.nz
- Entrance fee.

17. Wairarapa Wineries

One of New Zealand's smaller grape growing regions, Wairarapa produces only one percent of the country's wine, but has a huge reputation. Within the area there are three scattered sub-regions, Martinborough, Gladstone and Masterton, the last two have just four vineyards each, the best known of which the Gladstone Winery. However, it is the area around Martinborough that has made the region famous on the back of its award-winning pinot noir wines.

In 1979 the Department of Scientific and Industrial Research (DSIR) identified the Martinborough area as having climate and soil types similar to Burgundy, and by the early 1980s four vineyards were established: Ata Rangi, Chifney, Dry River, and Martinborough. The wine-growing area is small and compact (with a couple of exceptions) and within a short distance of the town. Cycle tours are popular and several places in town hire bikes. However be aware that many of the vineyards have very restricted opening hours, so, if you have a favourite vineyard it pays to check ahead to see if they are open. Toast Martinborough, a celebration of local wine and food (with several good olive growers in the district), is held each year on the third Sunday in November.

18. Putangirua Pinnacles

The Putangirua Pinnacles are the most extensive example of 'badlands' or hoodoos formations in the country and are reached by an easy walk up a rocky stream.

Over the many thousands of years, the Putangirua stream has eroded the loose gravel soils to form a series of deep gullies including tall gravel pinnacles called hoodoos. These pillars are topped by rock that protects the underlying soil from the rain and prevents the soft gravels from eroding, creating high fluted formations. The result is a fascinating landscape comprising of tall towers of loose gravel with deep gullies and channels in between, and the walk takes you deep inside the formations. The 'Paths of The Dead' sequence in 'The Lord of The Rings; The Return of The King' was filmed here. There is a picnic area and camping ground at the entrance to the walk.

📍 12 km south of the junction of the Cape Palliser Road and the Lake Ferry Road, south of Martinborough.

19. Ngawi, South Wairarapa Coast

Facing the wild Southern Ocean, with nothing much between Ngawi and the Antarctic, this rocky coastline is hammered with some of the fiercest weather in the country. This does not deter a small community of fishers from launching their boats into wild waters in search of fish. With no sheltered harbours, here the boats are hauled in and out of the water by a collection of bulldozers that are as varied as the boats they pull, necessary to make a navigable track in the ever-changing shingle beaches.

Five kilometres along the coast from Ngawi is a striking historic lighthouse, painted in red and white horizontal stripes in the most traditional manner. Located 78 metres above the sea, the 18-metre-tall lighthouse was built in 1897 to guide shipping around the perilous Cape Palliser, a coastline that combines rocky headlands and ferocious weather. From the lighthouse keeper's cottage, the steps lead straight up the rocky bluff with to a fantastic view along the coast. Succulents and coprosma thrive in the crevices of the raw hillside.

About half way between Ngawi and the lighthouse keep an eye out for the seal colony on the rocks below, but take care if you plan to take a closer look as many seals rest right beside the road and are not easy to spot until you are almost on top of them.

As with much of this coast, the area around Cape Palliser/Te Kawakawa has close associations with legendary explorer Kupe. The name of the cape refers to a garland that Kupe's daughter fashioned from the leaves of a kawakawa tree that she found growing here. Just to the west of Te Kawakawa is an area of cliff face notable for its lighter shade of rocks, called Nga Ra o Kupe, 'the sails of Kupe'. On the shore below is a large flat rock where Kupe stood to view the snow-capped Kaikoura mountains across the strait; this is called Matakitaki a Kupe, 'the watching place of Kupe'.

While today this exposed coastline would appear too inhospitable to support Maori agriculture, there are numerous rock walls on the flat land below the cliffs. These rock walls not only delineated one family's garden from another, but also broke the wind and raised the temperature for growing kumara by reflecting and absorbing heat from the sun.

The road to Ngawi is excellent. Sealed, mainly straight, it follows the coast with just one or two rough patches through the unstable terrain, though the last section from Ngawi is unsealed.

WELLINGTON

1. Kaitoke Regional Park
2. Mangaroa Rail Tunnel
3. Wallaceville Blockhouse
4. The Weeping Pagoda Tree
5. Wainuiomata Hill Tunnel Portal
6. Pencarrow Coastal Trail
7. Lower Hutt Council Building and Town Hall
8. Petone Wharf
9. Battle Hill
10. Pataka Art + Museum
11. Te Pa o Kapo
12. Second World War American Officer's Mess
13. Johnsonville Line - Wellington Rail
14. Matiu/Somes Island and Wellington Harbour/ Te Whanganui a Tara
15. Katherine Mansfield House and Garden
16. Tinakori Road Houses, Thorndon
17. Harry Holland's Grave, Bolton Street Cemetery
18. Pinus Radiata Botanic Gardens
19. Krupp Gun
20. He Tohu: The Declaration of Independence, The Treaty of Waitangi and Women's Suffrage Petition
21. Old Government Buildings
22. Old Bank Arcade, Animated Musical Clock
23. Paddy the Wanderer Memorial Fountain
24. The Board Room – Wellington Museum
25. New Zealand Academy of Fine Arts and New Zealand Portrait Gallery
26. Boat Sheds, Clyde Quay Boat Harbour
27. Cuba Street Bucket Fountain
28. Nairn Street Cottage
29. Otari-Wilton Bush's Native Botanic Garden and Forest Reserve

30. Mrs Chippy Monument
31. Wrights Hill Fortress
32. Makara Peak Mountain-bike Park
33. Makara Beach and Walkway
34. Brooklyn Wind Turbine
35. Carlucci Land
36. The Container House, Happy Valley
37. Wellington's South Coast
38. Island Bay Butchery
39. Wellington Airport
40. Ataturk Memorial

Hutt Valley

1. Kaitoke Regional Park

In 1939 large areas of virgin bush were purchased for the local water-supply catchment area and today half of Wellington's water is still drawn from the Hutt River from within the park. Now covering 2860 ha, the park has some of the finest untouched bush in the Wellington region, with magnificent stands of old rimu, rata and beech. As well as walks, there are great picnic sites and swimming holes in the river.

Most walks begin from Pukuratahi with the main walk, a loop along the Hutt River, starting over a long swing bridge from the car park. Immediately over the bridge is a short nature walk with interpretive panels that will take around fifteen minutes to complete. The main track continues through magnificent forest to the Flume Bridge, from which there are views down the Hutt River gorge. Over the bridge is the Kaitoke Strainer

House, which acted as an initial filter for the water system. Located on the wall of the house is a fascinating map of Wellington's impressive water system, which is well worth a good look.

Near the car park a short side path leads to the site of Rivendell from the Lord of the Rings films. Although nothing now remains, a helpful panel shows stills from the film of the river setting below.

📍 Waterworks Road, Kaitoke, Upper Hutt.

2. Mangaroa Rail Tunnel

Built between 1875 and 1877 at the foot of Mount Climie, this 253 m rail tunnel finally closed in 1955 with the opening of the new Remutaka Tunnel. Lined with a curious and inconsistent mixture of brick and stone, the path through the tunnel is very even, making this is the perfect adventure for young children (torch is helpful but not necessary). The walk is just ten minutes from the car park through lovely native bush. Nearby is a flat area with gum trees and this was the camp site for workers building the tunnel.

For the more adventurous there are long walks and bike tracks in the area known as Tunnel Gully Recreation Area, part of the much larger 8000 ha Pakuratahi Forest.

📍 Tunnel Gully, Te Marua. Turn right into Plateau Road off SH 2 at the Te Marua store just north of Upper Hutt.

Right: Manutahi Taxidermy Museum. (Taranaki #4)

Left: Manutahi Taxidermy Museum. (Taranaki #4)

Opunake Beach. (Taranaki #17)

The Len Lye Centre, New Plymoth. (Taranaki #8)

The Rewa Rewa Bridge. (Taranaki #6)

Right: New Plymouth Power Station Chimney. (Taranaki #10)

Paritutu Rock and the Islands. (Taranaki #11)

Manaia Blockhouse and Redoubt. (Taranaki #20)

Parihaka Village. (Taranaki #15)

Wairarapa Times Age Building, Masterton. (Wairarapa #10)

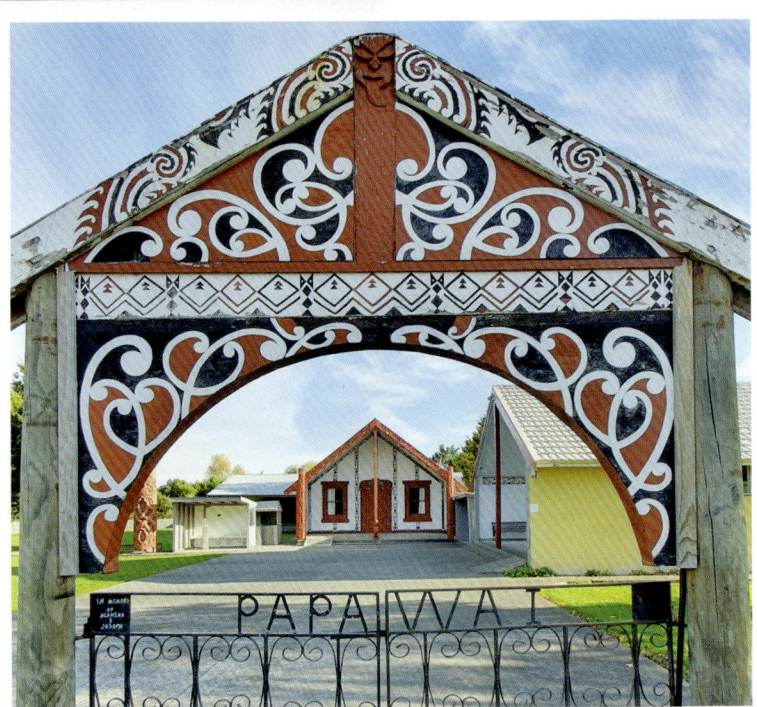

Papawai Marae. (Wairarapa #13)

Wallaceville Blockhouse, Upper Hutt. (Wellington #3)

Petone Wharf. (Wellington #8)

Povi, Pataka Art and Museum, Porirua. (Wellington #10)

Tinakori Road houses, Thorndon. (Wellington #16)

Harry Holland's Grave, Bolton Street Cemetery. (Wellington #17)

Krupp Gun, Wellington. (Wellington #19)

The Board Room, Wellington Museum, Jervois Quay. (Wellington #24)

Mrs Chippy Monument, Wellington. (Wellington #30)

Island Bay Butchery, Wellington. (Wellington, #38)

3. Wallaceville Blockhouse

In any other town or city, this blockhouse would be a local historical attraction, but here in Upper Hutt the local authorities have completely ignored this blockhouse. This is even more surprising as the area has few other historic buildings. The two-story building, complete with rifle loopholes, was built in 1860 for hostilities that never eventuated and is one of the very few wooden blockhouses to survive. Once the danger of war had passed, the blockhouse was the local Police Station from 1867 to 1880.

Built to an American design, like all blockhouses, Wallaceville had double wooden walls infilled with shingle to absorb any rifle fire, and was originally windowless (the windows were added in 1916). Now painted black, this colour reflects the original black stain from 1860. The blockhouse occupied one corner of a much larger complex with raised stockade earthworths that enclosed a well and magazine; these earthworks were destroyed during the construction of Heretaunga College in 1954.

Completely original, the building has no signage or any indication of its historical importance.

⚲ McHardy Street, by Heretaunga College, Upper Hutt.

4. The Weeping Pagoda Tree

In suburban Avalon, scattered among the gardens of several homes are several very old and curiously rare trees, clearly not contemporary with the 1950s houses of the area. These trees were planted sometime between 1840 and 1845 by Thomas Mason, who settled in the Hutt Valley when Petone (Pito-one) was the main settlement in the Wellington area. Mason, an avid gardener and horticulturalist, first planted gum trees to provide shelter for this 8 ha property (later known as The Gums) and then planted unusual trees from around the world.

The Weeping Pagoda Tree *Styphnolobium japonica 'Pendula'* is the only known weeping form of this species in New Zealand and it is not common even in its native China. Just 1.5 m high and compact in shape, the dense foliage disguises the twisted nature of the tree branches.

Suburban development eventually overwhelmed Mason's gardens, but many of the trees still survive in the gardens of neighbouring houses, including a golden-leaved chestnut of the property next door to the weeping pagoda tree.

The tree is right at the front of private property and is easily viewed from the street.

📍 7 Avalon Crescent, Avalon, Hutt Valley.

5. Wainuiomata Hill Tunnel Portal

Proudly emblazoned in bold letters 'Wainui-o-mata-Tunnel 1932', the western portal of an abandoned road tunnel is tucked up a driveway behind industrial buildings in Gracefield and protected by double prison-like gates.

In the late 1920s the Wainuiomata Valley was seen a logical urban extension to the rapidly expanding Hutt Valley and, to make the area more attractive, one of the first requirements was easy access via a road tunnel. Work began in earnest in 1932, but only 40 percent of the tunnel was completed before the money ran out and the project was stopped. Used as munition storage during the war, by the time attempts were made to resurrect the project in the 50s and 60s, a road tunnel was no longer a practical option.

Purchased by the Wellington Regional Water Board in 1975, work began again, this time on a more modest tunnel to carry water pipes and finally the tunnel broke through to the Wainuiomata side in September 1980. Today the tunnel also accommodates telecommunication cables and a sewer pipe.

📍 A concrete driveway to the left of NZ Safety-Blackwoods leads to the portal at the end of Tunnel Grove off Gracefield Road.

6. Pencarrow Coastal Trail

This coastal walk encompasses some of Wellington's wildest seascape, being wide open to the worst that the southerly weather can bring, but that very wildness is also its greatest appeal. There are great views of the harbour and, on clear days, across to the South Island and the Kaikoura mountains, snow-capped in winter; views enhanced by a short but steep climb up to the old lighthouse. The entrance to Wellington Harbour was even more treacherous in the days of sail than it is today, and from as early as 1842, lights to guide shipping were established here. However, it wasn't until 1 January 1859 that New Zealand's first lighthouse cast its light across the harbour entrance and this, in turn, was replaced by the lower lighthouse in 1906 still operational today. During the Wahine foundering in the storm of 1968 many of the survivors and bodies were washed up along this bleak stretch of coast.

While this track follows the coast from the road end right round to the Wainuiomata River mouth (three hours one way) most people only go as far as the lighthouse, a much more manageable one-and-a-half-hour one-way walk. The track is also very popular with mountain bikers.

📍 From Eastbourne following Muritai Road along the coast to the end, which is also known as Burdans Gate.

7. Lower Hutt Council Building and Town Hall

During the 1950s the Hutt Valley was the centre of a rapidly expanding population in the Wellington region with extensive areas of state and private housing, along with considerable new industry, taking advantage of large areas of flat land – a scare commodity in an area more notable for its hills. Between 1931 and 1951 the population of Lower Hutt tripled and by 1955 it was the fifth largest city in New Zealand.

To accommodate this, several civic buildings were built within a very short space of time, including the War Memorial Library, Cultural Centre, Horticultural Hall, Church of St James and the Council Building and Town Hall. Today this group of buildings represents the country's most extensive collection of post-modern architecture, though not all buildings have survived or are used for their original purpose. The Church of St James constructed in 1953 was described as the 'most radical modern church design in New Zealand' and won a New Zealand Institute of Architects Gold Medal in 1954.

Of these, the most striking today is the Lower Hutt Council Building and Town Hall. Predominately displaying Modern Movement attributes, along with elements of Art Deco, the building has strong horizontal and vertical lines, little ornamentation, extensive use of glass and simple but bold geometric shapes.

Designed by Keith Cook of King, Cook and Dawson and constructed by WM Angus Ltd, the building opened in April 1957 and the exterior has remained largely true to the original form. The adjoining Horticultural Hall also designed by Cook was demolished after earthquake damage in 2013, and has been replaced by the Events Centre. In contrast to the exterior, the interior has been completely remodelled.

📍 Laings Road, Lower Hutt.

8. Petone Wharf

Riddled with seaworm, in danger of collapsing during the next earthquake, not particularly attractive and costing a fortune to upgrade, locals are not letting their wharf go without a fight. It's not hard to see why, as there is something immensely appealing and thoroughly relaxing about strolling out far out over the water, whether it is to fish, swim or just sit taking in the grandeur of Wellington Harbour. Wrap up warm, it can be nippy out there.

Some sort of wharf has existed at Petone since a simple landing stage was built in January 1840, but it wasn't until 1884 that a substantial wharf was constructed by the Gear Meat Company to handle both the refrigerated ship the Jubilee and for landing coal. Substantial it may have been but by 1900 the wharf – built of wood, eaten away by marine life and in danger of collapse – was finally demolished in 1902.

Much sturdier, the current wharf was opened in 1909 and was used primarily as a cargo wharf, but also accommodated commuter ferries. Lasting a good deal longer, this wharf was damaged in the 2016 earthquake and it too was found to be eaten by sea life.

The local council now has the options of either demolishing the wharf, spending a small fortune to repair or replace the wharf or facing the ire of residents who have a deep attachment to their old jetty.

For those interested in local industrial history, the small but excellent Petone Museum just along the shore has excellent displays of one of New Zealand's most important industrial areas (like the Gear Meat Works, most large companies have long gone). Here is the history of companies such as the General Motors Plant, Wellington Woollen Mills, Colgate Palmolive and the Railway Workshops. The museum itself is housed in a striking Art Deco building opening in 1940 as part of New Zealand's Centennial celebrations.

📍 Wharf: The Esplanade opposite Victoria Street, Petone.

📍 Museum: The Esplanade opposite Buick Street, Petone.

North and Porirua

9. Battle Hill

Even today the site of this last engagement in the land wars around Wellington is relatively remote, but in 1846 this area was covered in dense bush; it was difficult to travel through at the best of times and in winter almost impossible.

After clashing with troops at Pauatahanui, Maori under the leadership of Te Rangihaeata (Te Rauparaha's nephew) drew back 6 kilometres to a position in steep and rugged hill country. They quickly but effectively fortified a hilltop in dense bush. The British troops, though heavily outnumbering the Maori, realised that a direct attack would be suicidal.

The first action against Te Rangihaeata began on 6 August in bitterly cold weather, with heavy gunfire from the 250 British soldiers as well as 150 Maori, mainly Te Ati Awa but also including some Ngati Toa men opposed to Te Rangihaeata. The musket fire made little impression and, after the death of three British soldiers, the attacking forces withdrew back down the hill. (Te Rangihaeata lost nine men on the same day.)

On 8 August two mortars were hauled up the steep hillside, through bush and mud, and began firing on the hilltop fort: eighty mortar rounds pounded the Maori positions. But still the British refused to move forward and eventually they withdrew completely on 10 August, leaving their Maori allies to continue the fight.

Over the next few days, the two sides skirmished inconclusively and finally Te Rangihaeata, realising that in the long run it was impossible to hold the fort, slipped away under cover of the rain and dark, leaving his enemies to find an empty shell on the morning of 13 August.

Today Battle Hill is farmland. The bush is mostly gone, replaced by grass and grazing sheep. The uphill walk is a good solid climb, and it can only be imagined what it was like pulling heavy iron mortars up the hill under fire. Only some minor earthworks remain of the Maori and British positions, but extensive interpretive panels make this a very worthwhile excursion.

A number of tracks start by the farm buildings. The best one to take is the Summit Loop Track (the first part of which is also the Farm Loop Track). This is all uphill, though it follows a farm track so the grade is steady rather than steep. Once you reach the top, enjoy the atmosphere and the view before taking the return track via the bush reserve.

> Battle Hill Farm Forest Park, Paekakariki Hill Road, 6 km from the intersection with SH 58 at Pauatahanui.

10. Pataka Art + Museum

Rather than create yet another local museum, Porirua City Council have cleverly opted for a more innovative approach and has linked several galleries and exhibitions to create an exceptional and original cultural experience. And it works, local love it and this is a busy place. Pataka (storehouse) is best described as a cultural centre, a combination of museum, galleries, library, café and art store. The twin hearts of the complex are the local library and a small museum and gallery, with fabulous temporary exhibitions that are usually themed and are inclusive of a wide range of art forms which in particular highlight the very best of contemporary Pacific- and Maori-inspired art. Next door is the Bottle Creek Gallery, and at the entrance to the complex is a small but excellent gift store and finally holding it all together is a great café. The single permanent display at the entrance to the complex is Michael Tuffery's 1998 sculpture entitled Povi, a large bull constructed entirely out of shaped corned beef tins.

> Corner Norrie and Parumoana Streets, Porirua.

🕐　Open daily 10 am to 4.30 pm Monday to Saturday,
　　11 am to 4.30 pm Sunday.

🌐　www.pataka.org.nz

11. Te Pa o Kapo

Regarded as the strongest and best fortified of the Ngati Ira pa in the Porirua area, Te Pa o Kapo may have been occupied for as long as 400 years. However, when Te Rauparaha invaded the area in 1819–20, of the three pa in the Porirua area, only Waimapihi was inhabited. Te Pa o Kapo had already been abandoned and was never subsequently reoccupied.

In 1901 the ethnographer Elsdon Best (who was born in Tawa) visited the pa and was impressed by the superb defences. He noted that at that time the stumps of the totara palisading were still visible.

Today the pa still retains the key elements of the defenses that made it so famous. The already narrow access to the small headland was accentuated by a deep trench and by steepening the cliffs on either side and even today it is a bit of scramble on to the main part of the pa.

Wide terraces remain and of course the view along the coast and across the strait remains undiminished by time.

📍　The small reserve is clearly marked on Terrace Road, Titahi Bay.

12. Second World War American Officer's Mess

For a short period from 1942 to 1944, the area north of Wellington hosted huge numbers of American soldiers. Those who came here to train were not impressed: it was cold, and they couldn't even get a hamburger. On the other hand, for those soldiers who had already seen action in the Pacific,

New Zealand was a peaceful haven, perfect to recover from the horrors of war.

The largest camp was at Camp Russell (Queen Elizabath II Park) and nearby Camp McKay, but 8000 men were also stationed at Porirua including 1400 at Titahi Bay. To provide for such large numbers of men, makeshift buildings were quickly erected with many of the buildings prefabricated in the South Island by the Public Works Department and then transported to the camps by the New Zealand Army. Titahi Bay Camp had platoons from the 'Special Troops' stationed there, including the Special Weapons Battalion, the Second Tank Battalion, the Second Parachute Battalion and the Second Scout Company.

Today just one building remains from this vast encampment along the coast, the Officer's Mess at Titahi Bay. Now used as a community building, this modest wooden building is plain and unremarkable, and its former use is neither commemorated or even acknowledged. However, at Queen Elizabeth Park there is an extensive display including many historical photos, giving a glimpse into the lives of thousands of Americans who briefly made this area home.

📍 Corner of Te Pene Ave and Tireti Road, Titahi Bay.

13. Johnsonville Line - Wellington Rail

Of all the cities in New Zealand, Wellington has the most extensive and best patronised rail network, linking the northern districts with the central station and for the visitor, and especially anyone interested in railways, the most interesting and scenic line is out to Johnsonville. Work began on the line in 1879, a project undertaken by the Wellington and Manawatu Railway Company as the main railway line from Wellington to Palmerston North. Now a branch line, this line weaves precariously along steep-sided valleys, trundles over small bridges and, although the line is only 10.5 km, it passes through no fewer than seven tunnels. Linking eight stations the trip takes twenty-one minutes and trains depart from the main Wellington Railway Station. Built in the Classical tradition with massive Doric columns and opened in 1937, it is believed that the huge entrance foyer in the Beaux Arts style was modelled on Pennsylvania Station in New York. When completed the station was the largest public building in New Zealand and employed in construction the latest earthquake protection technology available at the time.

Over 30 per cent of Wellingtonians use public transport, the highest percentage in New Zealand and about 17 per cent of Wellingtonians walk to work, more than three times higher than the New Zealand average of about five per cent.

⬥ Wellington Railway Station, Bunny Street, Pipitea.

14. Matiu/Somes Island and Wellington Harbour/ Te Whanganui a Tara

The harbour itself takes its name from Tara, who lived at Mahia and who, with his brother Tautoki, journeyed down to the area we now know as Wellington. So impressed were Tara and Tautoki that they convinced their father, the great chief Whatonga, that the harbour was an excellent place for a new settlement. Despite the abundance of kai moana (seafood), the cool summer climate restricted the growth of crops, and it is estimated that the pre-European population was well under 1000.

One of the best places to view the 'great harbour of Tara' is Matiu or Somes Island. This 25-hectare island has a long history of human occupation and is now an important nature sanctuary free from predators. Named Matiu by the legendary explorer Kupe, who discovered the harbour around 1000 AD, Maori have long occupied the island mainly as a refuge as the island lacked permanent fresh water. Purchased by the New Zealand Company and renamed Somes after the deputy governor of the company Joseph Somes, the island was used as a quarantine station from 1872 for both people and animals.

During both wars the island was a detention centre for alien residents. Oddly enough, among the WWI detainees were a Dutchman, a Swiss and a Mexican, all from countries that weren't even involved in the war. WWII detainees included members of Wellington's Italian, German and Austrian community, even though many were in fact refugees from Nazi Germany. Most of today's buildings are from the animal quarantine period though the barracks (1890) and a hospital (1915) remain. There are the remains of anti-aircraft gun emplacements from WWII, though the guns were never fired and have long been removed. Now an important native wildlife sanctuary the island is slowly being replanted in native bush and several bird species as well as tuatara have been reintroduced. In particular the rare kakariki is common on the island. The island circuit track is easy walking and for most part is high up on the island with excellent views all the way around and will take around two hours.

📍 East by West stops at the island on their cross-harbour ferry route.

📞 04 499 1282

🌐 www.eastbywest.co.nz

City

15. Katherine Mansfield House and Garden

The surprising thing about this house is that Kathrine Mansfield never had good memories of the place describing it as 'that dark little cubby hole', and yet the house regularly occurs in her writings, especially her short stories. Katherine was born in the house in 1888 and lived there until 1893 when the family moved to Karori. Eventually at the age of nineteen she left Wellington for Europe and died at Fontainbleau, France of tuberculosis in 1923.

Now recognised as one of New Zealand's greatest short story writers, the house has been immaculately restored to reflect a typical lower middle-class family home of the late Victorian period. With its dark stained wood, heavy drapes and furniture, and overly decorative wallpapers, the house has a somewhat overbearing and melancholic feel, but then so does Mansfield's writing. A useful handout relates each room of the house to Mansfield's writing, while the main bedroom has a detailed display of her life. For those not familiar with Katherine Mansfield's writing or life, an excellent range of books is available for purchase.

📍 25 Tinakori Road, Thorndon.
🕐 Open Tuesday to Sunday 10 am to 4 pm.
📞 04 4737268
🌐 www.katherinemansfield.com
💲 Entrance fee.

16. Tinakori Road Houses, Thorndon

Wellington's steep and hilly terrain has given rise to some intriguing local architecture as builders devised innovative ways to construct houses on some very difficult building sites. The main problem was the scarcity of flat land, and the obvious solution to this was to build close and build high. This approach is best expressed in the houses at 296 to 306 Tinakori Road in Thorndon. Here the six narrow wooden houses, built in 1903, are just one room wide but rise three to five stories above the road with steep steps climbing to the main entrance at the side of the house. While the fronts of the houses are ornate, several of these houses have corrugated iron cladding sides, a very common feature on many old Wellington buildings. The use of corrugated iron was primarily one of economy as it was light, inexpensive and easy to use, though it also acted as fire protection for Wellington's closely packed buildings. The grand frontage coupled with more modest sides and back led to the comment 'Queen Anne at the front, meat safe at the back'. Number 306 has a shop at street level that was once the local butcher's shop.

Diagonally across from these tall houses is the Shepherds Arms Hotel, built in 1870 and once a coaching on the way to Karori. Next to the hotel is Ascot St where small cottages are packed in tightly along the narrow street. The tiny cottage at 30 Ascot Street unbelievably housed a school run by Granny Cooper between 1867 and 1888.

The oldest house in the street, built in the 1860s, is at number 251 Tinakori Road, while the official Prime Minister's residence, Premier House, is at number 260 Tinakori Road.

17. Harry Holland's Grave, Bolton Street Cemetery

Established in 1840 to service the tiny settlement, this was Wellington's main cemetery until 1892 (though burials continued until 1967) and, as was usual practice at the time, was segregated by religion into Anglican, Jewish and public areas. The tall column near the rose gardens is the Seddon Memorial and just a few metres down the hill is the intriguing grave of Harry Holland, first leader of the Labour Party from 1919 to 1933. Curiously the grave is topped with a lithe and buff young man who apparently is a freshly emancipated youth, looking skyward to a prosperous future. Unfortunately, with his genitals smoothed to an androgynous lump, his love life is not going to be that bright. At the base grovel several contorted and semi-naked Gollum-like figures, two of which — a man and woman — have one arm thrust awkwardly into the base of the plinth. These are said to represent brutalised humans rising out of the grime of poverty.

📍 This part of the cemetery is most easily reached from the Botanic Gardens in Glenmore Street or the end of Kinross Street, off Bolton Street.

18. Pinus Radiata Botanic Gardens

The hilly nature of Wellington has led to the creation of a unique botanical garden with little hidden valleys and winding paths linking various parts. Although 5 hectares were set aside as a reserve as early as 1844, the garden was not formally established until 1868. Many existing trees date from this early period, planted to ascertain the economic potential of imported species in the southern climate. In 1871 the gardens were considerably expanded by the addition of a further 54 acres of remaining bush.

At first the garden was administered by the New Zealand Institute, an organisation whose prime interest was to assess the economic potential of important species, and many conifers in the garden today date from that period. One group of trees planted with forestry in mind were Monterey pines, better known in New Zealand as *Pinus radiata*. Seed was imported in 1869 and records report that radiata seedlings were planted in 1871 on the steep hillside along Glenmore Street. What makes these trees unusual is the seed was directly collected from pine trees in California, trees that today are close to extinction in the native habit, initially through urban development and more recently by a widespread fungal disease that has all but wiped them out in the wild. Trees from these gardens are now being re-exported back to California to improve the original stock.

📍 From the main entrance on Glenmore Street walk directly south for about 200 – 300 m and the pines streets are on the slope to the left.

Main entrance is at Glenmore Street, an extension of Tinakori Road, Thorndon. Top entrance from the Cable Car.

19. Krupp Gun

Located next to the old Dominion Observatory, this is the only surviving example of 190 such guns manufactured by F Krupp in Essen, Germany in 1907. The 8.2 metre long gun weighs 6.7 tonne and was captured by the Wellington Regiment near La Vacquiere in North-eastern France in 1918, and brought back to Wellington as a war trophy. The site of the gun is the old Botanic Garden Battery, established in 1894 and was one of six such batteries to defend the city during the 'Russian Scare' at a time when Russia was actively expanding into the Pacific. Naturally there are excellent views over the city and harbour from this vantage point.

📍 From the top of the Cable Car, head directly towards the Old Observatory and the gun is to the right.

20. He Tohu: The Declaration of Independence, The Treaty of Waitangi and Women's Suffrage Petition

In a purpose-built exhibition space, the National Library of New Zealand has on display just three documents precisely described as 'A Declaration, A Treaty, A Petition; Signatures that shape New Zealand'. In chronological order they are: 1835 Declaration of Independence Of Northern Chiefs, 1840 The Treaty of Waitangi, 1893 Women's Suffrage Petition.

Most widely known, it is odd seeing the actual treaty of Waitangi. For such an important document there is not too much to it, and the first page that contains the main text and the signatures of those who signed at Waitangi is battered and torn. Most of the document is made up of the signatures of the chiefs. At the time there were several copies circulating, though this is the main document and the only one remaining. After the northern chiefs signed the Treaty at Waitangi on February 6 1840, the document then travelled the length of the country to be signed by chiefs at various locations, though many refused to sign.

Along with the treaty, on display is New Zealand's earliest document, He Whakaputanga − the 1835 Declaration of Independence Of Northern Chiefs is all in Maori, penned by Eruera Pari Hongi. Reflecting a deep understanding of political changes both in New Zealand and internationally, the document was an innovative statement of how northern rangitira viewed the emergence of a new nation as one controlled and run by Maori.

The suffrage petition in 1893 was not the first such appeal to give women the vote, but it certainly was the largest. Described by leading activist Kate Sheppard as 'a monster', it was signed by 32,000 women – a quarter of all adult women in the country. Women (and many men) were galvanised into action by the election to be held later in 1893, knowing full well if the law wasn't changed before then, they would have to wait another three years. Signed into law in September 1893, New Zealand became the first country in the world to grant women the vote in parliamentary elections.

Along with the three documents is an excellent exhibition detailing the importance of each document accompanied by extensive illustrations and photographs.

National Library of New Zealand, corner Molesworth and Aitken Streets.

Open 9 am to 5 pm, Monday to Friday, 9 am to 1 pm, Saturday, closed on public holidays.

04 470 4541

www.natlib.govt.nz

21. Old Government Buildings

Wellington's Old Government Buildings is not only the largest wooden building in New Zealand, but also the largest in the southern hemisphere. Moreover, it is the second-largest wooden building in the world after the Great Buddha Hall in Nara, Japan.

Designed to house government departments, the building took 22 months to complete at a cost of PDS39,000 and was officially opened in 1876. Constructed mainly of kauri timber over a frame of Tasmanian hardwood, the Neo-Renaissance style of the building cleverly uses wood to imitate stone, a common practice in colonial buildings where the prestige of stone was more than offset by the cheapness of wood. Even though it is built entirely on reclaimed land, this large building is considerably more earthquake resistant than a building of concrete, stone or brick.

Extended in 1897 and in 1907, the building once housed the entire civil service and it served as government offices right up until 1990, after which the building underwent major restoration under the management of the Department of Conservation. It now houses the Law Faculty of Victoria University, though a section of the ground floor with displays is open to visitors (including a cutaway section of the wall to show construction), along with the Cabinet room on the first floor.

🕐 On Saturdays from 19 January to 30 March there are guided tours at 11 am and 2 pm.

22. Old Bank Arcade, Animated Musical Clock

Hanging from the ceiling of the Old Bank Arcade is a large bulbous clock, though the section that tells the time is relatively small and the reason why is revealed at the top of each hour. As the clock strikes the hour, the larger section opens to reveal four panels. Each panel depicts an historical scene from the site on which you are standing from the early nineteenth century to the mid-twentieth century. What makes this so appealing is that the tiny animated figures are very cute and funny. There is nothing sophisticated here with little silhouette figures performing little jerky movements. This will delight young children and adults, but teenagers will just roll their eyes. Maybe not a trip in itself, but certainly worth a minor detour if you are passing and timing is right.

📍 Old Bank Arcade, 233-237 Lambton Quay.

23. Paddy the Wanderer Memorial Fountain

Everyone loves a good dog story, but before you continue reading a small warning, this one is a very sad doggy tale.

Paddy started out life known as Dash, an Airedale terrier and the devoted pet of a young girl whose father was a seaman. Dash became familiar with the wharves from his many frequent visits with the family as they came down to the port to welcome their father home from a trip. When the small girl developed pneumonia and suddenly died, Dash ran away and began wandering the wharves, maybe hoping that the girl, like her father, would one day return by ship.

Now known as Paddy, he became a great favourite with local watersiders, seamen and taxi drivers who fed him and paid for his dog licence. The Wellington Harbour Board adopted him under the formal title of Assistant Night Watchman, whose job it was to keep guard for 'pirates, smugglers and rodents'. Frequently he joined seamen on board ships and travelled both around New Zealand and to Australian ports, and according to local legend even made it to San Francisco. His most famous moment was in December 1935 when he took a flight over Wellington in a Gyspy Moth biplane.

During a cruel cold snap, Paddy died on 17 July 1939 at Shed 1 and his funeral procession of twelve taxis led by a traffic officer brought central Wellington to a standstill. It wasn't until 1945 that a drinking bowl for dogs and a water fountain for people were erected on Queen's Wharf along with a bronze plaque of Paddy's doggy silhouette. The drinking fountain even includes stones from Waterloo Bridge, bombed during the blitz on London during World War II. RIP Paddy.

> Just inside Queen's Wharf Gates, opposite the Museum of Wellington.

24. The Board Room – Wellington Museum

Located in the historic Bond Store (built 1892), this excellent museum is often overlooked in a city well-endowed with galleries and museums. With a focus on Wellington maritime heritage the entry to and from the museum is through a recreation of the original 1890s Bond Store. The highlight is the incredible Wellington Harbour Boardroom. This was the meeting room of the Wellington Harbour Board from the 1920s through to 1987 and walking into this room the immediate thought is 'just who did these people think they were?' Forget about the usual image of a boardroom with a large central table around which board members meet in collegial fashion. This room is massive and is set out like a very grand courtroom. Beautiful wood panelling lines the walls and at the front of the room, arranged like thrones are three heavy carved leather chairs flanked by large Greek columns. In front of the chairs is a long table along which, no doubt, sat the lesser members of the board. Huge double height windows flood the room with natural light and the overall effect of the room is an opulent display of money and power.

- Queens Wharf, Jervois Quay.
- Open daily 10 am to 5 pm.
- 04 472 8904
- www.museumswellington.org.nz

25. New Zealand Academy of Fine Arts and New Zealand Portrait Gallery

These two galleries sit back to back on Wellington's waterfront and along with the Wellington Museum, which is right next door, make an excellent trio for a day out. All three are quite small and very different from each other so just when you have had enough, it is time to move on. The exhibitions are more geared to adult interests in contrast to Te Papa which now verges on infotainment.

Established in 1882, the Academy of Fine Arts gallery promotes the very best of New Zealand art by both new and established artists and is constantly changing. Professionally displayed in a modern and well-lit gallery, most of the art on show is for sale. The Academy is located in the Wharf Offices Building, an award-winning heritage building.

Directly behind the Academy is the New Zealand Portrait Gallery, housed in Shed 11 – also a heritage building. Although the Gallery has a permanent collection, only a few of these art works are on display, with most of the space given to revolving exhibitions which take a very wide view of what constitutes portrait art and what it means to be a New Zealander. The result is lively and frequently challenging exhibitions that are worth regular visits.

- Academy of Fine Arts, 1 Queens Wharf
- Open daily 10 am to 5 pm.
- www.nzafa.com
- Portrait Gallery, Shed 11 Queens Wharf,
- Open daily 10.30 am to 4.30 pm.
- nzportraitgallery.org.nz

26. Boat Sheds, Clyde Quay Boat Harbour

Virtually identical, simply constructed yet immensely appealing these boat sheds, with St Gerard's Monastery high on the hill above, create one of Wellington's most iconic images.

The earliest boat sheds were built in 1905 when the small boat harbour was constructed for the Royal Port Nicholson Yacht Club with further sheds built in 1909 and 1922. Unusual for the period, the sheds were built of concrete and back from the water as it was felt 'undesirable to build sheds on timber foundations over the water, as the ground would gradually shoal thereunder and become offensive and insanitary'.

During World War II, the harbour became an American base and the sheds were used for storage and, in some cases, temporary troop accommodation was built above the sheds.

Over 110 years later the sheds are virtually unaltered and are still used for storing boats by the yacht club.

📍 Clyde Quay, Oriental Bay.

27. Cuba Street Bucket Fountain

This fountain really divides Wellingtonians: they either loved or want it ripped out of the ground immediately. You can decide.

Originally called the Water Mobile, this fountain was part of the redevelopment of Cuba Street in the late 1960s when the tramlines were removed. Designed by architects Burren and Keen and erected in 1969, the fountain works a simple bucket system that in theory should merely fill and empty on a regular basis. In reality, however, the whole thing works erratically with the water missing the buckets altogether or tipping when partially full or swinging completely upside down, often splashing passersby. This gives the fountain enormous appeal as it is so unpredictable and it is immensely enjoyable just to sit, watch and wait. To others, it is poorly constructed, embarrassing and a waste of space.

While most of Wellington has embraced a modern future, Cuba Street has somehow clung on to its seedy past and, in some respects, is not a whole lot different to the time when opium dens operated in Haining Street in the 1920s, or when Wellington's most well-known transvestite ran Carmen's Coffee Lounge during the 1960s. The area, still, is an eclectic mix of budget hotels, snazzy cafes, offbeat shops, and the occasional strip joint. The street is named after an immigrant ship, not the country.

📍 Cuba Street Mall near the intersection with Dixon Street.

28. Nairn Street Cottage

Most historic houses tend to be large and grand but this, Wellington's oldest building, is a small family home where William and Catherine Wallis raised their ten children. Built in 1858, the house remained in the Wallis family until 1985, and both the garden and the house have been restored to reflect everyday life for ordinary New Zealanders in the second half of the nineteenth century. There are tours at 12 pm, 1 pm, 2 pm and 3 pm.

- 68 Nairn Street, Mount Cook.
- Open 12 pm to 4 pm, Summer open every day 1 January through to 19 March,
  Winter, Saturdays and Sundays only.
- Entrance fee.

Southern Suburbs

29. Otari-Wilton Bush's Native Botanic Garden and Forest Reserve

New Zealand has around 2500 plant species, 5800 fungi, 2000 lichens and 500 mosses, of which most are endemic and many confined to single location and this is the country's only public garden dedicated exclusively to native plants. Established in 1926 as the Otari Open-Air Plant Museum, the first director was pioneer botanist Dr Leonard Cockayne who was instrumental in collecting and classifying many native plants at a time when native plants held little interest to even the more enthusiastic gardener.

The gardens are beautifully laid out and easily accessible with the dramatic Canopy Walkway linking the two cultivated parts of the gardens. To the left of the information centre are the older gardens with impressive collections of hebe, flax, coprosma and threatened species (among others), while the fernery and alpine gardens in the themed area are equally worth visiting. The Nature Walk loop, which covers both gardens and an attractive section of bush between the two, takes around forty minutes, though it does have a steep section with steps. Beyond the Kaiwharawhara stream are several loop walks through original bush areas that can take up to one hour.

📍 160 Wilton Road, Karori.

🕐 Open daily dawn to dusk.

🌐 www.wellingtongardens.nz

30. Mrs Chippy Monument

Karori Cemetery is a vast expanse of steep banks and gullies with graves crowding the slopes and elegant mausoleums tucked into hillsides. Covering 40 hectares and containing over 80,000 graves, the cemetery opened in 1891 and was the first in New Zealand to erect a crematorium (1909).

Without the helpful map at the entrances, it would be impossible to find the Mrs Chippy Monument on the modest grave of Harry McNeish.

Not an explorer as such, Harry McNeish (more correctly McNish) was a Scottish carpenter by trade, but clearly with a yearning for adventure as he joined Ernest Shackleton's Endurance expedition to Antarctica in 1914. He was best known as Chippy, a common nickname given to carpenters. When the Endurance was crushed by ice, it was McNeish who built the small boats that were crucial to the survival of the crew. When he arrived on board, he had with him a cat called Mrs Chippy (though the cat was male) and it was most often seen curled up contently at the bottom of his bunk.

On January 24 1915 the Endurance became trapped by ice and remained firmly bound until on November 21 the ice finally crushed the ship and it was abandoned. Unfortunately during the long months marooned in an Antarctic winter, supplies became limited and Shackleton had given the order that all the sled dogs and poor Mrs Chippy be shot, naturally souring the relations between Shackleton and McNeish.

Later McNeish worked for the New Zealand Shipping Company and after visiting New Zealand five times he moved to Wellington in 1925, where he died destitute on 24 September 1930 and was buried in an unmarked grave. In 1959 the New Zealand Antarctic Society placed a headstone on the grave and then in 2004 the same organisation commissioned a bronze statue of his beloved Mrs Chippy lying on the grave as he once did on Harry's bed.

> The main entrance is off Karori Road, but it is quite a long walk from there to the grave (you can drive). The closest entrance is off Standen Street, Karori.

31. Wrights Hill Fortress

If you are looking for a place for a fortress, then the top of Wrights Hill is just the place. Though the elevation is a modest 358 metres, the harbour and the whole of the south coast is in view and in 1934 the British War Office advised the New Zealand Army that the whole of the Wellington harbour area could be protected from a single battery on the hill. However, it wasn't begun until 1942, and finally completed in 1947. Only two of the three guns were installed and, given the weather up here, most of the installation was sensibly underground. Today the most substantial remains above ground is the base of one of the guns, though underground, the installation is more intact with some of the older machinery still in place. Not to be missed, if you can make it, are the four open days each year held on public holidays.

Not surprisingly the views are superb and the summit is laced with tracks so you can decide just how much walking you want to do, but if the weather is not good or the cloud low, don't even waste your time thinking about a trip up here. Excellent information boards with historic photos make the trip even more worthwhile.

📍 Wrights Hill Road, off the end of Kano Street, Karori.

32. Makara Peak Mountain-bike Park

A mud-splattered heaven for mountain bikers, 40 km of track laces through the park's 250 ha, with over thirty bike tracks with something for every one, from children and the adult beginner, through to the hard-core and expert riders. Also used by walkers and runners, Makara Peak rises to 412 m with most of the park bush covered and is itself a conservation story. An army of volunteers not only maintains the tracks but have cleared the area of pests such as goats and possums.

If you don't have a bike you can hire one from Mud Cycles just down the road at 424 Karori Road (www.mudbikes.co.nz).

📍 116/122 S Karori Rd, Karori
🌐 www.makarapeak.bike

33. Makara Beach and Walkway

For many Wellingtonians Makara is a special place. Not the place for a dip in the sea, the bay, exposed to both northerly and southerly winds, opens directly on to the wild waters of Cook Strait and in summer or winter it is a place of solitude, wild winds, crashing waves and dramatic seascapes. It wasn't always as barren and devoid of vegetation as it is today. Several Maori pa sites in the area are testament to the richness of both sea and forest and even Captain Cook remarked on the din of the dawn chorus of bird song from the forest even though he anchored almost a kilometre offshore.

The Makara Walkway begins at the southern end of the beach and crossing farmland the track climbs solidly up hill, but the views along the way are magnificent, steadily unfolding as you climb. A track along a narrow ridge leads to an ancient Ngati Ira pa and higher still is Fort Opau, a WWII gun emplacement built to protect Cook Strait. The strategic value of the site to both Maori and Pakeha is immediately obvious. The whole of Cook Strait is in clear view, with Mana and Kapiti islands to the north, the Marlborough Sounds to the west, and the Kaikoura mountains to the south. The fort was extensive in its heyday, but now only the lookout posts, and the gun emplacements partially dug into the hillside remain.

📍 From the western end of Karori take the Makara Road 11 km to the beach.

34. Brooklyn Wind Turbine

Built as part of a research project in 1993, this was the site for New Zealand's first wind turbine, a modest machine, standing just 31.5 high, with blades 13.5 metres long and generating enough power to supply 60 to 80 homes. A firm Wellington favourite, when Meridan Energy proposed retiring the turbine, public affection was so high that Meridan replaced it with a newer model. Installed in 2016 the new turbine is 44 metres tall and has blades 20.8 metres, considerably larger than the old one, but a baby compared to the giants above the Manawatu gorge.

To say the site is windy is an understatement and the turbine is remotely controlled to adjust to the demanding conditions. Wellington is a windy city, with an average of 173 days a year experiencing winds over 60 km/h. From 1972 to 2016 Wellington had the largest average annual highest maximum wind gusts averaging 142 km/hr, and much higher than the second windiest location, Invercargill with just 118 km/hr. Within walking distance of the wind turbine is Hawkins Hill which on both 6 November

1959 and 4 July 1962 experienced wind gusts of 248 km/hr. The strongest wind recorded in New Zealand was at Mt St John near Tekapo in the MacKenzie Basin where on 18 April 1970 a wind gust reached 250 kph. To balance the record Wellington gets an average of about 2,050 hours of sunshine per year, about the same as Auckland.

An added bonus is the exceptional views from Poll Hill and the turbine borders Zealandia ecosanctuary so you never know what bird might pop over the fence.

And in case you are wondering the suburb of Brooklyn was named after the borough of New York City to which it bears absolutely no resemblance, though it also has a Central Park, and many of the streets are named after US Presidents.

📍 Ashton Fitchett Drive, Poll Hill, Brooklyn.

35. Carlucci Land

First impressions are that you have stepped into a set of a Mad Max movie, and quite honestly that is likely to be your middle and last impressions as well. Creative inventor Carl Gifford has taken metal recycling up a few notches and let his imagination run wild, building metallic sculptures both huge and tiny, most of which are now encrusted with a hue of orange, brown and red rust. Stuff is everywhere and you need to take time to find a tiny ferrous elephant, a delicately painted rock or the long forgotten road sign; the more you look, the more you find so be prepared to be surprised, intrigued, fascinated and especially entertained.

Added to that is an eighteen hole mini golf course that winds its way along a hillside hole kindly described as a junk yard and enormous fun.

Regularly unattended, mini golf visitors can use an honesty book or follow the instructions for using the eftpos machine.

📍 281 Happy Valley Rd, Happy Valley.
🌐 www.carlucciland.nz

36. The Container House, Happy Valley

The use of containers to extend living areas or as an entire house, while unusual, is not uncommon. Most such buildings are on a single level, but Wellington's topography is demanding and this house stacks the containers up a hill side, a style which reflects the old timber houses along Tinakori Road that creep with the hillside, one room wide and up to five stories.

Industrial designer Ross Stevens has stacked up three containers and along with all the features of a contemporary house, has used the close hugging hillside to create two large, sheltered and private outdoor spaces, one with a small waterfall. Stylish both inside and out, the house features three bedrooms and even a tiny cinema, and even better it is available to rent.

📍 173 Happy Valley Rd, Owhiro Bay.
🌐 www.wellingtoncontainerhouse.co.nz

37. Wellington's South Coast

If you are lucky enough to be in Wellington in a southerly gale, head off to the south coast which takes the full force of the wind and sea driving in directly from the Southern Ocean. In a storm, huge seas pound the rocky coast stripped of any substantial vegetation and waves often come over the road. While the wild weather can close the road at the southern end of the runway at Wellington airport, planes usually keep flying! At Lyall Bay, Wellington's best surf beach, hardy surfers take advantage of the conditions regardless of the season and the wind is so fierce that houses facing the ocean have small sand dunes in their front yards. Offshore the inter-island ferries lurch through the white-capped swells, though in these conditions the view from the shore is to be recommended. The only sheltered spot along the coast is Island Bay, where the small island of Taputeranga protects boats including a tiny fishing fleet.

This coast is home to blue penguins which cross the road at dusk to roost in the bushy cliffs or under houses, not popular with the homeowners who are kept awake at night by the nocturnal squawks of these noisy birds.

38. Island Bay Butchery

Taking pride of place under the main counter at the Island Bay Butchery are sausages. Not just a few little stacks of four or five varieties but massive piles of over thirty styles of sausage that should satisfy any taste. It is no surprise that this small butcher shop in suburban Wellington has carried off numerous awards and supplies cafes and restaurant, along with an army of local customers.

For sausage lovers this place is just heaven and it is genuinely impossible to know where to start. From the traditional Old English and Cumberland through to the more exotic Indian, and Thai pork, this is a sausage version of jetting around the world without leaving home. European sausages dominate and include Greek loukanika, French Toulouse, traditional Italian, Polish kiebasa and German bratwurst. Add to that boerewors from South Africa, black pudding and gluten-free sausages and you begin to the get the picture. The secret to success is simple: good quality meat, low-fat meat, quality additional ingredients and no fillers common in commercial sausages.

The Island Bay Butchery is a busy, lively place with great service from a gang of young butchers, and of course they supply a wide variety of other meats, equally good quality and prepared with care.

📍 127 The Parade, Island Bay.

🕐 Open Monday to Friday 7 am to 6.30 pm,
Saturday 7.30 am to 2 pm.

🌐 www.islandbaybutchery.co.nz

39. Wellington Airport

Everyone has a horror story of landing at Wellington airport and this single runway (1936 metre) is the busiest in New Zealand and just the best spot in the country to watch aeroplanes taking off and landing. For a close up, comfortable viewing, the main terminal has massive windows overlooking the runway and is complete with comfy chairs, food and drink, but if you want action then head to Wexford Road, just off Calabar Road on the north-eastern corner of the airport where there is a tiny carpark. Here the view is right down the runway and is at eye level with the planes taking off and landing. Just below is an odd block wall that runs for about 100 metres down the side of the side of the road and this is to prevent cyclists being knocked over from the back blast of jet engines as planes turn at the end of the runway. The wilder the weather the more interesting the experience and, especially in a turbulent northerly wind you'll be glad you are on the ground watching and not sitting in the plane.

📍 Wexford Road, Miramar.

40. Ataturk Memorial

War memorials are usually erected to commemorate victory, but in New Zealand (and Australia for that matter), it was a great defeat that seared itself into the national memory and today the country has an intriguing connection to its old WWI enemy Turkey. ANZAC Day was initially established to honour those who fought and died in the disastrous Gallipoli expedition in 1915, and today it is generally recognised that this military campaign was the birth of a strong and independent national identity for both New Zealanders and Australians. Rather than harbour bitter feelings towards the Turks (who were after all justly defending their homeland), a special and rare bond has formed between two old enemies. Equally surprising is that these feelings are reciprocated by the Turks and the Ataturk Memorial on Wellington's south coast is a tribute to Kemal Ataturk who lead the defence at Gallipoli.

The memorial is located on a rather bleak hill overlooking Cook Strait and the entrance to Wellington harbour; the site was deliberately chosen as a reminder of the harsh terrain faced by New Zealand soldiers landing on Anzac Cove on the rugged Gallipoli Peninsula. Unveiled on Anzac Day 1990, the monument was part of an agreement in which Turkey officially renamed Ari Burnu as Anzac Cove, and Australia and New Zealand created memorials to the conflict in both countries. Wreath laying ceremonies are held each year on both Anzac Day and in August to commemorate the battle for Chunuk Bair. It is a simple memorial, but it is the inscription of a statement penned in 1934 by Ataturk that is both moving and gracious and very hard to read with a dry eye …

'Those heroes who shed their blood and lost their lives, you are now lying in the soil of a friendly country. Therefore rest in peace. There is no difference between the Johnnies and the Mehmets to us where they lie side by side in this country of ours. You, the mothers who sent their sons from far away countries wipe away your tears, your sons are now lying in our bosoms and are in peace. After having lost their lives on this land they become our sons as well.'

📍 166 Breaker Bay Rd, Breaker Bay, Wellington.

Glossary

A & P Show: Agricultural and Pastoral Show

Bach: Small holiday house, usually by the sea or lake.

Crib: Same as bach, but more widely used in the South Island.

Dairy: Small general store

Domain: Public park usually with sport's fields

Gumboots: Tall rubber boots

Hokey Pokey: Ice cream flavour of honeycomb toffee

Hui: Meeting, gathering

i-SITE: Information site

Iwi: Maori community

Jandals: Flipflops, thongs

Kia Ora: Hello, very good

Koha: Donation

Marae: the courtyard in front of a meeting house, but occasionally used to mean a small Maori settlement

Pa: Historically a fortified Maori village but contemporary a Maori settlement

Pakeha: European New Zealander

Pounamu: Greenstone, jade

Rangatira: Chief

Tapu: Sacred, prohibited, forbidden, restricted

Togs: Swimsuit

Tohunga: Priest

Torch: Flashlight

Tramping: Hiking

Ute: Pickup truck

Waka: Maori canoe

Wairua: Spirit

Whanau: Family

Wharenui: Meeting house

Whitebait: young of six species of galaxiid fish, a New Zealand delicacy